The Wars of the Balkan Peninsula

Their Medieval Origins

Alexandru Madgearu

Martin Gordon, Consulting Editor

The Scarecrow Press, Inc.
Lanham, Maryland • Toronto • Plymouth, UK
2008

SCARECROW PRESS, INC.

Published in the United States of America
by Scarecrow Press, Inc.
A wholly owned subsidary of
The Rowman & Littlefield Publishing Group, Inc.
4501 Forbes Boulevard, Suite 200, Lanham, Maryland 20706
www.scarecrowpress.com

Estover Road
Plymouth PL6 7PY
United Kingdom

British Library Cataloguing in Publication Information Available

Library of Congress Cataloging-in-Publication Data

Madgeru, Alexandru.
   The wars of the Balkan Peninsula : their medieval origins / Alexandru
Madgearu ; Martin Gordon, consulting editor.
   Includes bibliographical references and index.
   ISBN-13: 978-0-8108-5846-6 (pbk. : alk. paper)
   ISBN-10: 0-8108-5846-0 (pbk. : alk. paper)
 1. Balkan Peninsula–History.   2. Balkan Peninsula–Ethnic relations–Political
aspects.   I. Gordon, Martin.   II. Title.

DR39 .M35 2008
949 .6–dc22   2007024653

∞™ The paper used in this publication meets the minimum requirements of
American National Standard for Information Sciences—Permanence of
Paper for Printed Library Materials, ANSI/NISO Z39.48-1992.
Manufactured in the United States of America.

"The Middle Ages is still living in the mind of those who claim conquests and desire empires. The memories of this Middle Ages, coming from an absolutely different world than the present one, are transformed in imprescriptible and exclusive national rights that fuel irreconcilable adversities. We must know this Middle Ages in order to explain the awful contemporary events that still could be provoked by it."

Nicolae Iorga, Sârbi, bulgari şi români în Peninsula Balcanic în evul mediu [1915], in *Studii asupra evului mediu românesc*, Bucureşti, 1984, 51.

Contents

Central Balkan Region

Preface to the English Translation

This is in fact a revised edition of the book first printed in Romania in 2001 by Corint Publishing House. A postdoctoral Fulbright grant at Ohio State University in Columbus (October 2002–March 2003) and research performed in several academic libraries in Rome (May–June 2005) gave me the opportunity to study many works not available in Romania. When I found out that Scarecrow Press intended to translate my book, I realized that it would be better to prepare a new edition, which would include a considerable amount of additions and corrections to reflect books and studies published in the past five years that have enriched our knowledge about the history of the medieval Balkans, some of them even changing old conceptions on ethnic identities and ethnogenesis.

I express my gratitude to those who supported the research work and publishing of this book: General (r) Mihail E. Ionescu and Colonel (r) Petre Otu and Dr. Sergiu Iosipescu from the Institute for Political Studies of Defense and Military History (Bucharest, Romania), where I work as a researcher; the Fulbright Commission Romania (especially former directors Ernest H. Latham, Archbishop Chrysostomos, and Ioana Ieronim); professor Timothy E. Grcgory (Ohio State University, Department of History); and Dr. Predrag Matejić (Ohio State University, Hilandar Research Library). My old friend and colleague Florin Curta (University of Florida, Gainesville) helped me not only with various publications, but also with some vital ideas and remarks. Paul Stephenson (University of Wisconsin,

Madison) introduced me to the amazingly rich library of the Dumbarton Oaks Center for Byzantine Studies in Washington, D.C., during my visit in the United States. Anton Cuşa from Paris provided me with copies of studies not existing in Romania. In Romania, I used the collections of the libraries of the Romanian Academy, the University of Bucharest, the Institute of History "Nicolae Iorga," the Institute of Archaeology "Vasile Pârvan," and the Institute for Southeast European Studies. Finally, I would like to thank Martin Gordon, who suggested I revise the book for Scarecrow Press, and Ms. April Snider, who assisted me in the editing process.

Introduction

In 1914 in Paris, the great Romanian historian Nicolae Iorga (1871–1940) published a book entitled *Notes of a Historian Concerning the Balkan Events*[1] (that is, the two Balkan wars of 1912 and 1913). Most of these pages remain illustrative of Iorga's ideas as historian and statesman. They do not concern, as one could think, the immediate causes of the Balkan wars. The book includes several studies that emphasize some features of the Byzantine period in the Balkans considered by Iorga to be useful for understanding the present. Iorga's present was not too different from ours, if we are thinking of the various real and potential conflicts that endanger Southeast European security. The work was written when it seemed that peace was installed, after the Treaty of Bucharest (August 10, 1913), when Romania had arbitrated the resolution of the Balkan Wars. Iorga explained the deep reasons for the conflicts, giving a historical background for the peace solutions. However, the adversities rose again the next year and are still alive in other forms. For this reason, I start this book with an extensive passage from Iorga's preface.

[The Bucharest Peace Conference] had to deal during the negotiations with all the problems that had risen from the last changes. Namely, it dealt with the Bulgarian and Serbian tradition that tends toward Constantinople, with the Serbian need to reach the Adriatic Sea, with the trend of the Montenegrins to create a larger state together with the Slavs and Albanians, with the aspirations of the Albanians, who wish a national state, with the desire of the Romanians from Pindus to preserve their ethnic identity, with the Greek dream of an entirely revived Byzantium. Next, on the other sides of the Danube and of the Adriatic Sea, with the Italian nostalgia for the colonization of the Balkan seashore, with the will of Austria to preserve its supremacy in the Balkans as well in the Carpathians, with the hope of the Russians that they will remain the protectors of their smaller Slavic brothers, and, finally, with the presence of Romania in Dobrudja and of the Romanian population on the right bank of the Danube. The spectator could be impressed by the anonymous noise of the popular demonstrations, by the fervent yells of the fanatic patriots, by the speculations of the sensational newspapers. He will be instead satisfied by the study of history, which shows that similar facts already happened and that they were resolved in a way that would guarantee that they arise again [that is, after the treaty of 1913].[2]

Indeed, facts from the recent past have close analogies in the remote history of the same region. What seems to be at first glance only the result of a transitory situation is in fact the consequence of a long historical evolution. The acknowledgment of the lessons provided by the study of the Balkan remote past could contribute to the anticipation and prevention of future conflict situations. An American strategist wrote in a documentary study prepared during the Yugoslavian crisis for the use of the U.S. Army that

Without a thorough understanding of the past political development of the region, policymakers may neither comprehend the complications of the present nor identify a successful path to the future [and that] the ongoing wars in the former Yugoslavia stem from multiple causes: fervent nationalism that springs from artificially heightened ethnic identity (religion, language, and an ethnic group's shared history, myths, and culture), economic disparities, regional differences, urban versus rural cultures, and preferred governmental structures, to name only the most prominent. Thus, solutions to the wars in the former Yugoslavia must address not simply one issue, but a large number of complex, interactive problems that exponentially increase the difficulties inherent in achieving a settlement. As a result, policymakers and interlocutors must be aware of the potential for short-term negotiating expedients to jeopardize long-term solutions to the conflict.[3]

Undeniably, the military conflicts of the Balkan states and the states that composed the former Yugoslavia were determined by the survival of nineteenth-century nationalism in the ideology of these nations, because "only since the late nineteenth and the beginning of the twentieth century have those conflicts acquired a distinct ethnic, national, and religious character."[4] The outstanding work of Noel Malcolm[5] demonstrates how the ethnic hate between the Albanians and Serbs and their fight for Kosovo was strongly influenced by of Western European ideology and politics in the age when modern nations emerged. However, this Balkan nationalism has searched and still searches for legitimation in medieval history, real or imaginary, and therefore we must examine that medieval history in order to understand why, for instance, Kosovo is a disputed area between Serbs and Albanians, or why Greece does not agree with the official name "Macedonia" for the present state that has its capital at Skopje. That is the purpose of this book.

The geographical term *Balkan Peninsula* was first coined by German geographer Adolph Zeune in 1808.[6] This expression is not very clear, since it refers to a relief element that covers only a small part of the peninsula: a mountain range of secondary importance in comparison with Rhodope, Pindus, or the Dinaric Alps.[7] The name *Balkan*, of Turkish origin ("wooded mountain"), replaced the Greek name *Haemus* in the sixteenth century. The first source that uses the new name is a report of an Italian diplomat from 1490.[8] The most suitable geographical name for the region is "Southeastern Europe," first used by another German geographer, Theobald Fischer, in 1893.[9] This term is more comprehensive, since it includes Romania.[10] However, this book will use the name "the Balkan Peninsula," due to the extrageographical significance acquired by this expression, and because all the conflict areas we will examine are located south of the Danube.

Being a book of history and geopolitics, this work concerns the political meaning of *Balkanism*, which could be defined in this respect as *a permanent state of cold or warm conflict between neighbor countries for territories with mixed populations*. It has been observed that the term *Southeastern Europe* is used in political context in association with ideas of stability and with European values, while the word *Balkans* is used when referring to conflicts.[11] In the 1950s, another scholar stated that Greece does not belong to the Balkan space, but to the Mediterranean area, because it is a bridgehead of the West in Eastern Europe.[12] The author of this affirmation, Robert Lee Wolff, was a great American medievalist who in 1956 published a synthetical history of Southeastern Europe, focused on contemporary events. During World War II, he was the chief of the Office of Strategic Services (OSS) research section for the Balkans. His opinion about the contents of the Balkan space (Romania, Bulgaria, Yugoslavia, Albania, but not Greece and Turkey) is obviously politically biased (it reflects the division between North Atlantic Treaty Organization (NATO) members and Communist countries), but it is also significant for the way that Balkanism is still perceived in certain circumstances. Namely, Balkanism is sometimes considered to be incompatible with Western values.[13] In fact, Wolff was wrong from both geographical and historical points of view.

The Balkan space can be defined by two criteria. The first, geographical, is based on the relief map and water streams. The second, cultural, takes into account the historical evolution of each territory of this space.

Some historians and geographers believe that the Balkan Peninsula includes a North Danubian area that encompasses Walachia, Moldavia, and even Transylvania and Hungary.[14] However, it seems that the best grounded opinion belongs to a famous expert in the physical and human geography of the Balkan Peninsula, Serbian Jovan Cvijić. He affirmed that the northern boundary of the peninsula is located on the Danube and on the Sava; in the northwest, the peninsula is limited by the Soča (Isonzo) River.[15] Another Serbian scholar, Traian Stoianovich, has published after half a century a basic work about the Balkans. A disciple of Fernand Braudel, Stoianovich gives a comprehensive view of the Balkan world, which takes into account economic history, history of culture, cultural and physical anthropology, and historical geography. Stoianovich agrees with the northern limit on the Sava and the Danube, but with the correction that this line was surpassed by some Balkan civilizations that penetrated the steppe regions and the Carpathian area. Because of this, he includes Romania in the Balkan space.[16] Nevertheless, it is clear that the Balkan Peninsula is a bridge between Europe and Asia, between West and East, with all the good and all the evil that result from this ambiguous position.

In my view, the present states that belong to the Balkan space are (in alphabetical order): Albania, Bosnia, Bulgaria, Croatia, the Former Yugoslavian Republic of Macedonia (FYROM), Greece, Montenegro, Serbia, and Turkey (the European part). Slovenia is not included in the Balkan Peninsula, if we apply the definition given by Cvijić, because only a third of its territory is located south of that limit. Slovenia is excluded from the Balkan area, especially from the cultural point of view, because it belongs to the Central European space of German civilization. The Slovenians were from the very beginning a part of the Western world. They were converted to Christianity between the seventh to the ninth century by missions organized by bishops from Aquilea and Bavaria. Previously mastered by the Avars, today's Slovenia and Carinthia were conquered by the Franks in 788 and came under the jurisdiction of the Archbishopric of Salzburg.[17] Slovenia remained in the Germanic space for a millennium, until it was included in the Yugoslavian federacy (1920–1991).

Romania does and does not belong to the Balkan Peninsula. Strictly geographically, the area north of the Danube is out of the Balkan Peninsula. Only Dobrudja is a prolongation of the Balkan space, a kind of isthmus that links this peninsula with the region north of the Black Sea. If we take into account the ethnic, historical, and geopolitical situation, then Dobrudja could be defined as a part of the Romanian space, attached to the North Danubian territory. From the cultural, historical and geopolitical points of view, *Romania is a space of transition and convergence between three areas: Southeastern Europe, Central Europe, and Eastern Europe.* Romania is fully integrated in none of these areas, but shares with each of them one or another feature of its history, civilization, and economy. The modernization of Romania and its unification with the provinces previously included in Austro-Hungary (1918) accented the Western orientation, while the Communist regime led to a reverse phenomenon.[18] The intermediary position of the Romanian society and civilization between southeast, east, and center contradicts all those reductionistic conceptions that include Romania only in the Balkans, or only in Central Europe, or only in Eastern Europe, without taking into consideration the necessary hues.

There are many geographical and historical works that present Romania as a part of the Balkan space. Moreover, they make a clear distinction between the Old Romania (the frontiers before 1918) and Transylvania, Banat, and Crişana, included in Central Europe. To the same view belongs the concept of the "Carpathian Basin," which separates Transylvania from Walachia and Moldavia, linking it to the Pannonian Plain rather than to the rest of Romania. This concept does not take into account the unitary shape of Romania given by the centrifugal flowing of rivers from Transylvania and by the existence of many gorges that link this region with the areas south and east of Carpathians.[19] Romania also differs from the Balkan space in its ethnic configuration. It is true that Romania has many national minorities, but not one of its provinces has an ethnic mosaic like the Balkan Peninsula. This does not concern the number of minorities, but the way they are settled within the territory. "The Balkan Peninsula displays an ethnic composition that has no analogy in Europe and even in the rest of the world": Victor Papacostea argues this assertion by the interpenetration of all the populations in the peninsula, in each of its regions. The climax of this interpenetration is reached in Albania and Macedonia, where "Slavic, Greek, Vlach, Albanian and Turkish villages are interlaced."[20]

It has been observed that this interpenetration, which has existed since antiquity, makes the establishment of clear interethnic limits impossible:

> The successive superpositions of peoples along the centuries and the continuous interpenetration from a part to another [explains why] the central part of the Balkan Peninsula was and continues to be a place of turmoil and endless conflicts, [resulting] from the mixture of various ethnic elements, with different features and with even different trends, that are giving to this area the shape of a mosaic of peoples: Vlachs, Bulgarians, Greeks, Serbs, Albanians, Turks etc.[21]

The ethnic mosaic is the deepest cause of the endemic state of conflict in the Balkan Peninsula. It is therefore necessary to clarify the circumstances that led to such an unique ethnic configuration.

The ethnic configuration of the Balkan Peninsula is the result of the interaction of several geographical and historical factors. Although the role of geographical factors in historical processes should not be overestimated, understanding of geographical determinations is necessary for any historical inquiry into the medieval Balkans. As Jovan Cvijić has affirmed, the most important feature of the Balkan Peninsula is the fragmentation of this space into many small regions, which are in fact depressions set between mountain ranges. Communication between these depressions was quite difficult before modern times because of the dense forests that covered the mountains. The most inaccessible and isolated areas are the Rhodope, Pindus, and the Dinaric chains.

Circulation across the peninsula was instead facilitated by the existence of long longitudinal and transversal depressions. The most important is the corridor shaped by the Morava and Vardar valleys, which played a noteworthy economic and military role during the centuries. This road connected Belgrade with Thessaloniki and Constantinople (by the Maritza River). The main transversal way is Via Egnatia, the Roman road that crossed the peninsula from west to east, from Dyrrachion (Durrës) to Thessaloniki.[22] Interaction between the fragmented populations in many depressions and the existence of these roads resulted not only in isolation and separation trends, but also unification and penetration trends.[23] Mastership over these two great roads was a goal for all conquerors. The cities Constantinople and Thessaloniki connected these roads with the sea, essential for mastery of the entire Balkan Peninsula.[24]

Romanian geographer Vintilă Mihăilescu[25] has remarked that the Balkan Peninsula could be divided into three regions: western, central, and eastern. "Central Balkania" is the region where the highest mountain ranges of the peninsula (Pirin, Crna Gora, Šar Planina, Olympus) are concentrated, separated by many depressions communication among which is made by passages and gorges (Ochrid, Prespa, Tetovo, Skopje, Metohia, Kosovo, Niš, Leskovac, Pirot, etc.). "Central Balkania" is divided by the corridor shaped by the Morava and Vardar valleys. The highlands, peopled by pastoralists, alternate with agricultural depressions. The two kinds of human communities are complementary in that region. Two of the three conflict areas studied in this book (Kosovo and Macedonia) are located in "Central Balkania."Geographers agree that the fragmentation of the Balkan landscape favors ethnic diversity, regional particularism, and conflicts.[26] An American historian hypothesized that the mountain relief of the peninsula led to the isolation of communities, hindering the establishment of larger states, and gave suitable places for refuge, brigandage, and nomadic pastoralism.[27] The extreme heterogeneity of the anthropological features of the Balkan population since the Neolithic Age is another remarkable fact.[28]

The historical factors that caused the Balkan ethnic mosaic are:

- invasions by and next settlement of populations that came from the north (Slavs, Protobulgarians) and east (Turks);
- colonizations made by the three empires that mastered the peninsula (Roman, Byzantine, Ottoman);
- flight of several communities in times of crisis (wars, epidemics, starvation).

Significant population movements took place in the Balkan Peninsula during the Middle Ages. The outcome was an ethnic diversity without analogies in Europe. There is no zone with a true autochthonous population. Not even in Greece, because the present Greeks have among their ancestors Slavs, Albanians, and Vlachs, assimilated after the ninth century. A specific Balkan feature is the preservation of the ethnic identity of all these peoples, although some parts of them were absorbed by others.[29]

The geographical conditions of the central and western Balkans were always propitious for nomadic mountain pastoralism. This way of life is attested to since classical antiquity in regions like Epirus, Dardania, and Thrace. The settlement of the Slavs in agricultural lands compelled some sedentary communities to become nomadic, such as the Latin-speaking population from which descended the Vlachs (Aromanians); the Albanians; and also some Greek communities (the Sarakatsanoi). Later, the huge demand for sheep meat during the Ottoman domination was a stimulus for the pastoral economy in the Balkans. The transhumant and nomadic pastoralists enjoyed special advantages on the Ottoman estates.[30]

Mountain nomadism differs in an essential way from the usual nomadism of the steppe peoples. The former kind of nomadism is a permanent feature of Balkan history, because it is a consequence of geographical and economic conditions, and not of ethnic origins.[31] The testimony brought by Arrianus (*Anabasis*, VII. 9. 2), who described the ancient Macedonians who lived before King Philip II (359–336 BCE) as shepherds who wandered between mountains and valleys, just like the Aromanians and the Albanians in medieval and modern times, is often quoted. The same way of life is attributed to the Thracian tribes Bessi and Dardani during the Roman period.[32] This mountain nomadism was not transhumance pastoralism, because the latter meant the permanent settlement of families in the lowland villages. Mountain nomadism is well-known in other parts of the Mediterranean world besides the Balkans (Spain, Italy).[33] Among the Aromanians, this way of life was practiced until the twentieth century by the Farserots from Albania, Pindus, and Thessaly. The communities, called *fălcări*, wandered over long distances with their entire population and belongings. The tents were installed in the mountains during the summer, and when winter came they descended with the flocks to the lowlands.[34] Mountain nomadism was responsible for many demographic and ethnic changes along the centuries. These changes led further to the heterogeneity of the Balkan world.

Jovan Cvijić has introduced a basic concept for understanding the Balkans: the so-called metanastic movements, which concerned the sedentary communities, expelled from their homeland by certain economic, political, or military reasons. The medieval metanastic movements were mostly the consequence of the Ottoman expansion that disturbed the eastern and central Balkan space and led, for instance, to the migration of the Serbs to the north. Other communities took refuge in the highlands. The dry and harvest periods provoked the displacement of many communities toward more fertile areas, especially toward the Danube valley. Transhumance pastoralism also has an important role in the metanastic movements of the Vlachs and Albanians. The final result of these multiple population movements was the ethnic mosaic that defines the Balkan Peninsula.[35]

The first part of this work examines the historical evolutions that led to the genesis of several conflict areas in the Balkans. The second part studies how history was used in political propaganda and the nationalist ideologies of the Balkan states in order to support territorial claims, ethnic cleansing actions, and conflicts with other countries.

The author of one of the best studies written about the Romanian-Bulgarian state founded by the Asan brothers in 1186, American historian R. L. Wolff, said that

> in the Balkans medieval data accumulated by scholars are often regarded as providing strong arguments for the settlement of present-day controversies. For this reason the contributions of the Bulgarian and Romanian historians must be used with great care, and the sources themselves examined afresh.[36]

For this reason, the contributions of Balkan historians need to be considered with great care when they concern sensitive aspects of the history of their countries. Even if some of our conclusions would be awkward, the truth must be expressed, because only so will the errors of the past be acknowledged by decision makers. Unfortunately, in most cases they do not follow the lessons of history.

The Balkan Peninsula as a whole is not a conflict area. What makes it the "gunpowder keg of Europe" is the existence of several inner conflict areas. American geographer Huey Louis Kostanick defined in a very important study a series of "problem areas" within the Balkan space (in his view, this space included Romania and Bessarabia).[37] These "problem areas" were those able to raise territorial clashes with neighboring states, such as Istria, Voivodina, southern Dobrudja, the Popular Republic of Macedonia, or southern Albania. Kostanick had in mind only the areas where the interests of at least two states clashed (the tensions between Yugoslavia, Greece, Bulgaria, and Albania). He did not study the conflicting potentiality of internal regions like Bosnia, because the political situation of his time (the beginning of the 1960s) made any prediction that the Yugoslavian federation would shatter sometime in the future unthinkable. Kostanick believed that the delimitation of frontiers was very difficult in the most mixed regions, and that this fact could bring irredentism and conflicts. The solution he proposed was change of populations between the disputed areas.

The "problem areas" defined by the American geographer are not the same as the areas dealt with in the present book. Some of them provoked only temporary tensions and conflicts (Istria, southern Dobrudja, that rose from the need of neighbor states to reach strategic frontiers or to control points and zones with high economic or strategic value. The real conflict areas are those where ethnic, political, and religious conditions developed along several centuries, explaining the warm or cold conflicts. If, for instance, we look over one of those "problem areas," Dobrudja, we can remark that the tensions between Romania and Bulgaria have no such background. History has shown that Dobrudja, although it has more national minorities than Macedonia, was not an area of interethnic conflicts. The incidents provoked in the interwar period by the so-called Bulgarian *comitagii* (terrorist groups) were incited by Bulgaria, whose irredentist policy after 1920 aimed to recover at least the southern part of Dobrudja, recognized as belonging to Romania by the Treaty of Neuilly (November 27, 1919). The secession of Dobrudja was also supported by the Comintern until 1940, when Bulgaria obtained the southern part of the province in the favorable conditions created by the Soviet–German Pact of August 23, 1939 (by the Treaty of Craiova, September 7, 1940). Therefore, the dispute for Dobrudja was only a matter of international relations, and was not based on domestic interethnic conflicts. There is no reason to include Dobrudja in the list of Balkan conflict areas. In this case, the only regions that we can consider without any doubt as real conflict areas are *Bosnia, Kosovo, and Macedonia*.[38] All of them illustrate the same potential for internal conflict based on historical conditions and on historical arguments invoked by belligerents in support of their territorial claims.

The causes of the present conflicts in the Balkans are deep rooted in history, but it would be an exaggeration to search for them in Greek or Roman antiquity. The real origins of the present ethnic, political, and religious situations can be found in the Middle Ages, when the states emerged from which the states involved in the modern and present conflicts descend or claim to descend from. However, a short overview of the more ancient background is nevertheless necessary.

In classical antiquity, Southeastern Europe was peopled by three large ethnic groups: Greeks, Thracians, and Illyrians. None of them was able to establish states including all their tribes (or cities, in the case of the Greeks). The Greek cities and the Thracian and Illyrian tribes were virtually common peoples, with a common language, but they were never united under a single political organization. The so-called unified and centralized state of the king Burebista, which included northern Thracians (Getae, Dacians), Celts, and some Greek cities from the Black Sea shore, existed only during the life of its creator. On the contrary, what is specific about the ancient history of the Balkan populations (including the Greeks) is the discord. Herodotus (*Histories*, V. 3) wrote that the Thracians are

> the most powerful people in the world, except, of course, the Indians; and if they had one head, or were agreed among themselves, it is my belief that their match could not be found anywhere, and that they would very far surpass all other nations. But such union is impossible for them, and there are no means of ever bringing it about. Herein therefore consists their weakness.

In fact, this discord was a general feature of Balkan ethnies and it could be also observed in the Greek world. The divergent orientation toward sea and not toward the inner land of the Greek city-states, as in medieval Italy, explains this lack of cohesion.[39] On the other hand, the forms of organization of the Illyrian and Thracian tribes were determined by a geographic framework, namely the depressions and small plains divided by many mountain ranges, which caused a similar divergent orientation.

The entire pre-Roman history of the Balkan Peninsula displays the existence of a great number of small power centers that only in few and ephemeral cases were able to unify larger spaces. Even the empire of Alexander the Great, born in the central Balkans, was shattered after the death of its founder, being replaced with a Macedonian kingdom and with several Thracian states, among which the Odrysian was the most important. The Greek world returned to the same policentrism of the period before the Macedonian conquest. The first true unification of the Balkan Peninsula was realized by an external power, Rome. The Roman expansion was favored by the decline of the Hellenistic kingdoms that inherited the empire of Alexander the Great. The Romans first occupied territory on the Dalmatian shore in 219 BCE. Epirus and Macedonia were conquered after the battle of Pydna, when the Macedonian king Perseus was defeated (168 BCE). Macedonia was organized as a province in 148 BCE (the capital city was Thessaloniki). The same province included Epirus and Greece. Mastership over Macedonia assured a valuable base for future Roman expansion toward the northern and eastern parts of the Balkan Peninsula. (The same function was fulfilled by Macedonia during the Byzantine reconquista and during the Ottoman expansion.) The kingdom of the Thracian Odrysi, located in the east of present-day Bulgaria, resisted for a longer time, becoming a client state. Next, the Roman domination extended in several stages up to the Middle Danube. This process occurred in the first years of the Christian era, during the reign of Augustus (27 BCE–14 CE), when the province of Dalmatia was organized. In the last phase of the Roman conquests the Lower Danube was reached, the natural limit of the empire, after the inclusion of the Odrysian kingdom in the provinces of Moesia and Thrace, in 46 CE. In this way the integration of the Balkan Peninsula into the Roman Empire was accomplished.[40]

The Roman conquest led to a partial homogenization of the Balkan space, through Romanization. It was partial, because Romanization of the Greeks was impossible, since they were the creators of that superior civilization that was the model followed by the Romans themselves. Those regions from the Balkan Peninsula where Romanization succeeded were the ethnogenetic area of the Romance peoples (the Romanians and the disappeared Dalmatians). But these regions (located mainly north of a line established by linguists Constantin Jireček, Alexandru Philippide, and Haralambie Mihăescu on the basis of the spreading of Latin inscriptions versus Greek inscriptions) included only a part of the Balkan Peninsula, namely the former early Roman provinces Dalmatia, Moesia Superior, and Moesia Inferior. South of this line Romanization was successful only along Via Egnatia. The existence of this enclave of Romanization in Macedonia is highlighted in the research of Emanuelle Banfi, Haralambie Mihăescu, and Cicerone Poghirc.[41] Its importance will be emphasized in the discussion of the origin of the Vlachs or Aromanians, the southern branch of the Romanian people.

In the Balkan Peninsula, the Middle Ages started with a return to heterogeneity, caused by the conversion to mountain nomadism and by the occasional movements of the different communities. The plains were for the most part occupied by the Slavic newcomers. In the ninth and tenth centuries the return to the lowlands of some communities previously converted to nomadism began. At the same time, Byzantine offensives led to a new Hellenization of the territories previously occupied by the Slavs. *This new ethnic diversity and the trend toward the emergence of many power centers are the ethnic premises of the endemic state of conflict in the Balkans, which can be observed along the entire Middle Ages, and which was the ultimate background of the modern interethnic conflicts.*

NOTES

1. N. Iorga, Notes d'un historien relatives aux événements des Balcans, re-published in N. Iorga, *Études Byzantines*, I, Bucarest, 1939, 1–48.

2. Iorga 1939, 1.

3. W. T. Johnsen, *Deciphering the Balkan Enigma: Using History to Inform Policy*, Strategic Studies Institute of the US War College, November 1995, 43, 64 (www.dtic.mil/doctrine/jel/research_pubs/enigma.pdf).

4. S. Pavlović, "Understanding Balkan Nationalism: The Wrong People, in the Wrong Place, at the Wrong Time," *Southeast European Politics* (Central European University, Budapest), 1, 2 (2000), 119 (www.seep.ceu.hu).

5. Malcolm 1998, XXIX–XXX.

6. M. Todorova, *Imagining the Balkans*, Oxford, 1997, 25; G. Mintsis, The Balkans: A Term Bearing a Heavy Politico-Historical Load, AIESEEB, 30 (2000), 137.

7. J. Cvijić, *La Péninsule Balkanique. Géographie humaine*, Paris, 1918, 2–3. See also V. Papacostea, La Péninsule Balkanique et le problème des études compares, *Balcania, 6*, III–XXI (1943), III–IV.

8. Todorova 1997, 26.

9. Todorova 1997, 28; Mintsis 2000, 141.

10. C. C. Giurescu, "România, stat al ariei balcanice?," in Idem, *Probleme contro-versate în istoriografia română* (pp. 76–79), Bucureşti, 1977. As an unitary space that includes Romania, the expression "Southeastern Europe" was frequently used by Nicolae Iorga. See A. Pippidi, Changes of Emphasis, Greek Christendom, West-ernization, South-Eastern Europe, and Neo-Mittel Europa, *Balkanologie, 3,* 2 (1999), 103–104.

11. A. Drace-Francis, "The Prehistory of a Neologism, 'South-Eastern Europe,'" *Balkanologie* (Paris), 3 2 (1999), 127. The author has shown that the word was first introduced in historical and linguistic studies by Slovenian philologist B. Kopitar (1813). See also Mintsis 2000, 141: the "negative historical burden, which was al-ways born by the name Balkans, provoked many historians and political scientists who tried its replacement by a new, and without any 'bad' burden name, i.e. the pure geographical and neutral term South-East Europe."

12. R. L. Wolff, *The Balkans in our Time*, Cambridge, MA, 1956, 8.

13. See the remarkable work of Todorova 1997.

14. For instance: L. S. Stavrianos, *The Balkans since 1453*, New York, 1959, 2; F. W. Carter, "Introduction to the Balkan Scene," *Carter 1977*, 1–24. See other view-points quoted by Todorova 1997, 29–30 and Mintsis 2000, 138–139.

15. Cvijić 1918, 6–7.

16. T. Stoianovich, *A Study in Balkan Civilization*, New York, 1967, 3–4.

17. For the Christianization of the Slovenians and for their first polities, see M. Kos, "L'Etat slovène en Carantanie," *Europe 1968*, 123–132; S. Vilfan, "La cris-tianizzazione delle campagne presso gli Slavi del sud occidentali: organizzazione, resistenze, fondo sociale," in *Cristianizzazione ed organizzazione ecclesiastica delle campagne nell'alto medioevo: Espansione e resistenze (Settimane*, 28, 1980), Spoleto, 1982, II, 889–918; S. Vilfan, Evoluzione statale degli Sloveni e Croati. *Gli Slavi*, 106, 126–136.

18. Pippidi 1999, 106.

19. See the basic work of S. Mehedinți, *Qu'est-ce que la Transylvanie?*, Bucarest, 1943.

20. Papacostea 1943, VII.

21. I. I. Russu, Granița etnică între traci și illiri. Cercetări epigrafice și onomastice. *Anuarul Institutului de Studii Clasice* (Cluj-Sibiu), IV (1944), 73.

22. See the analysis of the strategic value of Via Egnatia and of other roads from the southwestern Balkan Peninsula in N. G. L. Hammond, *Migrations and Invasions in Greece and Adjacent Areas*, Park Ridge, NJ, 1976, 21–33. For the Middle Ages, see especially N. Oikonomides, The Medieval Via Egnatia, in E. Zachariadou (ed.), *The Egnatia under Ottoman Rule (1380–1699). Halcyon Days in Crete II: A Symposium Held in Rethymnon (9–11 January 1994).* Rethymnon (Idem, *Social and Economic Life in Byzantium*, Variorum, Ashgate, 2004, XXIII), 1996, 9–16 and K. Belke, "Roads and Travel in Macedonia and Thrace in the Middle and Late Byzantine Period," in R. Macrides (ed.), *Travel in the Byzantine World. Papers from the Thirty-Fourth Spring Symposium of Byzantine Studies, Birmingham, April 2000*, Aldershot, 2002, 73–90.

23. Cvijić 1918, 17–35.

24. Stavrianos 1959, 5–6.

25. V. Mihăilescu, "La 'Balcania' centrale," *Balcania*, 6, 1943, 1–13.

26. H. Kostanick, The Geopolitics of the Balkans, *Balkans 1963*, 3–5; G. W. Hoffman, The Evolution of the Ethnographic map of Yugoslavia, *Carter 1977*, 437, 439.

27. J. V. A. Fine Jr., *The Early Medieval Balkans. A Critical Survey from the Sixth to the Late Twelfth Century*, Ann Arbor, MI, 1991, 1–2.

28. Stoianovich 1967, 120–21.

29. Stavrianos 1959, 12–13.

30. D. Antonijević, Cattlebreeders' Migrations in the Balkans through Centuries, *Migrations 1989*, 153–155.

31. M. Gyóni, La transhumance des Valaques balcaniques au Moyen Âge, ByzSl, 12 (1951), 40–42; J. Matl, "Hirtentum und Stammesverfassung als Kulturfaktor," *Völker 1959*, 108–110; W. C. Brice, "Nomadism in Thrace—Its Nature and Origins," Thracia (Sofia), 2 (1974), 99–101; Antonijević 1989, 147–156; A. Madgearu, *Continuitate și discontinuitate culturală la Dunărea de Jos în secolele VII–VIII*, București, 1997, 135–137.

32. By Strabo (VII. 316, 318, 331) in the first century BCE and by St. Paulin of Nole (fifth century CE). See Gyóni 1951, 40–41; Antonijević 1989, 150.

33. F. Braudel, *La Méditerranée et le monde méditerranéen a l'époque de Philippe II*, Paris, 1966, I, 76–85; P. Garnsey, *Mountain Economies in Southern Europe. Thoughts on the Early History, Continuity and Individuality of Mediterranean Upland Pastoralism*, in C. R. Whittacker (ed.), *Pastoral Economies in Classical Antiquity* (The Cambridge Philological Society, Supplementary Volume nr. 14), Cambridge, 1988, 196–209.

34. Th. Capidan, Românii nomazi. Studiu din viața românilor din sudul Peninsulei Balcanice, *Dacoromania* (Cluj), 4, 2 (1927), 183–352.

35. Cvijić 1918, 112–52.

36. R. L. Wolff, The "Second Bulgarian Empire." Its Origin and History to 1204, *Speculum*, 24 (1949), 175.

37. Kostanick 1963, 1–55. His PhD dissertation, written in 1947, was entitled "Macedonia—A Study in Political Geography."

38. By Macedonia we do not mean here the present state called "The Former Yugoslavian Republic of Macedonia," but the historical Macedonia, which is now divided between Greece, FYROM, and Bulgaria.

39. C. Carras, Greek Identity: A Long View, *Balkan Identities* (2004), 296.

40. N. G. L. Hammond, Illyrs, Rome and Macedon in 229–205 BC, *Journal of Roman Studies*, 5, 1–2 (1968), 1–21; R. Syme, *Danubian Papers*, Bucharest, 1971, 13–25; Lazarou, 1986, 25–35.

41. E. Banfi, Aree latinizate nei Balcani e una terza area latino-balcanica (Area della Via Egnazia), *Rendiconti dell'Istituto Lombardo di Scienze e Lettere, Classe di lettere*, 106 (1972), 215–230; Poghirc 1989, 16–44; H. Mihăescu, *La romanité dans le Sud-Est de l'Europe*, București, 1993, 169–76.

Part I

THE PAST

Chapter 1

The Ethnic Aspects

In the Balkans, the Middle Ages began with the Avarian and Slavic invasions that step-by-step and inevitably ruined the Roman domination and civilization. The downfall of the Danubian frontier was quite a long process that lasted from circa 576 to circa 614.[1] The abandonment of most of the Balkan part of the empire by Heraklios (610–641) was the starting point of the events and processes studied in this book. The vanishing of the structures of the Late Roman state caused a power vacuum that favored the revival of the old pre-Roman policentrism, which this time was a Slavic one.

THE SLAVIZATION OF THE BALKAN PENINSULA

The time and significance of the Slavic colonization of the Balkans are protracted disputed matters. The extreme idea that the Slavs came from the northern Balkan Peninsula in the fifth century or in the first decades of the sixth century has no foundation. The single proof claimed in this respect—the supposed Slavic derivation of some place-names from Dacia Mediterranea (southern Serbia), Dardania (Kosovo), and Macedonia recorded by Procopius in 560 CE (Bourdopes, Bratzista, Doubrouliana, Triskíana, Trivo etc.)[2]—is not suitable, because it was shown that their Slavic origin is not sure.[3] This early date has obvious political significance,

17

since it would confer increased rights over Macedonia and Kosovo, regions which are considered by some historians and linguists as part of the Albanian ancient homeland (see chapter 2), to the Slavic population.

The supposition that some Slavic enclaves appeared around Naissus (Niš) and in Bosnia after the invasion of 550/551[4] was contradicted by the careful research of Serbian archaeologist Vladislav Popović.[5] The real date of the Slavic settlements and cremation graves from Bosnia (Dvorovi, Bosanska Rača, Biščepolje, Mušici, Batković, and Brestovik) is the seventh century.[6] For the sixth century, only the settlement of some small Slavic groups around the Iron Gates just after 585, when this sector of the *limes* was conquered by the Avars (the settlements from Korbovo, Dunav, Ljubičevac, Kula etc.), can be traced. However, the interpretation put forward by D. Janković,[7] that this group could be identified with the Serbs colonized by Heraklios as frontier guards, is not valid, since it is clear that the settlements were earlier than the alleged colonization of the Serbs (see p. 20). They belonged more probably to the Slavic soldiers from the Avarian army.

The traditional theory about the Slavic ethnogenesis, based on archaeological research and linguistic interpretations, maintained that the homeland of the proto-Slavic people was somewhere in Ukraine, near the northern Carpathians, or in the Dnieper and Pripyat basins, or perhaps in Galicia.[8] However, this theory was challenged by another one, expressed in the last two decades by several linguists. Russian scholar O. N. Trubačev held that Indo-European comparative linguistics proves the location of the primary Slavic homeland to be on the Middle and Lower Danube, where they returned in the sixth century.[9] Omeljan Pritsak, a remarkable Ukrainian specialist in Slavic and Türkic philology, has introduced the ideas that the Proto-Slavic language was the common idiom (*lingua franca*) used by all the subjects of the Avarian kaganate, and that the first meaning of the name Sclavini was a class of pedestrian and river boat frontier warriors.[10] By consequence, the Slavic homeland should be located within the Avarian territory, namely on the Middle Danube. This conclusion was shared by Johanna Nichols, who accepted that "the ultimate Slavic homeland" was "north of the Carpathians, stretching from southern Poland to the Ukraine," but added that "the ultimate epicenter of the Slavic spread" was the Danubian area mastered by the Avars. The Slavic expansion was merely a spreading of this language, and not a series of population movements.[11] This theory is the most plausible.

In his recent monograph on Slavic migrations and ethnogenesis, Florin Curta has developed the ideas previously expressed by Pritsak and Nichols. The traditional view of a large-scale and sudden migration from a primary homeland is replaced with a theory of short-distance movements of itinerant communities, which covered the Balkan Peninsula during the seventh and eighth centuries. The new Slavic ethnicity appeared through a process of group identification that occurred among the barbarian populations north of the Danube during the sixth century, in relation to the rise of a military elite. The emergence of Slavic political organization was the result of contacts with the Byzantine state.[12] Curta agrees that the Proto-Slavic language spoken by these warriors became a lingua franca in the Avarian kaganate. The spreading of this language over the areas dominated by the Avars was the other side of the Slavic expansion that occurred in the seventh–eighth centuries north and south of the Danube.[13] For the Balkan Peninsula, Curta has established a clear chronology of the Slavic and Avarian raids, including the much disputed siege of Thessaloniki (dated in 586). The migration of the Slavs south of the Danube can be dated since only 614, when a wave of Avarian and Slavic invasions destroyed many cities in the Balkan Peninsula. It is certain that the years 614–626 were the real gap between antiquity and the Middle Ages in Southeastern Europe.[14]

Some historians maintain that the Slavs began settling in Greece after the Avarian attack of 586, following information preserved in the so-called *Chronicle of Monemvasia* (a short text composed around 900 in Patras).[15] Archaeological excavations from Argos, Corinth, Isthmia, and other Greek sites revealed that these places were indeed attacked by barbarians in 581–586, but also that the town life survived.[16] In fact, the decline of cities from Greece, Macedonia, and other regions of the Balkan Peninsula was mainly a result of the general economic crisis of the late Roman Empire.[17] It would consequently be wrong to ascribe great importance to destruction caused by the Slavs and the Avars in the transition from urbanized ancient society to the more ruralized one of the seventh–ninth centuries. The cultural discontinuity that can be observed in the Danubian area as well as in continental Greece was the result of a combination of internal and external causes. The barbarian invasions were only a supplementary factor in the process. A Slavic dwelling spot appeared at Argos, just after the destruction of the city in 585.[18] The pottery found there is not from the sixth or seventh century, but from the eighth–ninth, perhaps even from the tenth century.[19] Similar shards were found nearby, at Tyrins.[20] It is otherwise true that a small seventh-century Slavic settlement was identified at Isthmia.[21] All Slavic pottery found in Peloponnesus is dated no earlier than the seventh century, while the cremation cemetery from Olympia, the single such site from Greece that could be ascribed to the Slavs,[22] is dated with certainty to the eighth century.[23]

In conclusion, archaeology shows that the Slavs did not settle in Greece before the seventh century, or more precisely, before 614. Slavic settlement in Greece was a protracted process that lasted until the middle of the

eighth century. According to information recorded by Constantine Porphyrogenitus, Peloponnesus was entirely Slavized during the plague of
745–747, but it was proven that this would mean the occupation of some
Greek territories by Slavs already settled in the peninsula. However, this
does not exclude the arrival of a new wave from the north.[24]

Moesia, the intensively Romanized region between the Danube and the
Balkan range, did not evolve into an ethnic mosaic like Macedonia, where
Slavs, Greeks, Vlachs, and Albanians are mingled everywhere. Very suitable for agriculture, Moesia was a great attraction for the Slavs, who expelled a large part of the native Latin-speaking population to the south
and north. Remnants of this population survived between Timok and
Morava and in the Balkan Mountains. The Thracian plain was another
agricultural area where the Slavs settled in great numbers.[25] The higher
regions were instead shelters for the natives, regardless of their ethnic origin, in the period of the Slavic advance in the Balkan Peninsula, and also
later, during the Ottoman conquests, when many Greeks took refuge in
the mountains, in Pindus, Epirus, and Acarnania.[26] We can thus understand why the landscape of Kosovo and Macedonia favored the extreme
ethnic mosaic: the high zones are interlaced with depressions settled by
the last comers.

Other refuges for the Greeks were the cities of the seashores and the islands, and also Sicily and southern Italy. In the western part of the Balkan
Peninsula, Slavic waves pushed the Romance population to the seashore,
where some towns resisted after the seventh century.[27] The complete Slavization of the inner parts of the former Illyricum (Croatia, Bosnia, and Serbia) began after the first two decades of the seventh century. The Romanians recorded by the medieval sources west of Morava valley were
not the offspring of a native Latin-speaking population. They arrived
there by immigrations started in the ninth century, in circumstances discussed below.

Following information recorded around the middle of the tenth century by Constantine Porphyrogenitus in *De Administrando Imperio*, c. 32,
the emperor Heraklios colonized the Serbs and the Croats in Illyricum,
in order to use them as allies against the Avars,[28] but a careful study has
shown that this tradition is wrong. Heraklios was in no way interested
in the recovery of the Balkan provinces, and he did not summon the
Serbs and the Croats. His attention was focused on the Persian war.[29] It
is otherwise true that both peoples gained freedom after the decline of
the Avarian kaganate that followed after the failed siege of Constantinople (626). In the 630s several inner rebellions against the Avarian
power occurred, which also led to the migration of these Slavic groups
from Pannonia to the present lands of central Serbia, Montenegro,
Bosnia, and Croatia.[30]

The population of the plains occupied by the Slavs was estimated on the basis of the supposed density for that period at about four hundred thousand to six hundred thousand people,[31] but it cannot be inferred how many Slavs and how many Romance peoples or Greeks there were. However, it is certain that the demographic and ethnic configuration of the low regions of the Balkan Peninsula has radically changed, because the Slavs settled in the agricultural lands. The few surviving cities were islands in a Slavic sea. This is the image displayed by sources like the *Miracula of St. Demetrios* and the *Chronicle of Monemvasia*. The newcomers filled the spaces that remained deserted after the invasions and epidemics that caused a significant decrease of the native Greek and Roman populations.[32] They spread all over the area between the Danube and Peloponnesus and between the Adriatic and the Black Seas, but they were not able to build large polities around the cities. The Slavic communities remained exclusively rural and their political organization did not surpass the low level of the so-called *Sclaviniae*, small territories ruled by competing chiefs. Such Slavic polities are attested to by the Byzantine sources in Macedonia, Moesia, and Greece from the seventh and eighth centuries, until they were absorbed or annihilated by the conquerors, Protobulgarians or Byzantines.[33]

In the former Moesia, the assimilation of the Proto-Bulgarians, a people of Türkic origin, and the development of the state created by them led to the genesis of the medieval Bulgarian people. The Bulgarian ethnic identity was further consolidated by Christianization and by the use of the Slavonic language in the Church. In the central and western Balkan Peninsula (the former Illyricum), Slavic tribes arriving from Pannonia were recorded in ninth- and tenth-century sources with different names like Slavoni, Croats, and Serbs. All these were regional names, as well as Moravljani, Zachlumi, and others. In Dioclea, the name of the Serbs was imposed by the Nemanja dynasty, which began the unification of the central Balkan Peninsula from its homeland located in Raška at the end of the twelfth century. If the state created in the eleventh century in Dioclea by the Vojslav family would have survived longer, it is possible that another regional name would come to cover a larger area. In the western part of the peninsula, the first unification of a Slavic people was achieved even earlier by the Croats, in the tenth century. Their regional name (first time recorded in 852) was later extended over a territory that is nearly the same with the present states of Croatia and Bosnia. The Croats inherited the name of a group of warriors from the Avarian kaganate, who gathered around them the subjected Slavs, like the Protobulgarians. In fact, several ethnogenetic processes took place in the western and central Balkan Peninsula in the early Middle Ages, in the areas where the *sclaviniae* evolved toward a more stable political organization. The Serbs and the

Croats were those ethnic groups that were able to build such states. Once these Slavic groups acquired distinct names that reflected the existence of a specific political organization, they evolved as different ethnicities. Other potential ethnies from the ex-Yugoslavian space vanished because they did not achieve this stage of evolution.[34] The increasing disparity between the Serbs and the Croats was the consequence of the divergent religious and cultural orientations, conditioned by the geographical and political circumstances that will be analyzed in the following chapters.

Different ethnogenesis does not mean different language. There are no significant linguistic disparities between Serbs and Croats (Slovenian is instead another language). The scientific name of their language is "Serbo-Croatian," an idiom with several dialects that cannot be regarded as different languages. The literary language was developed from the dialect called Stokavian, by Croatian and Serbian linguists. Still, nationalist Croatian scholars tried to argue that Croatian should be treated as a distinct language.[35] After 1990 a "Bosnian" language was also invented. This brings to mind the issue of the so-called "Moldavian language," invented by the Soviet authorities and academics in order to justify domination over Bessarabia. In fact, there is no significant difference between the Romanian language and the language spoken in the Republic of Moldova.

A researcher from the Institute for Balkan Studies in Belgrade[36] has distinguished four types of reasons for the conflict that led to the shattering of Great Yugoslavia: structural, ideological, political, and geopolitical. We are interested here only in the structural causes that express the divergent historical evolution of the Serbs and Croats. These structural causes are: economic and cultural disparities; religious differences and intolerance; nationalism; lack of a common democratic culture; and preservation of cultural relations with the centers of the former empires that mastered the Yugoslavian territories. The origins of separatism should be searched for in the Middle Ages.

The religious differences between Serbs and Croats were not so great and clear in the beginning. They emerged and evolved during medieval and modern history, and the result was a cultural cleavage that explains the endemic state of conflict between Serbs and Croats (and Bosnians). The Serbs became part of the Orthodox and Byzantine commonwealth, while the Croats remained Catholics and oriented toward Western Latin civilization. Between 1102 and 1918, Croatia survived as an autonomous polity within Hungary and later within the Habsburg Empire, while the Serbs became subjects of the Ottoman Empire after the disappearance of their state. This long political and cultural separation, which reflects the tensions between West and East, is the ultimate reason for the conflicts that have occurred in the ex-Yugoslavian space.

The territory that was Slavized in the seventh and eighth centuries was larger than the present Slavic Balkan states. Some regions were peopled again by the old inhabitants, or acquired a new ethnic configuration in the Middle Ages and in modern times. For instance, the lowlands of Albania were intensively Slavized. Most of the Slavic place-names from Albania are not Serbian, but Bulgarian. They appeared during the Bulgarian domination, in the ninth and tenth centuries. The ancestors of the Albanians lived in the highlands only until the twelfth century, afterward descending to the plains.[37] In Macedonia, the Greeks gained more and more field, pushing the Slavs to the higher places during the tenth–thirteenth centuries.[38]

The almost four thousand Slavic place-names analyzed by German linguist Max Vasmer (*Die Slaven in Griechenland*, Berlin, 1941) show that it was a time when the Slavs occupied all of Greece, especially western Thessaly, Epirus, Aetolia, Acarnania, and Peloponnesus. However, some of these place-names are in fact of Albanian or Aromanian origin.[39] Vasmer made an important contribution, but he followed a political agenda (see chapter 2). Byzantinist Johannes Koder concluded that the presence of a great amount of Slavic place-names in the highlands could be explained by a later retreat of the Slavs to these areas, after the return of the Greek population to the lowlands in the ninth century.[40] In 1978, Michael Weithmann published a thorough research of Slavic toponymy in Greece in a monograph,[41] which shows that large parts of present-day Greece were peopled by Slavs in the early Middle Ages. However, the great number of Slavic place-names in Greece does not reflect the situation from a certain time, because those from the mountains were given in a later period by the same communities that had dwelled in the lowlands.

The expansion of the new Slavic states caused other ethnic changes. The first was the strengthening of the Slavic population in Macedonia after the Bulgarian occupation of a part of this region in 842.[42] The most important Slavic expansion toward the south of the Balkan Peninsula occurred in the fourteenth century, when Macedonia was colonized by Serbs during the reign of Tzar Stephen Dušan (1331–1355). They did not overcome the natives, but in this way Macedonia became a Serbian land.[43] The process started with the granting of many estates, confiscated by Stephen Dušan from the Byzantine monasteries and landlords after the conquest of Macedonia in 1343–1348, to Serbian feudals. The Serbian colonization was also a result of the installation of several garrisons in the cities (at Serres, Vodena, Verria, Servia, etc.). It seems that these Serbs settled by the state in Macedonia numbered around five thousand by 1350,[44] but there are no data about those who arrived there by free migration. In Macedonia, the Serbs came to live together with the Greeks, Bulgarians, Albanians, and Aromanians. In the previous period, Macedonia was not a part of the

Serbian area. After the Ottoman conquest, the percentage of the Serbian population in Macedonia decreased dramatically.[45]

The Ottoman conquests led to a reverse movement, from Macedonia and Kosovo toward the north. The refugees arrived in northern Serbia and beyond the Danube, in Hungary. These demographic changes started just after the battle of Kosovopolje (1389). Among the waves of Serbian refugees in Hungary, the most important was that of 1459, when the Serbian state disappeared; it seems that around two hundred thousand people departed to Hungary. Even before, the number of Serbs who took refuge in southern Hungary was quite large. In 1433, the Serbs were already the largest part of the population in some places from southern Banat like Cuvin, Hram, and Bela Crkva. According to a source from 1437, most of the inhabitants of Srem (the land between Danube and Sava) were Serbs.[46]

The Ottoman domination also caused other population movements within Serbo-Croatian space. For instance, in the seventeenth century people from the mountain regions of Bosnia, Herzegovina, and Montenegro migrated to the Adriatic seashore, to areas controlled by Venice. In this way the Croatian population in Dalmatia was strengthened, finally replacing the Dalmatian Romance population in the cities. To these Venetian possessions also came Orthodox Serbs, who enhanced the ethnic and religious diversity of the Dalmatian lands.[47] Other Serbs, Croats, and southern Romanians took refuge in the Habsburg Empire in the sixteenth and seventeenth centuries. They entered military service on the frontier, in the northern parts of the present Croatia.[48]

The last large Slavic population movements occurred during the wars between the Ottoman and Habsburg Empires at the end of the seventeenth century. The retaliations of the Turks against the Serbs who supported the Austrian offensive of 1688–1689 led to the emigration of a large part of the local population from Kosovo and Serbia to southern Hungary, under the direction of the Serbian patriarch of Peć, Arsenije III Čarnojević (in 1690–1691). The number of refugees is unknown, but it could be estimated at some tens of thousands.[49]

In conclusion, the present ethnic configuration of the Balkan Peninsula was mainly determined by the settlement of Slavs in all parts of this area. The historical evolutions occurring along the Middle Ages and in modern times led to the contraction of the Slavic area, and the final result was *the increase of the ethnic mosaic*, in such a way that the different ethnies are interlaced in many zones. Albania, Kosovo, and especially Macedonia are examples of how *the same area was peopled by different ethnies, one after the other, which cannot claim absolute historical rights over the disputed regions because none of them was truly "the first."* This is the lesson of history, which should be acknowledged by present-day political and military decision makers when they try to resolve the territorial disputes.

THE EXPANSION OF THE ALBANIANS

The origin of the Albanians was and continues to be an intricate problem discussed by historians and linguists. Whatever the truth about the origin and homeland of the Albanians, it is certain that they were recorded for the first time in literary sources in the eleventh century. They had no political and military role before this period, and therefore no Byzantine historian has mentioned them. The fragment from the chronicle of Michael Attaliates that speaks about the participation of some Albanoi in the rebellion led by General Georgios Maniakes in 1042 was doubted by Hera Vranoussis, because the form *Albanoi* is different than the usual names mentioned by Byzantine authors in the eleventh and twelfth centuries (*Arbanitai, Arbanoi*). Even the same chronicler used the name *Arbanites* in another fragment. Because of this, it was supposed that those Albanoi from 1042 were Normans from Sicily, called by an archaic name (the Albanoi were an ancient tribe from southern Italy).[50] The following instance is indisputable. It comes from the same Attaliates, who wrote that the Albanians (Arbanitai) were involved in the 1078 rebellion of Nikephor Basilakes. After a few decades, Albanians and the region Arbanon were recorded in Anna Comnena's *Alexiada*.[51] The Albanian language was mentioned for the first time in 1285.[52]

Arbanon was a small region located in the mountain areas of central present-day Albania, in the northern part of the Shkumbin river valley.[53] This river was always a dividing line between northern and southern Albania, from linguistic and cultural points of view. The *Via Egnatia* was built along it. The two Albanian dialects (Geg and Tosk) are separated by this line. The geographical fragmentation determined by this river was considered one of the reasons why no unitary Albanian state could be established during the Middle Ages.[54]

At the end of the twelfth century, the Albanians were attested to as a compact group in the mountain zones around Shkoder Lake, in northern Albania (in the foundation deed for the Athonite monastery of Hilandar issued by the great župan of Serbia, Stephen Nemanja, in 1198–1199). According to several Serbian scholars, before the middle of the thirteenth century the Albanians lived between the northern bank of Shkoder Lake and the Devolli River, and migration toward the plains of Metohija began after the end of the twelfth century.[55]Albanians are attested to in Epirus in the same period (twelfth-thirteenth centuries), and it can be supposed that this area also belonged to their primary homeland, where they lived together with the Greeks.[56]

The Albanians preserved until modern times a tribal organization that had some analogies with that of the Aromanians (*fălcări*) and Serbs (*zadruga*). The population increase in the poor mountain regions caused migration of Albanian tribes to the lowlands. In the thirteenth century, they began to spread from the region between Shkumbin and Mati to the west, south, and east. A significant cause of the emigrations was the rise of a greedy local aristocracy that left many Albanians without land; in this way the number of nomadic Albanians and the area of their expansion increased.[57] Some Albanians were assimilated by the Serbs. Montenegrins have among their ancestors Slavized Albanians and Aromanians.[58] The presence of both populations is attested to in Serbian documents from 1222–1223, when King Stephen Părvovečani (1196–1227) issued a deed for the Žiča monastery.[59]

The Albanians wandered up to Thessaly, especially after 1318, when the Byzantine Empire occupied the Thessalian principality after the death of the *sebastokrator* John II Angelos. The first mention of the Albanians in this region comes from 1325 (inserted in a report of Venetian Marino Sanudo, who wrote that the Albanians had occupied a large part of the Thessalian Vlachia and attacked the cities). The expansion toward the south continued peacefully in the fourteenth and fifteenth centuries. The despots of Morea Manuel Cantacuzenus (1348–1380) and Theodore I Paleologos (1383–1407) settled large Albanian groups in Peloponnesus (during the reign of the latter around ten thousand people).[60] Thessaly, Peloponnesus, and other Greek regions, however, remained at the periphery of the spreading area of the Albanians. These colonists were almost entirely assimilated by the Greeks. During the fourteenth century, the Albanians spread especially in Kosovo and to a lesser extent in Macedonia, under the favorable circumstances of the expansion of Serbia during the reign of Stephen Dušan (they came with the Serbian troops in 1348).[61] The Albanian population of Epirus increased in the second half of the fourteenth century; they searched for new places for pastoralism in the area of Gjirokastër.[62]

Serbian historians tried to minimize the Albanian presence in Kosovo and Macedonia, but sources issued during the Serbian domination and next those from the Ottoman domination recorded the existence of Albanian communities in Kosovo (Albanian place-names and person names). It is difficult, however, to determine what the percentage of Albanians was at different moments of this period (fourteenth–seventeenth centuries).

In Kosovo and Macedonia, the expansion was brought about by the same economic reasons as those of other methanastic movements of Albanians. Albanians and names of Albanian origin have been recorded in Serbian and Ragusan deeds since the thirteenth century. The first document that lists an Albanian place-name in Kosovo was issued in 1253 by the Serbian *knez* Miroslav. Many people with typical Albanian names are mentioned in the chrysobull issued in 1330 by Serbian king Stephen Dečanski (1321–1331), which describes the estates owned by the monastery of Dečani in Kosovo, and in other similar documents granted in 1348 and 1355 for the monasteries of Prizren and Dobrušta.[63]

However, the decisive role in the increasing of Albanian penetration in Kosovo and Macedonia was played by the Ottoman domination, which favored the Albanians, who more easily accepted the Islamic religion (unlike the Serbs). Generally speaking, the Albanians were faithful to the Ottoman domination after the end of the resistance led by the national hero Skanderbeg. Sources published in the last decades show that the Muslim Albanian populations of Kosovo and Macedonia constantly increased from the fifteenth to the eighteenth century. This is especially reflected by fiscal registers (*defters*) preserved since 1455. They show that Kosovo (divided between the *sangeaks* of Vučitrn, Prizren, and Shkodra, established after 1459) was a mosaic of Albanian and Serbian villages, while cities like Prishtina and Prizren were inhabited especially by Muslim Albanians. Albanian expansion also had some particular catalysts in the fifteenth century: Albanians went to the north to work in the mines of Srbrenica and Novo Brdo in Kosovo. Another wave of Catholic Albanian colonists came to the mining area in the seventeenth century, to the towns of Prishtina and Gjakova. A report from 1638 from the Roman archbishop of Antivari Georgius Bardhi (of Albanian origin) said about Gjakova and Prizren that "these places are Albanian and have [an] Albanian speaking population."[64] In Macedonia, the same *defter* from 1455 records the presence of Albanians in the region of Tetovo.[65]

The permanent increasing of the Albanian population combined with significant emigrations of Serbs from Kosovo to the north after the wars of 1690 and 1738. Serbian historians usually state that Albanians became the major part of the population in Kosovo only after the Ottoman retaliations of 1690 when this region was wasted. Such ideas are expressed by authors like Jovan Trifunovski and Atanasije Urošević.[66] Another Serbian historian wrote that

> once the Serbs withdrew from Kosovo and Metohia, Islamized Albanian tribes from the northern highlands started settling the area in greater number, mostly by force, in the decade following the 1690 Great Migration of Serbs, ethnic Albanian tribes (given their incredible powers of reproduction) was posing a grave threat to the biological survival of the Serbs in Kosovo and Metohia.[67]

On the other hand, Albanian historians minimize the amount of the Serbian exodus, holding that Albanians represented the majority in Kosovo before 1690.[68] Some of these historians even affirm that Serbians did not flee from the region during that war, which is obviously exaggerated.[69]

It is very possible that Albanians became the majority in Kosovo only after 1690, but this fact does not contradict their presence in earlier times, attested to by various sources. *The whole truth does not belong to any of the factions involved in this quarrel, and the present fate of Kosovo cannot be decided by its medieval history, or according to the wishful thinking of Albanians or of Serbians.*

THE VLACHS (AROMANIANS)—A PEOPLE WITHOUT A STATE

The South-Danubian Romanians are divided into three groups, which speak specific dialects of the Romanian language: the Aromanians (or Macedo-Romanians), the Megleno-Romanians, and the Istro-Romanians. The last group, now almost vanished, inherited a larger group that was living in Croatia and Bosnia during the Middle Ages (the so-called "western Romanians," an expression coined by Romanian linguist Sextil Puşcariu.)[70]

The Romanians are the heirs of the Thracian and Dacian Romanized population from the Lower Danubian Roman provinces (Dacia, Moesia Superior, Moesia Inferior), mixed with the colonists brought by the Roman administration and later with other ethnic groups that settled in this area, north and south of the Danube, in the fourth–sixth centuries. The Slavs shattered this Romance bloc in the seventh century, when they arrived in the fertile lands between the southern Carpathians and the Balkan Mountains. They expelled most of the natives from this area to the higher regions.[71] One of these areas of concentration of Romance population, located in the west of present-day Bulgaria and southeast Serbia, became the buffer zone between the Bulgarian and Serbian languages (dialectological research established this zone on the line Timok–Breznik–Ovčepolje–Skopje–Shar Palanka). In this mountain region are preserved archaic Romanian place-names like Vakarel, Pasarel, and Ursul.[72]

It is not true that this central Balkan region, which includes the upper Morava basin and Kosovo, was the single ethnogenetic region of the Romanians, as several historians and linguists have claimed.[73] They explain the common features of the Romanian and Albanian languages by the habitation of these peoples in this area. However, those common features are due to the Dacian substratum of the Romanian language. Linguistic research proves that the ancestors of the Romanians survived not only in the Balkan Peninsula, but also in Transylvania and in the highlands of both sides of the western and southern Carpathians.[74] A mosaic of Romance zones intermingled with Slavic zones resulted. Romanian historian

Petre P. Panaitescu defines this kind of habitation with the suggestive expression "webs of Romance and Slavic population." These webs were interlaced within a large space, from Transylvania to the Balkan Mountains and later to Pindus.[75]

The Romanian population from the regions south of the Balkan Mountains descended from immigrants from this northern space, and also from some Romance groups that survived in Macedonia and Albania. The preservation of some words like *hicu* (from Latin *ficus*), and *pălur* (from Latin *paliurus*) in the Aromanian dialect would not be possible without a Roman continuity in Macedonia, because these words concern plants not existing in the Danubian area. Place-names like Sărună (Salonic) and Lăsun (Elasson) testify to the existence of a local Latin-speaking population in Macedonia and Albania, namely in the zones crossed by the Via Egnatia, which were Romanized, unlike most of the region south of the Balkan range that remained Greek. Some cities have names borrowed by the Slavs from the Romance population, not from the Greeks: Ser (Serres), Kostur (Kastoria), Solun/Selun (Salonic, that is Thessaloniki), Ber (Verria). Toponymy proves the existence of an area of continuous Romance habitation around the 41° parallel.[76]

Another Romance group has survived in present-day Montenegro. Place-names like Visitor and Durmitor (mountains from this area) are evidence of this.[77] A twelfth-century chronicle composed by an anonymous priest from Dioclea (the medieval name of Montenegro) recorded that during the Slavic invasions many Roman Christians from the seashore and from the plains took refuge in the mountains, where they built forts. The chronicler maintained that these Latini were the ancestors of the Dalmatian Morovlachi. Serbian archaeologist J. Kovačević agrees with this opinion, supposing that one of those forts was that from Martinić.[78] These refugees could not be the same as the speakers of the disappeared Dalmatian language (the last one died in 1898), because they were exclusively an urban population that survived in the cities along the Adriatic seashore. The Dalmatians were called *Romanoi* by Constantine Porphyrogenitus, in order to emphasize their Roman origin, but also to distinguish them from the Byzantines (Romaioi). The Dalmatians were a Romance population distinct from the Romanians. Their language suffered an intensive Italian influence that finally led to its extinction. In the famous trading center Ragusa (Dubrovnik), the Dalmatian language was already forgotten in the fifteenth century.[79]

The Aromanians call themselves Armân or Arămân, but the neighbors gave them the name *Vlach* (*Vlachoi*, *Vlahi*, *Vlasi*). This word meant in fact "Roman," because the Slavs called the Latin-speaking populations by it. The word was borrowed from the Slavs by the Byzantines.[80]

The survival of several Romance groups in the central and western Balkan Peninsula was possible because they were strengthened by population movements from north to south. It has been theorized that these movements started in the eighth century with the so-called Vlachorynchinoi, but the single source that records that migration has no value. A manuscript from the Athonite monastery Kastamonitou written in 1698, which speaks about the invasion of this people in the period of the iconoclast emperors, was found upon comparison to be closely related to a ninth-century source (*Miracula St. Demetrii*), which remembers in a similar context the Slavic tribe of Rynchinoi, with the name of the tribe seemingly erroneously changed by the author of the text written in 1698.[81]

Another alleged example of information about the northern origin of the Vlachs is preserved by *Descriptio Europae Orientalis*, a short work written in 1308 for Charles of Valois (pretender to the title of emperor of Constantinople) and for the Hungarian king Charles Robert of Anjou. It was demonstrated that the author, long unknown, was Andreas Hungarus, archbishop of Antivari in Albania between 1307 and 1308, formerly a Hungarian priest.[82] He was quite familiar with Hungary and Albania, but he had a confused image of other Balkan regions. We must regard with circumspection his data about the Balkan Vlachs:

> *Notandum [est hic] quod inter Machedoniam, Achayam et Thesalonicam est quidam populus valde magnus et spaciosus qui vocantur Blazi, qui et olim fuerunt Romanorum pastores, ac in Ungaria ubi erant pascua Romanorum propter nimiam terre viriditatem et fertilitatem olim morabantur. Sed tandem ab Ungaris inde expulsi, ad partes illae fugierunt.* [It should be noted that between Macedonia, Achaia and Thessaloniki there is a certain people much numerous and spread called Blazi, who were once the shepherds of the Romans and who formerly settled in Hungary, where the pastures of the Romans were, on account of the exceeding lushness and fertility of the land. But they were eventually driven out of the area and fled to these parts].[83]

The expression *pascua Romanorum* indicates that Andreas Hungarus was inspired by the Hungarian sources that call the Pannonian Romanians (Blaci) *pastores* Romanorum. Knowing something about the Balkan Vlachs, he supposed they were the same people, and he proposed an explanation for this identity. In fact, he distorted the data taken from Hungarian sources.[84] The Pannonian origin of the Balkan Vlachs was invented by Andreas Hungarus, who thus found the way to link data about Blachii from Hungarian sources with those about the Balkan Vlachs. This confusion is not surprising. Even one of the most learned Byzantine writers, John Zonaras, mixed up Pannonians with Paeons, in his *Lexicon*: "Paeoni, Latin or Thracian people. Some call them Macedonians, while others are thinking they are the present Pannonians. The Pannonians are Bulgarians."[85] In fact, these Paeoni were the Aromanians. As Stelian Brezeanu has remarked, Byzantine authors (like the Hungarians) established a relationship between the Romance people from the Balkans and the ancient Romanized populations (Bessi, Dacians, or Pannonians).[86] The wrong identification Pannonians = Bulgarians is not unique in Byzantine sources.[87] Zonaras made an association between the so-called Pannoni and Aromanians from Macedonia, on the basis of the similarity of *Pannoni* and *Paeoni*. Here, *Paeoni* are not the Pannonians, but the ancient Paeoni, who lived in exactly the same places where the Vlachs dwelled in the time of Zonaras, that is in Macedonia. Zonaras has invented another archaic name for the Vlachs. A confusion like Paeoni = Pannoni = Vlachs could be the source of inspiration for Andreas Hungarus.

Some researchers[88] accepted the trustworthiness of the data recorded in *Descriptio Europae Orientalis* about the homeland of the Balkan Vlachs, especially because it seems that a Byzantine source confirmed it. In his *Strategikon* (composed between 1075 and 1078), Kekaumenos, dealing with the origin of the Thessalian Vlachs, wrote that "they lived before near Danube and Saos, the river now called Sava, where the Serbians lived more recently, in defended and difficult to reach places." For the history of the southern branch of the Romanian people, Kekaumenos is indeed a valuable source, but only for contemporary events, not for the legend about their arrival from the Danube, because it has been demonstrated that the latter was in fact inspired by the work of Cassius Dio. He identified the Vlachs with the Dacians, ignoring the fact that Dacia was not the same as the south Danubian Dacia created by Aurelianus, better known by Byzantines.[89] Therefore, the fragment from Kekaumenos does not prove the migration of the Balkan Vlachs from north to south or their Pannonian origin.[90] Some Greek authors preferred to accept the trustworthiness of this source because this would imply that the Aromanians were not autochthonous in Macedonia,[91] while others—who aimed to demonstrate that the Aromanians were Romanized Greeks, natives in Macedonia—denied its value.[92]

The first certain information about the Balkan Romanians comes from 980. In that year, the duke of the Hellas province, which included Thessaly, Pindus and Achaia, Niculitzas, was appointed by Basil II (976–1025) as ruler (*archon*) over the Vlachs from that province. It is possible that this function meant command over a military unit composed of Vlachs.[93] However, there is another testimony that could concern the presence of the Aromanians in Macedonia more than one century ago. Greek linguist Phaedon Malingoudis[94] supposed that the place-name Subdelitia (a region near Amphipolis, east of Thessaloniki) recorded by Constantine Porphyrogenitus (*De Caerimoniis*, ed. Bonn, 1829, I, 634–635) is composed from the words *sub* ("under," of Latin origin) and *del* (Romanian *deal*, "hill"), of alleged Thracian origin. Therefore, the place (located near a mountain) had the Romanian name *sub deal* ("under hill"). Malingoudis emphasized that this name borrowed by the Slavs from the Romanized natives could represent the first mention of the Vlachs in Macedonia.

In the Middle Ages, the highest concentration of Vlach communities was in Pindus and Thessaly. Pindus was officially called Great Vlachia when it belonged to the despotate of Epirus, in the thirteenth and four-teenth centuries. In Thessaly, the name Vlachia was attested to by Jewish traveler Benjamin of Tudela in 1165–1171.[95] This region was located in the mountain area between the Spercheios valley and the Thessalian plain. The authors of a monograph of historical geography suppose that a province called Blachia existed in the twelfth century.[96] In the thirteenth–fifteenth centuries, the name Great Vlachia was applied to all of Thessaly. Even if most of the Aromanians were nomad shepherds, some of them had lived in the Thessalian towns since the eleventh century, for instance at Larissa and Trikkala, while other were farmers.[97]

In 1332, the Byzantine emperor Andronikos III Paleologos (1328–1341) made a treaty with tribes called Malakasioi, Buioi, and Mesaritoi (a total of 12,000 men). At that moment, Andronikos III was at war with Serbia, while the Albanians from Albania rebelled against the domination of the Serbian tzar Stephen Dušan, with the help of the Angevine kingdom of Naples. These Thessalian tribes lived outside of any mastership (*abasileu-toi*, as wrote John Cantacuzenus), as nomad shepherds in the mountains. Some of them descended to the lower areas of Thessaly, but remained no-mads.[98] These three tribes were often considered to be of Albanian stock, but they were in fact of Aromanian origin, as French traveler François Charles Pouqueville observed at the beginning of the nineteenth century. The Aromanian family Buia had a leading place in the fourteenth–eighteenth centuries in Epirus and Thessaly, while a Vlach village from northern Thessaly was named Mălăcaşi. The similarity between the Al-banian and Aromanian ways of life could explain the confusion of some Byzantine authors, who were not so well informed about the intricate ethnic configuration of the Balkan Peninsula.[99]

Other areas peopled by Aromanians are located in the north, in Mace-donia and Kosovo. In Macedonia, they are mentioned for the first time in an event that happened in 976. Several Vlachs called *hoditai* ("travelers") killed David, the brother of the future Bulgarian tzar Samuel, on the road between Prespa and Kastoria. This testimony comes from an interpolation in the chronicle of Skylitzes made by an unknown copyist at the end of the eleventh century, who was obviously familiar with the local history of Macedonia. This information is not the first record of the Aromanians, as is often maintained,[100] because it was written at the end of the eleventh century. The word *hoditai*, which does not mean "nomads," concerns the same people who are recorded in Serbian sources with the name *kjelatori* as involved in military transportation. The name *kjelatori* renders the Romanian word of Latin origin *călători* ("travelers"). M. Gyóni, R. C. Lăzărescu, and A. Lazarou hold that the Vlachs involved in that murder were guards of the military road and that they acted as representatives of the Byzantine authority against the rebellious Bulgarians. This hypothesis is seductive, but not proven.[101]

Many place-names of Aromanian origin exist in Macedonia, some of them attested to since very early times. For instance, Kimbalongon (from the Romanian Câmpulung, "long plain"), is recorded in an account of the Byzantine–Bulgarian battle of July 20, 1014, that took place in the Strymon valley, near Mount Belasica.[102]

The first record of the Vlachs in Serbian medieval sources is from Kosovo: the donation charter issued by the great župan Stephen Nemanja in 1198–1199 for the Athonite monastery Hilandar, which mentions the Vlachs near Prizren as peasants tied to the land of this monastery. Other documents show that the same monastery possessed two more Vlach villages in Kosovo (Petrače, Goračevci). Other Vlach villages are recorded in Kosovo in the fourteenth century: Proilovci, Vlasi Sremljane, Dragoljevci. The Vlach population is mentioned in different deeds issued by Serbian rulers for the monasteries that owned estates in Kosovo. The Aromanians that dwelled in Kosovo between Prizren and Peć were ruled by local chiefs called *primikeri*.[103] A Vlach gentry was also recorded in Montenegro in a document issued in 1280 by the Serbian queen Helena.[104] Fifteenth- and sixteenth-century Ottoman sources show that the Vlachs continued to live in Kosovo, in towns like Kruševac, Prizren, and Priština.[105]

The Megleno-Romanians, very few today, live northwest of Thessaloniki. Romanians from the region of the Balkan range who founded the state of the Asan dynasty in the late 1100s spoke the same Megleno-Romanian dialect, as is shown by the names of the villages Cercel, Văcărel, Cerbul, Păsărel, Singurel, Banişor, Cârnul, and of the mountain Vlahinja.[106] A recent study of their dialect suggests that the Megleno-Romanians are a Daco-Romanian colony originating from the Morava and Vardar Rivers.[107]

An important Romanian concentration existed in the region between the Timok and Morava Rivers. Their speech was closer to the Daco-Romanian dialect. This Romanian group was included in the state created by the Asan dynasty in 1186 (they were first mentioned in 1189, when they entered into contact with participants in the third crusade on the road between Branicevo and Niš). The region was taken by Serbia in 1291 or 1292 from two Cuman chiefs, Darman and Kudelin, that were first under Hungarian vassalage. Only then did the Serbization of this region previously peopled by Romanians and Bulgarians begin. Romanians continued to live in the Timok region during the Ottoman domination, when many of them were recruited into the army.[108]

The region between Morava and Drina is the southwestern limit of the area where the Romanian language has emerged. The ancientness of Romanian settlements from that area is proved by archaic place-names like Taor, Ursule, Bukor, and Krnule. This was the cradle of the "western Romanians," whose speech is closer to the Daco-Romanian dialect than to the Aromanian.[109] The first migrations from this area were caused by the Bulgarian aggression of 818, in the Timok-Morava area, when a part of the population took refuge in Frankish Pannonia (they are called Timociani in the Frankish sources).[110] The region of Srem and the eastern part of the area between Sava and Drava were also occupied by Bulgaria, in 827–828. Bulgaria continued to master Srem after the establishment of peace with the Franks in 832.[111] The expansion toward the west and northwest of the Balkan Peninsula began in the tenth and eleventh centuries, when the Romanians are recorded on the Dalmatian coast, in Istria and even in northeastern Italy.[112]

Bosnia and Herzegovina had a quite large Romanian population in the thirteenth–fifteenth centuries. The "western Romanians" migrated to Croatia and even Istria, where they survive until now (the Istro-Romanians). The first certain mention of Romanians in Istria comes from 1329 (a Vlach called Pasculus), but another document from the second half of the twelfth century preserves the name of a person, Radul, who looks too Romanian. In Dalmatia, these western Romanians were called Morovlachi or Morlaci, that is "Black Romanians."[113] The first Vlachs were reported in Croatia in 1322, in Bosnia in 1344, and in Dalmatia in 1357. In 1475, the prince Nicholas de Ujlak titled himself "Bosniae et Valachiae Rex." This title suggests not only the great number of Romanians, but especially the survival of Romanian forms of autonomous organization within Bosnia (in the region that was united with Hungary). A mountain zone near Sarajevo is called Stari Vlah ("The Old Vlach"). In 1373, a region from the southwestern Croatia was named Maior Vlachia.[114]

All these "western Romanians" came from Serbia as shepherds, or because they were driven away by the Turks. In the south, the western Romanians spread up to Kosovo, where they met the Aromanians, already present in that region. This penetration is proven by some phonetic features of Romanian place-names from Kosovo.[115] On the other hand, some of the Kosovar Aromanians migrated toward the north in the fourteenth and fifteenth centuries, together with the Serbs, consolidating the Romanian element from northern Serbia and the Timok region.[116]

Serbian and Croatian deeds record Romanians with the names Vlahi and Vlasi. Most of them were transhumant or nomad shepherds. They sold milk, cheese, and wool in the Dalmatian cities. However, documents show that other Vlachs were involved in agriculture and viticulture. The settlements of these sedentary Vlachs were called *katun*. They lived according to their traditional laws, recognized by the authorities (Zakon Vlahom, Jus Valachicum), being autonomous. They were ruled by chiefs called *cnezi, celnici,* or *primikeri.* A special category of Vlachs was recorded in the Serbian documents with the name of *kjelatori.* Other Vlachs from Serbia, Bosnia, and Croatia were the so-called *voinuks* or *voinici*—soldiers who guarded the roads. Their villages were exempted from the usual taxes in exchange for this military service, which continued during the Ottoman domination. Two Ottoman deeds from 1477 and 1490 specified that Romanians from Herzegovina were exempted from the capitation (*harach*) because they were enlisted in the light cavalry. They owned inalienable lots of land and preserved a specific military and social organization. As in other parts of the Balkan Peninsula, these Romanians were ruled by *cnezi* and *primikeri,* who enjoyed certain privileges. The *primikeri* were the chiefs of the Romanian villages (*cătune*), while the *cnezi* were leaders of clusters of villages. Quite unusually for the Christian subjects of the Ottoman Empire, the *cnezi* were not only tax exempted, but they also owned a small number of dependent peasants to work the estates (*timar*) granted for their military service. These more important chiefs who possessed *timar* estates had the duty of organizing light cavalry detachments from their villages. They were appointed by the sultans. The forms of autonomous life of the Vlachs in the Ottoman period were inherited from the Serbian state.[117]

This does not mean that all the Vlach population enjoyed a good situation during the Ottoman domination. Others chose to take refuge in the west, on the Dalmatian seashore, where they were recorded with the name Morovlachi until the eighteenth and nineteenth centuries. The last remnant of this population is represented by the few thousands of so-called Istro-Romanians, who dwell in some villages in Istria.

Aiming to exclude the Vlachs from the history of Macedonia, Kosovo, and Serbia, different Serbian authors state that the word Vlach had only a social and professional meaning (transhumant or nomad shepherds).[118] It is true that the word has this meaning in the Serbian and modern Greek languages, but the oldest sources confirm that the primary meaning was ethnic: a Romance population (Romanians or Aromanians). The gradual Slavization of some of them led to change of the meaning, but the Vlachs recorded in the eleventh–fifteenth-century sources are without any doubt western Romanians or Aromanians.[119] The author of a reference work about the history of Bosnia points out that the use of the name Vlach for Bosniac Orthodox believers could be explained by the high percentage of this Romanian element in the medieval Bosnian population.[120]

Sometimes, Yugoslavian historians agree with the Roman origin of the Vlachs and with their autochthony in the central and western Balkan Peninsula. According to Jovan Kovačević, the Vlachs descended from a part of the Latin-speaking Dalmatian population that took refuge in the mountains in the seventh century and converted to pastoralism. Others remained sedentary, living in the seashore towns like Zadar and Trogir, the ancestors of the Dalmatian Romance population.[121] This theory cannot explain the strong differences between the Romanian southern dialects and the Dalmatian language. Istro-Romanian and Macedo-Romanian are closer to Daco-Romanian than to Dalmatian. In addition, the data presented above suggest that the Romanians arrived quite late in Croatia, Bosnia, and Dalmatia (in the thirteenth–fourteenth centuries).

Scattered in almost all the parts of the Balkan Peninsula in smaller or greater enclaves, the South-Danubian Romanians were not able to establish their own state. When some of them succeeded in acquiring power in the aftermath of the uprisings against the Byzantine authority, these polities had a short life as Romanian forms of organization. The Romanian–Bulgarian state created by the Asan brothers after a short time became exclusively ruled by Bulgarian aristocrats, while the small principality established by the Vlach Dobromir Chrysos in Macedonia at the end of the twelfth century disappeared after a few years.

Living in all the medieval and modern Balkan states, Aromanians became a problem when modern nations emerged. The existence of the Aromanian minority in Greece and Bulgaria became a source of conflict, which had a certain role in the fulfillment of the Balkan Wars of 1912–1913, although the territories inhabited by the Aromanians could not be united with Romania. The partial assimilation of the Aromanians (started in the Middle Ages) lessened the possibility of conflicting situations. On the other hand, with this assimilation they lost the position they had in Macedonia and Thessaly in the Middle Ages.

DEPORTATIONS AND COLONIZATIONS MADE BY THE BYZANTINE AND OTTOMAN EMPIRES

The demographic and ethnic situation of the Balkan Peninsula was seriously affected by the deportations made by aggressors. The first period of large deportations was the seventh century, when the Avars and the Slavs took tens of thousands of prisoners from Southeastern Europe. Sometimes, they or their descendants come back (like the Byzantine prisoners from Avaria led by the Bulgarian chief Kuver who returned to Macedonia in 685),[122] but overall these attacks diminished the native Greek and Roman populations. In this way, the Slavs who settled in the same areas became the majority.

The Byzantine Empire applied in several instances a policy of deportation toward rebellious or unsure populations, combined with the forced colonization of foreign groups. The population transfers had not only military, but also economic reasons, because they were intended to develop wasted regions.[123] The Byzantine authorities settled several groups of Armenians and Syrians in Thrace and Macedonia in the second half of the eighth century and in the first decades of the ninth century, and next during the reigns of John Tzimiskes (969–976) and Basil II (in 988). Their mission was the strengthening of defenses against Bulgaria. On the other hand, the recovery of central and southern Greece in the eighth century made possible the return of the descendants of the Greeks who took refuge in Sicily and southern Italy when continental Greece was plundered by barbarian invaders. The result was the strengthening of the Greek element, which was thus able to assimilate the Slavs. This process was enforced by massive deportations from Asia Minor to inland Greece ordered by Emperor Nikephor I (802–811).[124]

In other instances, the Byzantines moved the hostile Slavic population from dangerous regions. After campaigns led by Constans II in 657–658 and Justinian II in 688–689, tens of thousands of Slavs from the area near Thessaloniki were deported to Asia Minor.[125] When Basil II occupied all of Bulgaria, a large part of the Bulgarian population from Macedonia was expelled to southern Thrace and Armenia and replaced with Byzantines and Armenians. The emperor wanted to consolidate Byzantine domination over a territory that had to be pacified.[126] Manuel I Comnenos (1143–1180) acted in the same way after crushing the Serbian rebellion of 1149–1151 (thousands of prisoners were deported from Raška to the zone around Sofia).[127] Similar deportations were made by the Protobulgarians just after their settlement in the former Roman province, in 681. They moved some of the Slavic tribes to the east and northwest, in order to "guard the places near the Avars," as wrote Byzantine chronicler Nikephor.[128] Later, in 813, khan Krum took around twelve thousand prisoners from Macedonia, establishing them north of the Danube, in a region dominated by Bulgaria. They returned to their homeland after twenty-five years.[129]

The policy of colonization for defense purposes was also applied by the Ottomans. The people of the Serbian villages that had military tasks were moved from Slavonia to Bosnia in the first half of the sixteenth century, on the new frontier with the Habsburg Empire.[130] The main action undertaken by the Ottoman Empire was, however, the large-scale enslavement and deportation of people from conquered territories. These operations started a short time after their expansion in Europe. After the battles of Cernomen (1371) and Kosovopolje (1389), many surviving Serbs were enslaved. Greece was also affected. During the campaign of 1397, 30,000 prisoners were taken from Argos to Anatolia. Other deportations were made in Thessaly, after 1393. In Serbian lands, similar actions took place during the wars of 1439, 1444, 1451–1454, and 1458–1459. The enslavement of the conquered population then reached its climax. For instance, when Serbia was finally occupied in 1459, all of the 8,000 inhabitants of the Smederovo fortress were captured.[131]

In southern Thrace (the European part of Turkey), the place of deported Christian prisoners was taken by Anatolian Turks sent there during the reigns of Murad I (1359–1389) and Bayazid I (1389–1402). They received the name Yürüks. In Macedonia, the installation of the Turks began just after the battle of Kosovopolje (1389). Colonization was made especially in the cities and along the main roads, but there are some early cases of villages peopled by Turks near Thessaloniki and in Thessaly. Because of the intensive colonizations made by Bayazid I, the city of Skopje, a former Serbian capital, became the center of Ottoman power in Macedonia. After 1402, colonizations were scarce, but in 1415–1430 there was settlement of a group of Anatolian Turks in Albania, who received *timar* estates there.[132]

After the conquest of Kosovo in 1455, the Ottoman administration granted lands to the *spahis* and started the colonization with Turks. In this way, the lowlands of Macedonia and Kosovo again changed their ethnic composition, with settlement by Turks and Muslim Albanians. Some of the Slavic inhabitants took refuge in the highlands.[133] The Anatolian Turks received estates in the conquered zones that were previously depopulated by wars and epidemics. Many Serbian villages were plundered and deserted, while other settlements were established by the Turkish colonizers.[134] At the same time, the Ottoman domination was strengthened by the conversion to Islam of some of the new subjects.[135] These processes of population transfer and Islamization radically changed the ethnic and religious configuration of the Balkan Peninsula, increasing the diversity and the potential for future ethnic conflicts.

The various events and historical processes turned the Balkan Peninsula into a space of ethnic mosaic, where *no population is a majority in a large zone and where no region preserved a fixed ethnic configuration for any length of time.* No other European area displays such features. In these circumstances, the ethnic changes that occurred during the Middle Ages in the Balkan Peninsula can be taken as a premise for the understanding of what happened later, in the nineteenth and twentieth centuries: *the ethnic mosaic became one of the reasons for the interethnic conflicts in the age of the national awakening of the Balkan peoples and of the emergence of their national ideologies, when this ethnic configuration became a risk factor.*

NOTES

1. A. Madgearu, The Downfall of the Lower Danubian Late Roman Frontier, RRH, 36, 3–4 (1997), 315–336.

2. See, for instance: I. Popović, Die Einwanderung der Slaven in der Ostromische Reich im Lichte der Sprachforschung, *Zeitschrift für Slavistik*, 4, 5 (1959), 705–721.

3. V. Beševliev, *Zur Deutung der Kastellnamen in Prokops Werk "De Aedificiis,"* Amsterdam, 1970, 1–2, 17–18.

4. M. Ljubinković, Les Slaves des régions centrales des Balkans et Byzance, *Berichte 1973*, vol. 2, 184.

5. V. Popović, Les témoins archéologiques des invasions Avaro-Slaves dans l'Illyricum Byzantin, *Mélanges de l'École Française de Rome. Antiquité*, 87, 1 (1975), 449.

6. M. Ljubinković, La nécropole slave de Brestovik, *Archaeologia Iugoslavica*, 2 (1956), 131–137; I. Nestor, Les éléments les plus anciennes de la culture matérielle slave dans les Balkans, in *Posebna Izdanija, XII. Simpozijum. Predslavenski etnički elementi na Balkanu u etnogenezi južnih slovena*, Sarajevo, 1969, 147; I. Čremošnik, Die ältesten Ansiedlungen und Kultur der Slawen in Bosnien und der Herzegovina im Lichte der Untersuchugen in Mušići und Batkovići, BSl, 1 (1972), 59–64.

7. D. Janković, The Slavs in East Serbia in VI and VII Century, in M. Lazić (ed.), *Archaeology of Eastern Serbia*, Belgrade, 1997, 148–149.

8. For instance: K. Godlowski, Zur Frage der Slawensitze vor der grossen Slawenwanderung im 6. Jahrhundert, in *Gli Slavi*, 257–284; J. Udolph, Kamen die Slaven aus Pannonien?, in G. Labuda (ed.), *Studia nad etnogeneza Slowian i kultura Europy wczesnosredniowiecznej: Praca zbiorowa*, I, Wroclaw, 1987, 167–173; Z. Golab, *The Origins of the Slavs. A Linguist's View*, Columbus, 1991, 236–305; H. Birnbaum, On the Ethnogenesis and Protohome of the Slavs: The Linguistic Evidence, *Journal of Slavic Linguistics*, 1, 2 (1993), 352–374; A. M. Schenker, *The Dawn of Slavic. An Introduction to Slavic Philology*, New Haven, CT: Yale University Press, 1996, 1–7.

9. O. N. Trubačev, Linguistics and Ethnogenesis of the Slavs: The Ancient Slavs as Evidenced by Etimology and Onomastics, *The Journal of Indo-European Studies*, 13, 1–2 (1985), 203–256.

10. O. Pritsak, The Slavs and the Avars, in *Gli Slavi*, 353–432 (especially 399–424).

11. J. Nichols, The Linguistic Geography of the Slavic Expansion, in R. Maguire & A. Timberlank (eds.), *American Contributions to the Eleventh International Congress of Slavists (Bratislava, August–September 1993). Literature, Linguistics, Poetics* (quotation at 386), Columbus, 1993, 377–391.

12. F. Curta, *The Making of the Slavs. History and Archaeology of the Lower Danube Region c. 500–700*, Cambridge, 2001, 307–308, 335–346.

13. F. Curta, The Slavic Lingua Franca (Linguistic Notes of an Archaeologist Turned Historian), *East Central Europe* (Budapest), 31, 1 (2004) (*Research Dossier. East European Dark Ages: Archaeology, Linguistics and the History of the Early Slavs*), 134–148.

14. I. Nestor, La pénétration des Slaves dans la Péninsule Balkanique et la Grèce continentale. Considèrations sur les recherches historiques et archéologiques, RESEE, 1, 1–2 (1963), 62–63; V. Popović, Aux origines de la slavisation des Balkans: La constitution des premières Sklavinies Macédoniennes vers la fin du VIe siècle, *Académie des Inscriptions et Belles-Lettres. Comptes Rendus des séances de l'année 1980*, 1 (Paris) (Janvier–Mars 1980), 246–248; P. Lemerle, *Les plus anciens*

recueils des Miracles de Saint Démétrius et la pénétration des Slaves dans les Balkans,
vol. II, *Le commentaire,* Paris, 1981, 85–94; R. J. Lilie, Kaiser Heraklios und die Ansiedlung der Serben. Überlegungen zum Kapitel 32 des "De Administrando Imperio," SOF, 44 (1985), 20–23; J. F. Haldon, *Byzantium in the Seventh Century. The
Transformation of a Culture,* Cambridge, 1997, 43–45; Curta 2001, 90–108.

15. P. Charanis, Observations on the History of Greece during the Early Middle
Ages, BS, 11, 1 (1970), 15– 23; Popović 1975, 451; J. Koder, Zur Frage der Slavischen
Siedlungsgebiete im mittelalterlichen Griechenland, BZ, 71, 2 (1978), 315– 316; M.
W. Weithmann, *Die Slawische Bevölkerung auf der griechischen Halbinsel. Ein Beitrag
zur historischen ethnographie Südosteuropas,* München, 1978, 85– 97; P. Charanis, On
the Demography of Medieval Greece, a Problem Solved, BS, 20 (1979), 196– 214;
Popović 1980, 234, 244–245, 256–257; J. Ferluga, Gli Slavi del Sud ed altri gruppi
etnici di fronte a Bisanzio, *Gli Slavi,* 1983, 312–314; M. W. Weithmann, Interdisziplinäre diskrepanzen in der "Slavenfrage" Griechenlands, ZB, 30, 1 (1994), 89–90.

16. P. A. Yannopoulos, La pénétration slave en Argolide, BCH, Supplément VI
(*Études argiennes*), 1980, 353–357; G. L. Huxley, The Second Dark Age of the Peloponnese, *Lakonikai Spoudai,* 3 (1977), 93; J. Karayannopulos, Zur Frage der Slave-
nansiedlung im griechischen Raum, in A. Hohlweg (ed.), *Byzanz und seine Nachbarn* (Südost-Europa Jahrbuch, 26), München, 1996, 208–209.

17. D. A. Zakythinos, La grande brèche dans la tradition historique de l'Hel-
lénisme du septième au neuvième siècle, in *Charisterion eis Anastasiou K. Orlandou,*
vol. III, Athens, 1966, 300–327. For the economic causes of the urban decline see:
T. Gregory, Cities and Social Evolution in Roman and Byzantine South East Europe, in J. Bintliff (ed.), *European Social Evolution. Archaeological Perspectives,* Brad-
ford, 1984, 267–276; S. J. B. Barnish, The Transformation of Classical Cities and the
Pirenne Debate, *Journal of Roman Archaeology,* 2 (1989), 385–400; W. Liebeschuetz,
The End of the Ancient City, in J. Rich (ed.), *The City in Late Antiquity,* London/
New York, 1992, 1–49.

18. P. Aupert, Céramique slave à Argos (585 ap. J-C.), BCH, Supplément VI
(*Études argiennes*), 1980, 373–394; Idem, Les Slaves à Argos, BCH, 113 (1989), 1,
417–419.

19. Curta 2001, 233–234.

20. A. Avraméa, *Le Peloponnèse du IVe au VIIIe siècle. Changements et persistances,*
Paris, 1997, 86.

21. T. Gregory, An Early Byzantine (Dark-Age) Settlement at Isthmia: Preliminary Report, in T. Gregory (ed.), *The Corinthia in the Roman Period Including the Papers Given at a Symposium Held at the Ohio State University on 7–9 March, 1991,* Ann
Arbor, MI, 1993, 149–159.

22. T. Vida & T. Völling, *Das Slawische Brandgräberfeld von Olympia,* Rahden,
2000, 15, 26, 93.

23. Curta 2001, 234.

24. Constantino Porfirogenito, *De Thematibus,* ed. A. Pertusi, Roma, 1952, 91;
Jenkins 1963, 27; Charanis 1970, 21; M. W. Weithmann, Politische und ethnische
Veränderungen in Griechenland am Übergang von der Antike zum Frühmittelal-
ter, *Die Kultur Griechenlands,* 1994, 23–24; F. Curta, Barbarians in Dark-Age Greece:
Slavs or Avars? in Ts. Stepanov & V. Vachkova (eds.), *Civitas divino-humana. In hon-
orem annorum LX Georgii Bakalov,* Sofia, 2004, 525.

25. P. Charanis, Ethnic Changes in the Byzantine Empire in the Seventh Century, DOP, 13 (1959), 39, 43; G. Cankova-Petkova, L'etablissement des Slaves et des Protobulgares en Bulgarie de Nord-Est actuelle et le sort de certaines villes riveraines du Danube, EH, 5 (1970), 224; H. Ditten, Zur Bedeutung der Einwanderung der Slawen, in *Byzanz im 7. Jh. Untersuchungen zur Herausbildung des Feudalismus* (BBA, 48), Berlin, 1978, 107–112; J. D. Howard-Johnston, *Urban Continuity in the Balkans in the Early Middle Ages*, in A. G. Poulter (ed.), *Ancient Bulgaria. Papers presented to the International Symposium on the Ancient History and Archaeology of Bulgaria*, Part 2, Nottingham, 1983, 249–251.

26. T. Stoianovich, *A Study in Balkan Civilization*, New York, 1967, 112–113. For the runaway of the Greeks in the fifteenth–seventeenth centuries, see A. Vacalopoulos, La rétraite des populations Grécques vers des régions éloignées et montagneuses pendant la domination Turque, BS, 4, 2 (1963), 265–276.

27. J. Herrin, Aspects of the Process of Hellenization in the Early Middle Ages, *The Annual of the British School of Archaeology at Athens*, 68 (1973), 118; J. Kovačević, Les Slaves et la population dans l'Illyricum, *Berichte 1973*, vol. 2, 150; P. Koledarov, Zur Frage der politischen und ethnischen Veränderungen auf dem Balkan im 7. Jahrhundert, EH, 10 (1980), 78–81; G. Schramm, Frühe Schicksale der Rumänen. Acht Thesen zur Lokalisierung der lateinischen Kontinuität in Südosteuropa (II), ZB, 22, 1 (1986), 110; H. Ditten, Ethnische Verschiebungen zwischen der Balkanhalbinsel und Kleinasien vom Ende des 6. bis zum zweiten Hälfte des 9. Jahrhunderts (BBA, 59), (1993), 46–52; Weithmann 1994a, 90; Weithmann 1994b, 20–21; W. J. H. G. Liebeschuetz, The Refugees and Evacuees in the Age of Migrations, in R. Corradini, M. Diesenberger, & H. Reimitz (eds.), *The Construction of Communities in the Early Middle Ages. Texts, Resources and Artifacts* (Transformation of the Roman World, 12), Leiden, 2003, 71–73. For Karst as a refuge zone on the Adriatic seashore see also G. W. Hoffman, The Evolution of the Ethnographic Map of Yugoslavia, *Carter 1977*, 466–467.

28. S. Guldescu, *History of Medieval Croatia*, The Hague, 1964, 44–46; I. Božić, La formation de l'Etat serbe aux IXe–XIe siècles, *Europe 1968*, 133–134; Ljubinković 1973, 191; Kovačević 1973, 149; Popović 1975, 503; I. Tomljenović, *Wann begegneten die Kroaten den Christentum?* in P. Urbanczyk (ed.), *Early Christianity in Central and East Europe*, vol. I, Warszaw, 1997, 43–46; Haldon 1997, 47; N. Malcolm, *Kosovo. A Short History*, New York, 1999, 24; J. V. A. Fine Jr., Croats and Slavs: Theories about Historical Circumstances of the Croats' Appearance in the Balkans, BF, 26 (2000), 206–208; O. Karatay, Ogur Connection in the Croatian and Serbian Migrations, in G. H. Celâl, C. C. Oguz, & O. Karatay (eds.), *The Turks*, vol. 1, Ankara, 2002, 556–558.

29. Lilie 1985, 17–43; M. Whittow, *The Making of Byzantium, 600–1025*, Berkeley, CA, 1996, 263. R. Katičić (Die Anfänge des kroatischen Kroatischen Staatesstaates, in H. Friesinger & F. Daim, *Die Bayern und ihre Nachbarn*, I [DAW, 179], Wien, 1985, 309) remarked that the legend of the colonization of the Croats organized by Heraklios is tendentious, because it provides reasons for the Byzantine domination in Dalmatia. For the Balkan policy of Heraklios after 614, see W. E. Kaegi Jr., *Heraclius, Emperor of Byzantium*, Cambridge, 2003, 95, 118–121.

30. V. Popović, Koubrat, Kouber et Asparouch, *Starinar* (Belgrade) 37, (1986), 127–128; W. Pohl, *Die Awaren. Ein Steppenvolk in Mitteleuropa, 567–822 n. Chr.*, München, 1988, 261–268.

Chapter 1

31. S. Kurnatowski, Demographische Aspekte hinsichtlich slawischer Migratio-
nen im 1. Jahrtausend, CIAS III, vol. I, 470–471.

32. Charanis 1959, 25–44.

33. D. Angelov, *Die Entstehung des bulgarischen Volkes*, Berlin, 1980, 62; Ferluga
1983, 318–319; L. Maksimović, Verwaltungsstrukturen in Byzanz und in den
Balkanländern, in A. Hohlweg (ed.), *Byzanz und seine Nachbarn* (Südost-Europa
Jahrbuch, 26), München, 1996, 48–50; Curta 2001, 107–119.

34. N. Budak, Die südslawischen Ethnogenesen an der östlichen Adriaküste im
frühen Mittelalter, in *Typen der Ethnogenese unter besonderer Berücksichtigung der
Bayern*, I (DAW, 201), Wien, 1990, 129–136.

35. See a well-documented approach to this problem in B. Zelić-Bučan, The
National Name of the Croatian Language throughout History, *Folia Croatica-
Canadiana*, 2 (1999), 63–121.

36. D. Bataković, *La crise Yougoslave: Les aspects historiques*, BS, 33, 2 (1992),
274–292.

37. A. Ducellier, L'Arbanon et les Albanais au XIe siècle, TM, 3 (1968), 354; S.
Anamali, Des Illyriens aux Albanais, AIESEEB, 10, 2 (1972), 117; Angelov 1980,
144–145; S. Pollo & A. Puto, *The History of Albania from Its Origins to the Present Day*,
London, 1981, 30; V. Popović, Byzantins, Slaves et autochtones dans les provinces
de Prévalitaine et Nouvelle Epire, in *Villes et peuplement dans l'Illyricum proto-
byzantin. Actes du colloque organisé par l'École Française de Rome (Rome, 12–14 Mai
1982)* (Collection de l'École Française de Rome, 77), Rome, 1984, 211–213;
V. Popović, L'Albanie pendant la Basse Antiquité, *Les Illyriens 1988*, 268; B.
Gjuzelev, *Die Bulgarisch-Albanische Ethnische Grenze während des Mittelalters (6.–15.
Jh.)*, EB, 27, 3 (1991), 79–84; A. Ducellier, Have the Albanians Occupied Kosova?
Kosova 1993, 64; R. Elsie, Hydronimica Albanica—A Survey of River Names in
Albania, ZB, 30, 1 (1994), 42. The presence of a Serbian Slavic population in the
Albanian plains (Cvijić 1918, 159–160) has not been proven.

38. J. Lefort, Toponymie et anthroponymie: Le contact entre Grecs et Slaves en
Macedoine, in *Frontière et peuplement dans le monde Méditerrannéen au Moyen Âge.
Actes du colloque d'Erice—Trapani (Italie) tenu du 18 au 25 Septembre 1988, recueillis et
présentés par Jean-Michel Poisson* (Castrum, 4), Rome, Madrid, 1992, 161–171.

39. Ph. Malingoudis, Toponymy and History. Observations Concerning the
Slavonic Toponimy of the Peloponnese, *Cyrillomethodianum* (Thessaloniki), 7
(1983), 103–106.

40. Koder 1978, 315–331. See also M. Graebner, The Slavs in Byzantine Empire.
Absorption, Semi-Autonomy and the Limits of Byzantinization, BB, 5 (1978),
48–51, 53; Weithmann 1994a, 91.

41. Weithmann 1978, 132–197.

42. P. Ivić, Balkan Slavic Migrations in the Light of South Slavic Dialectology,
Aspects 1972, 77–78; Gjuzelev 1991, 80.

43. Ivić 1972, 73; A. E. Vacalopoulos, *History of Macedonia, 1354–1833*, Thessaloniki, 1973, 15–21.

44. M. Bartusis, The Settlement of Serbs in Macedonia in the Era of Dušan's
Conquests, in H. Ahrweiler & A. E. Laiou (eds.), *Studies on the Internal Diaspora of
the Byzantine Empire*, Washington, DC, 1998, 153–158.

45. Vacalopoulos 1973, 9, 15.

46. Hoffman 1977, 475; D. Dragojlović, Migrations of the Serbs in the Middle Ages, *Migrations 1989*, 63.

47. R. Samardžić, Migrations in Serbian History (the Era of Foreign Rule), *Migrations 1989*, 85–86; D. Živojinović, Wars, Population Migrations and Religious Proselytism in Dalmatia during the Second Half of the XVIIth Century, in *Migrations 1989*, 77–82.

48. Samardžić 1989, 85–86; M. Cazacu, Les Valaques dans les Balkans occidentaux (Serbie, Croatie, Albanie, etc.). La Pax Ottomanica (XVème–XVIIème siècles), *Les Aroumains*, 1989, 88–90.

49. G. Stadtmüller, Die Islamisierung bei den Albanern, *Jahrbücher für Geschichte Osteuropas*, 3, 4 (1955), 421; S. Skendi, Religion in Albania during the Ottoman Rule, SOF, 15 (1956), 317; L. S. Stavrianos, *The Balkans since 1453*, New York, 1959, 98; P. F. Sugar, *Southeastern Europe under Ottoman Rule, 1354–1804*, Seattle, WA, 1977, 222; Hoffman 1977, 476; Ducellier 1993, 65–66; Malcolm 1999, 161.

50. H. L. Vranoussis, Les termes Albanoi et Arbanitai et la première mention des Albanais dans les sources du XIe siècle, in *Actes du IIe Congrès International des Études du Sud-Est Européen* (Athènes), 2, (1972), 387–396. The information was considered reliable by other historians, such as Ducellier 1968, 357; A. Ducellier, Les Albanais du XIe au XIIIe siècle: Nomades ou sédentaires? BF, 7 (1979), 24; and G. Schramm, *Anfänge des Albanischen Christentums. Die frühe Bekehrung der Bessen und ihre langen Folgen*, Freiburg im Briesgau, 1994, 235–236.

51. Ducellier 1968, 357–364; A. Ducellier, Nouvel essai de mise au point sur l'apparition du peuple Albanais dans les sources Byzantines, SA, 9 (1972), 2, 300–304; K. Bozhori, À propos de l'extension du nom Arbanon à l'époque Byzantine, CIEB XIV, vol. II (1975), 307–308; B. Ferjančić, Les Albanais dans les sources Byzantines, *Les Illyriens 1988*, 306–307; M. Tadin, Les "Arbanitai" des chroniques byzantines (XIe–XIIe s.), CIEB XV, vol. IV (1980), 316–322.

52. R. Elsie, The Earliest References to the Existence of the Albanian Language, ZB, 27, 2 (1991), 102.

53. Ducellier 1968, 353–368; Bozhori 1975, 308; Ducellier 1984, 4; K. Frashëri, The Territories of the Albanians in the XVth Century, *Albanians 1985*, 211; Ferjančić 1988, 305–307; Gjuzelev 1991, 82–83; Schramm 1994, 157–167.

54. Ducellier 1981, 645–651 (see also 76–80, for Via Egnatia); Popović 1984, 208–210; Popović 1988, 252.

55. S. Ćirković, Les Albanais à la lumière des sources historiques des Slaves du Sud, *Les Illyriens 1988*, 346–352; B. I. Bojović, Le passé des territoires, Kosovo-Metohija (XIe–XVIIe siècle), BS, 38, 1 (1997), 41.

56. K. Giakoumis, Fourteenth-Century Albanian Migration and the 'Relative Autochthony' of the Albanians in Epeiros. The Case of Gjirokastër, BMGS, 27 (2003), 174–176.

57. Ducellier 1979, 27–36.

58. C. Jireček, Albanien in der Vergangenheit, in L. von Thallóczy (ed.), *Illyrisch-Albanische Forschungen*, I, München-Leipzig, 1916, 69; N. Iorga, *Ilusii și drepturi naționale în Balcani. Lecție de deschidere la Institutul de Studii Sud-Ost Europene*, Vălenii de Munte, 1916, 23; M. E. Durham, *Some Tribal Origins, Laws, and Customs in the Balkans*, London, 1928, 13–59; I. Ajeti, Contribution to the Study of

the Medieval Onomastics in the Territory of Montenegro, Bosnia and Hercegovina, and Kosova, in *Albanians 1985*, 287–296.

59. S. Gashi, The Presence of the Albanian Ethnos in Kosova during the 13th–14th Centuries in the Light of the Serbian Church Sources, *Albanians 1985*, 278–281; Malcolm 1999, 55.

60. G. Ostrogorsky, *Histoire de l'État Byzantin*, Paris, 1956, 565; R. Jenkins, *Byzantium and Byzantinism*, University of Cincinnati, 1963, 35; A. E. Vacalopoulos, *Origins of the Greek Nation: The Byzantine Period, 1204–1461*, New Brunswick, NJ, 1970, 10; T. Jochalas, Über die Einwanderung der Albaner in Griechenland, in *Dissertationes Albanicae in honorem Josephi Valentini et Ernesti Koliqi septuagenariorum* (Beiträge zur Kenntnis Südosteuropas und des nahen Orients, 13), München, 1971, 91–101; Ferjančić 1988, 319–321; Giakoumis 2003, 177.

61. Vacalopoulos 1970, 8; Jochalas 1971, 94; Malcolm 1999, 48.

62. Giakoumis 2003, 178–181.

63. Gashi 1985, 250–261; H. Islami, Anthropogeographic Research in Kosova. An Aperçu on the Work "Kosovo" by Academician Atanasije Urosevic, *Albanians 1985*, 487; M. Tërnava, Albanians in the Feud of Dečan in the 30's of the 14th century According to the Chrysobull of Dečan, *Albanians 1985*, 227–246; S. Pulaha, *L'autochtoneité des Albanais en Kosove et le prétendu exode des Serbes à la fin du XVIIe siècle*, Tirana, 1985, 23–24.

64. Islami 1985, 488–489; S. Pulaha, The Altun-Ilia Province and Its Population at the End of the 15th Century, *Albanians 1985*, 354–365; (Idem), The Northeastern Regions of the Sandjak of Dukagjin-Hass and Its Population during the Second Half of the 16th Century, *Albanians 1985*, 366–393; Čirković 1988, 354–355; O. Zirojević, Les premiers siècles de la domination étrangère, *Kosovo 1990*, 42–43, 68–72; Gjuzelev 1991, 87; S. Pulaha, On the Presence of Albanians in Kosova during the 14th–17th Centuries, *Kosova 1993*, 35–44; Ducellier 1993, 66.

65. Gashi 1985, 277.

66. Islami 1985, 484; Pulaha 1985, 4–7.

67. D. T. Bataković, *The Kosovo Chronicles*, Belgrade (online version: members .tripod.com/Balkania/resources/history/kosovo_chronicles), 1992 (chapter "The Age of Migrations").

68. M. Tërnava, Migrations to the Present-Day Territory of Kosova during the 14th–16th Centuries, *Albanians 1985*, 435–475.

69. S. S. Juka, *The Albanians in Yugoslavia in Light of Historical Documents*, New York (online version at www.alb-net.com/juka2.htm), 1984, 16–17; Pulaha 1985, 80–81; Pulaha 1993, 44; A. Doja, Formation nationale et nationalisme dans l'aire de peuplement Albanais, *Balkanologie* (Paris), 3, 2 (1999), 39.

70. S. Puşcariu, *Studii istro-române*, vol. II, Bucureşti, 1926, 3–5. See C. Tagliavini, *Le origini delle lingue neolatine*, Bologna, 1972, 357–364 for the areas of the Romanian dialects.

71. For the Romanian ethnogenesis, see E. Gamillscheg, Zur rumänischen Frühgeschichte, in *Die Kultur Südosteuropas. Ihre Geschichte und ihre Ausdrucksformen*, Wiesbaden, 1964, 45–73; E. Condurachi & G. Ştefan, La romanité orientale, *Nouvelles Études d'Histoire* (Bucarest), 4, (1970), 7–22; A. Niculescu, Le dacoroumain—Romania antiqua, Romania nova et la continuité mobile. Une synthèse,

in *Actes du XVIIIe Congrès International de Linguistique et de Philologie Romanes* (Trier, 1986), I, Tübingen, 1992, 86–104.

72. Ivić 1972, 66–68.

73. For instance: M. Gyóni, La transhumance des Valaques Balcaniques au Moyen Âge, ByzSl, 12 (1951), 41–42; Schramm 1994, 185–190; Malcolm 1999, 26–27, 38–40.

74. G. Reichenkron, Die Entstehung des Rumänentums nach den neuesten Forschungen, SOF, 22 (1963), 75–77; I. Conea, L. Badea, & D. Oancea, Toponymie ancienne, témoignant de la continuité daco-roumaine dans les Carpathes Méridionales de l'ouest de l'Olt, in *VIIo Congresso internazionale di scienze onomastiche*, Firenze-Pisa, 1961, 327–362.

75. Stoianovich 1967, 112–113; P. P. Panaitescu, *Introducere la istoria culturii româneşti*, Bucureşti, 1969, 120–121, 210; A. Rosetti, *Istoria limbii române, I. De la originii până la începutul secolului al XVII-lea. Ediţie definitivă*, Bucureşti, 1986, 200–201; N. Djuvara, Sur un passage controversé de Kekaumenos, RRH, 30, 1–2 (1991), 64; A. Madgearu, *Continuitate şi discontinuitate culturală la Dunărea de Jos în secolele VII–VIII, Bucureşti*, 1997, 133–134, 196–197.

76. Th. Capidan, *Limbă şi cultură*, Bucureşti, 1943, 161–164, 181–211, 283–290; E. Scărlătoiu, The Balkan Vlachs in the Light of Linguistic Studies (Highlights and Contributions), RESEE, 17 (1979), 1, 17–37; Schramm 1986, 104–108; Djuvara 1991, 60–66; C. Poghirc, Romanisation linguistique et culturelle dans les Balkans. Survivances et evolution, *Les Aroumains*, 1989, 36–39; P. Ş. Năsturel, Les Valaques de l'espace byzantin et bulgare jusqu'à la conquête Ottomane, *Les Aroumains*, 1989, 46–48; Madgearu 1997, 134–135.

77. S. Dragomir, La patrie primitive des Roumains et ses frontières historiques, *Balcania*, 7, 1 (1944), 71; Dragomir *Vlahii din nordul Peninsulei Balcanice în evul mediu*, Bucureşti, 1959, 37, 165, 173.

78. Presbyteri Diocleatis, Regnum Sclavorum, in I. G. Schwandtner, *Scriptores Rerum Hungaricarum*, III, Vindobonae, 1748, 479 (c. VII); Kovačević 1973, 151; Djuvara 1991, 63–64; Madgearu 1997, 133, 135. For the value of the Chronicle of the Priest of Dioclea, see J. Ferluga, Die Chronik des Priesters von Diokleia als Quelle für die Byzantinische Geschichte, Byzantina, 10 (1980), 429–460; M. Hadžijahić, Das "Regnum Sclavorum" als historische Quelle und als territoriales Substrat, SOF, 42 (1983), 11–60.

79. Tagliavini 1972, 374–377; S. Brezeanu, *Romanitatea orientală în evul mediu. De la cetăţenii romani la naţiunea medievală*, Bucureşti, 1999, 61–62, 167–168.

80. Poghirc 1989, 9–15; Brezeanu 1999, 101–105.

81. M. Gyóni, Les Vlaques du Mont Athos au début du XIIe siècle, *Études Slaves et Roumaines*, 1, 1 (1948), 30–42; Madgearu 1997, 191–193.

82. H. Sulyok, Quasi Latini, Acta Universitatis de Attila József Nominatae. Opuscula Byzantina (Szeged), 9 (*Byzance et ses voisins. Mélanges à la mémoire de Gyula Moravcsik à l'occasion du centième anniversaire de sa naissance*) (1994), 98.

83. O. Górka, *Anonymi descriptio Europae orientalis. Imperium Constantinopolitanum, Albania, Serbia, Bulgaria, Ruthenia, Ungaria, Polonia, Bohemia. Anno MCCCVIII exarata*, Cracoviae, 1916, 12–13.

84. A. Madgearu, *The Romanians in the Anonymous Gesta Hungarorum. Truth and Fiction*, Cluj-Napoca, 2005, 55–56.

85. Ioannes Zonaras, *Lexicon ex tribus codicibus manuscriptis . . .*, ed. J. A. H. Tittmann, II, Leipzig, 1808, 1495.
86. S. Brezeanu, Mésiens chez Nicétas Choniate. Terminologie archaïsante et réalité ethnique médiévale, *Études Byzantines et Postbyzantines*, vol. II, Bucarest, 1991, 109–110.
87. See G. Moravcsik, *Byzantinoturcica, II. Sprachreste der Türkvölker in dem byzantinischen Quellen*, Berlin, 1958, 244, to which can be added a fragment from the "Geography" of Nikephor Blemmydes (C. Müller, *Geographi Graeci Minores*, Paris, 1861, II, 460).
88. The most recent is M. Pillon, L'exode des "Sermésiens" et les grandes migrations des Roumains de Pannonie dans les Balkans durant le Haut Moyen Âge, EB, 38, 3 (2002), 113–115.
89. M. Gyóni, L'oeuvre de Kekauménos, source de l'histoire roumaine, RHC, 23, n.s., vol. 3, 1–4 (1945), 148–180; Djuvara 1991, 23–66.
90. The same conclusion is made in a recent paper of N. Saramandu, On the Establishment of Aromanians in the South of the Balkan Peninsula. Kekaumenos' "Evidence," RESEE, 42, 2004, 1–4, 293–303 (who ignores some recent historical works on the subject).
91. P. Charanis, John Lydus and the Question of the Origin of the Vlachs in the Greek Lands, in *Byzance et les Slaves. Études de civilisation. Mélanges Ivan Dujcev, Association des amis des études archéologiques des mondes Byzantino-Slaves et du christianisme oriental*, Paris, 1979, 106–107.
92. A. Lazarou, *L'aroumain et ses rapports avec le Grec*, Thessalonique, 1986, 88, 103.
93. Gyóni 1945, 101, 118; P. Ş. Năsturel, Vlacho-Balcanica, BNJ, 22 (1978), 229; G. Murnu, *Studii istorice privitoare la trecutul românilor de peste Dunăre*, Bucureşti, 1984, 67–77; Năsturel 1989, 50–52.
94. Ph. Malingoudis, Frühe slawische Elemente im Namengut Griechenlands, in *Die Völker 1987*, 54–56. For Subdelitia, see also J. Karayannopoulos, Les Slaves en Macédoine. La prétendue interruption des communications entre Constantinople et Thessalonique du 7ème au 9ème siècle, *Centre d'études du sud-est européen* (Athènes), 25, (1989), 26.
95. *The Itinerary of Beniaminde Tudela* (critical text, translation and commentary by N. M. Adler), London, 1907, 11.
96. J. Koder, F. Hild, & P. Soustal, *Tabula Imperii Byzantini*, 1. *Hellas und Thessalia* (DAW, 125), Wien, 1976, 40–41
97. Murnu 1984, 85–94, 130–151, 189–193; G. Soulis, The Thessalian Vlachia, ZRVI, 8, 1 (1963), 271–273; D. M. Nicol, Refugees, Mixed Population and Local Patriotism in Epiros and Western Macedonia after the Fourth Crusade, CIEB XV, vol. I, 8 (1976), 3–33 (Idem, *Studies in Late Byzantine History and Prosopography*, London, Variorum Reprints, 1986, IV); E. Stănescu, Premisele răscoalei Asăneştilor. Lumea românească sud-dunăreană în veacurile X–XII, *Răscoala 1989*, 21–23; Năsturel 1989, 52–54; A. G. C. Savvides, Splintered Medieval Hellenism: The Semi-Autonomous State of Thessaly (A.D. 1213/1222 to 1454/1470) and Its Place in History, *Byzantion*, 68, 2 (1998), 407–408; Brezeanu 1999, 164–165, 170.
98. Ostrogorsky 1956, 520, 530; Vacalopoulos 1970, 7–8; Jochalas 1971, 93; A. Ducellier, *La façade maritime de l'Albanie au Moyen Âge. Durazzo et Valona du XIe*

au XVe siècle, Thessalonique, 1981, 349; G. Soulis, *The Serbs and Byzantium during the Reign of Tsar Stephen Dushan (1331–1355) and His Successors*, Washington, DC, 1984, 110; Ferjančić 1988, 315–316; Gjuzelev 1991, 85; J. V. A. Fine Jr., *The Late Medieval Balkans. A Critical Survey from the Late Twelfth Century to the Ottoman Conquest*, Ann Arbor, MI, 1994, 253.

99. I. Caragiani, *Studii istorice asupra românilor din Peninsula Balcanică*, București, 1929, 5–6; N. Iorga, *Études Byzantines*, I, Bucarest, 1939, 41, 43; N. G. L. Hammond, *Migrations and Invasions in Greece and Adjacent Areas*, Park Ridge, NJ, 1976, 39, 42; T. J. Winnifrith, *The Vlachs, the History of a Balkan People*, London, 1987, 120.

100. A. J. B. Wace & M. S. Thompson, *The Nomads of the Balkans. An Account of Life and Customs among the Vlachs of Northern Pindus*, London, 1914, 257; S. Dragomir, La patrie primitive des Roumains et ses frontières historiques, *Balcania*, 7, 1 (1959), 162; Năsturel 1978, 228–229; Schramm 1986, 105; Năsturel 1989, 49.

101. V. Bogrea, Sur les Vlaques "oditai" de Cédrenus, *Bulletin de l'Institut pour l'Étude de l'Europe Sud-Orientale*, 7 (1920), 7–9, 51–52; Gyóni 1951, 29–42; Dragomir 1959, 110–134; R. C. Lăzărescu, Din nou despre vlahii din cronica lui Skylitzes, BBRF, 7 (11) (1979), 357–368; A. Tanașoca, Autonomia vlahilor din Imperiul Otoman în secolele XV–XVII, RdI, 34, 8 (1981), 1516; A. Lazarou, *L'Aroumain et ses rapports avec le Grec*, Thessalonique, 1986, 67–69; A. and N. Ș. Tanașoca, Ancienneté et diffusion du "cătun" vlaque dans la Péninsule Balkanique du Moyen Âge, RESEE, 27 (1989), 1–2, 139–144; Stănescu 1989, 19–20; Poghirc 1989, 25; Năsturel 1989, 49.

102. See P. Ș. Năsturel, Les Valaques Balkaniques aux Xe–XIIIe siècles (Mouvements de population et colonisation dans la Romanie Grecque et Latine), BF, 7 (1979), 107.

103. Dragomir 1959, 17, 31–32, 113–116, 162; Winnifrith 1987, 113; M. Cazacu, Les Valaques dans les Balkans occidentaux (Serbie, Croatie, Albanie, etc.). La Pax Ottomanica (XVème–XVIIème siècles), *Les Aroumains*, 80; Malcolm 1999, 54; A. Tanașoca & N. Ș. Tanașoca, *Unitate romanică și diversitate balcanică. Contribuții la istoria romanității balcanice*, București, 2004, 43–44. The name Sremljane indicates an immigration from Srem (the area between Danube and Sava).

104. Gashi 1985, 269.

105. N. Beldiceanu, Sur les Valaques des Balkans slaves à l'époque ottomane (1450–1550), *Revue des Études Islamiques*, 34, 1961 (1966), 90–91; Tanașoca 1981, 1517.

106. Dragomir 1959, 13–14, 159; G. Ivănescu, *Istoria limbii române*, Iași, 1980, 309, 369, footnote 1; Schramm 1986, 123; Năsturel 1989, 55.

107. P. Atanasov, La position du Mégléno-Roumain par rapport au Daco-Roumain et l'Aroumain, AIESEEB, 31 (2001), 159–168.

108. Th. N. Trâpcea, Contribuțiuni la istoria românilor din Peninsula Balcanică. Românii dintre Timoc și Morava, *Balcania*, 5 (1942), 230–233; S. Dragomir, La patrie primitive des Roumains et ses frontières historiques, *Balcania*, 7, 1 (1944), 89–94; N. Beldiceanu, La région de Timok-Morava dans les documents de Mehmed II et de Selim I, *Revue des Études Roumaines*, 3–4 (1957), 111–129; Dragomir 1959, 34–35, 171. For the events, see also L. Mavromatis, *La fondation de l'Empire Serbe. Le Kralj Milutin*, Thessalonique, 1978, 18, 22; Ș. Papacostea, *Românii*

în secolul al XIII-lea. Între cruciată și imperiul mongol, București, 1993, 124; Fine 1994, 220.

109. Pușcariu 1926, 338–366; Capidan 1943, 281–283; N. Drăganu, Ancienneté et expansion des Roumains d'après la toponymie, l'onomastique et la langue, Balcania, 6 (1943), 426–428; Dragomir 1959, 157–160, 171–180; Ivănescu 1980, 70–71; Rosetti 1986, 324.

110. *Annales Regni Francorum*, a. 818 (*Fontes ad Historiam Regni Francorum Aevi Karolini illustrandam*, Berlin, 1960, I, 116, 118).

111. V. Gjuzelev, Bulgarisch-Fränkische Beziehungen in der ersten Hälfte des IX. Jhs., BB, 2 (1966), 25–34; H. Bulin, Aux origines des formations étatiques des Slaves du Moyen Danube au IXe siècle, *Europe 1968*, 169–170; C. Beševliev, *Die protobulgarische Periode der bulgarischen Geschichte*, Amsterdam, 1981, 285–286.

112. Pușcariu, 3–13, 342–366; D. Găzdaru, Romeni Occidentali stanziati in Italia nel medioevo, *Cultura Neolatina* (Modena), 6–7 (1946–1947), 141–163; Dragomir 1944, 75–76; Dragomir 1959, 157–158; Panaitescu 1969, 224–227.

113. A fantastic ethymology from Mauri, which suggests descent from the Roman soldiers brought from Mauritania, was put forward by the Croatian priest Dominik Mandić in 1956. See N. Malcolm, *Storia di Bosnia dalle origini ai giorni nostri*, Milano, 2000, 114–115.

114. Pușcariu 1926, 3–32; Dragomir 1959, 36–109; Dragojlović 1989, 65; Winnifrith 1987, 115; Cazacu 1989, 83; Brezeanu 1999, 164–166; Malcolm 2000, 115–123; Tanașoca 2004, 46–47.

115. Dragomir 1959, 157–159.

116. Cazacu 1989, 83.

117. See note 105 and H. Inalcik, Ottoman Methods of Conquest, *Studia Islamica*, 2 (1954), 114–115; Dragomir 1959, 110–136; N. Beldiceanu & I. Beldiceanu-Steinherr, Quatre actes de Mehmed II concernant les Valaques des Balkans slaves, SOF, 24 (1965), 103–111; Beldiceanu 1975, 122–130; Tanașoca 1981, 1513–1530; N. Beldiceanu, Românii din Herțegovina (XIII–XVI), BBRF, 14 (18) (1987–1988), 83–102; Cazacu 1989, 86–88; Zirojević 1990, 49–50; Malcolm 2000, 111–112.

118. Dragojlović 1989, 65; Dj. Janković, *The Serbian Questions in the Balkans*. Faculty of Geography, Belgrade (www.rastko.org.yu/arheologija/djankovic-serbs_balkans.htm), 1995. See also other opinions mentioned by Dragomir 1959, 141–142; Tanașoca 1981, 1515–1516, footnote 13; Tanașoca 2001, 116–117; Tanașoca & Tanașoca 2004, 56–72.

119. A. Tanașoca, Caracterul etnic al vlahilor nord-vest Balcanici, *Cercetări de istorie și civilizație sud-est Europeană*, 5 (1988), 41–47; Tanașoca & Tanașoca 2004, 64–76.

120. Malcolm 2000, 111.

121. Kovačević 1973, 150–151.

122. Beševliev 1981, 159–168; Ditten 1993, 69–70; Pillon 2002, 103–141.

123. P. Charanis, The Transfer of Population as a Policy in the Byzantine Empire, *Comparative Studies in Society and History*, 3, 2 (1961), 140–154; J. C. Cheynet, Les transferts de population sous la contrainte à Byzance, *Travaux et Recherches de l'Université de Marne-la-Vallée*, 7 (2001), 46–47; Liebeschuetz 2003, 65–79.

124. Charanis 1961, 144–146, 152; Jenkins 1963, 29–30; Herrin 1973, 117, 119–120; Graebner 1978, 47; Ferluga 1979, 41; Angelov 1980, 97; Ditten 1993, 177–207, 331–353; Weithmann 1994a, 93; Cheynet 2001, 54; Liebeschuetz 2003, 76–77.

125. Ostrogorsky 1956, 161–162; Charanis 1961, 143–144; S. Antoljak, Die Makedonische Sklavinien, *Macédoine 1970*, 36–37; Graebner 1978, 44–45; Ditten 1993, 209–212, 216–234; Cheynet 2001, 51–52, 55; Liebeschuetz 2003, 76.

126. Charanis 1961, 148–149; Ferluga 1979, 39–41; V. Tăpkova-Zaimova, Les mouvements de populations en Mésie et en Thrace entre le début du XIe et le début du XIIIe s., BF, 7 (1979), 196.

127. Dragojlović 1989, 62–63.

128. Beševliev 1981, 180–181.

129. Beševliev 1981, 259; W. Treadgold, *The Byzantine Revival, 780–842*, Stanford, CA, 1988, 203, 290–291; Ditten 1993, 72, 89, 117. For the location of the deportation area, see D. G. Teodor, Quelques aspects concernant les relations entre Roumains, Byzantins et Bulgares aux IXe–Xe siècles n.e., *Anuarul Institutului de Istorie şi Arheologie 'A. D. Xenopol*, 24 (1987), 2, 9–12; O. Damian, Considérations sur la citadelle en brique de Slon-Prahova, *Studia Antiqua et Archaeologica*, 9 (2003), 485–487.

130. Hoffman 1977, 476; R. Samardžić, Migrations in Serbian History (the Era of Foreign Rule), *Migrations 1989*, 84–85.

131. Inalcik 1954, 122–123; D. Angelov, Certains aspects de la conquête des peuples balkaniques par les Turcs, ByzSl, 17, 2 (1956), 249–259; Dragojlović 1989, 63.

132. Inalcik 1954, 123–128; Angelov 1956, 263–268; F. Babinger, Die Osmanen auf dem Balkan, *Völker 1959*, 203–204; Stavrianos 1959, 97; Vacalopoulos 1970, 64–65, 162–165; Vacalopoulos 1973, 52–58 (and map nr. 4); R. I. Lawless, The Economy and Landscapes of Thessaly during Ottoman Rule, *Carter 1977*, 508; M. Vasić, *Der Islamisierungsprozess auf der Balkanhalbinsel* ("Zur Kunde Südosteuropas", II/14), Graz, 1985, 7; S. Runciman, *The Fall of Constantinople, 1453*, Cambridge, 1990, 37.

133. Hoffman 1977, 476.

134. See J. Kalić, La région de Ras à l'époque byzantine, in *Géographie historique du monde Mediterranéen* (sous la direction de H. Ahrweiler), Paris, 1988, 133 for central Serbia after 1455.

135. G. Palikruševa, Islamisation de la région Reka dans le nord-est de la Macédoine, *Macédoine 1970*, 138.

Chapter 2

The Political Aspects

THE DOWNFALL AND RECOVERY OF THE BYZANTINE DOMINATION AND THE RISE OF BULGARIA

The political map of the Balkan Peninsula dramatically changed at the beginning of the Middle Ages after the victories of the Avars and Slavs against the Byzantine army. Although it seemed that the Byzantine Empire would rescue the Danubian frontier in 601, the mutiny of the officer Phokas turned the course of the war in 602. The army that was supposed to remain north of the Danube during the winter marched toward the capital to proclaim this rebel as emperor, leaving undefended large parts of the frontier. The shattering of the *limes* continued in the following years. Very dangerous were the Avarian and Slavic invasions of 614–619, resumed in 623 and in 626, when Constantinople was besieged by a large Persian and Avarian coalition.[1] After the failure of this siege, Avarian power declined, but the Balkan Peninsula was almost abandoned by the Byzantine Empire. The emperor Heraklios applied a realistic policy, which consisted in the defense of the Asiatic part of the state, where he moved the troops that had retreated from the Balkan provinces. Aware that the western part of the empire could not yet be recovered, he chose to preserve what was more important for the survival of the state, namely, two-thirds of the army.[2]

A power vacuum appeared in many zones of the Balkan Peninsula after the re-treat of the Byzantine army. The small Slavic tribal organizations (Sclaviniae) were not able to fill it, and the Avars did not preserve their domination over this space after 626, with the exception of the present Croatia and Serbia. However, the retreat of the Byzantine administration was not total. The empire kept a zone west and north of the capital and some enclaves in Greece, among which the most important was around Thessaloniki. Urban life continued in these enclaves that were sur-rounded by Slavic tribes. Relations between these tribes and the Byzan-tines in the seventh and eighth centuries are described by a very valuable source that gathers accounts of the miracles said to be made by St. Demetrios, the patron of Thessaloniki. This text shows how the inhabi-tants of this city fought several times against the Avars and the Slavs. The Macedonian metropolis remained an island in the Slavic sea, a refuge for people who arrived there from endangered areas. The city survived be-cause it kept maritime relations with Constantinople.[3] The continuity of other cities like Thessaloniki, Corinth, Edessa, and Adrianople was a fa-vorable condition for the future Byzantine *reconquista*, achieved in the eighth and ninth centuries, when they became centers of the new military and administrative structures.

The Byzantine *reconquista* was a gradual and long process that started with the offensive led by Constans II (641–668) in 658 against the Slavic polities from Macedonia (the tribes of Draguvitoi, Rynchini, Sagudatoi, and Velegesitoi). After some decades, Byzantine domination in northern continental Greece was consolidated by a new campaign directed against the Slavs settled near Thessaloniki, launched by Justinian II (685–695, 705–711) in 688–689.[4] In the same years a type of organization of the Byzantine territory in the Balkan Peninsula appeared, based on provinces called *themes*, commanded by *strategoi*. This was decisive for the recovery of the lost positions, because it implied the military colonization of the ter-ritories occupied by the Slavs with Greeks.[5] The Thracian *theme* was es-tablished around 680, on the Black Sea shore north of Constantinople, in order to protect the capital against the aggressions of a new enemy, Bul-garia. Until the end of the eighth century, this province was extended up to Mesembria. Another *theme*, Hellas, was created in central and eastern Greece between 687 and 695.[6]

Bulgaria was founded by a group of Türkic warriors, called Protobul-garians by historians in order to distinguish them from the people that emerged from their mixture with the Slavs. They settled in 680 in the for-mer province Moesia Secunda near Varna, after a victory over the Byzan-tine army, which tried to prevent their aggressions launched from the area of the Danube Delta. In 681, the emperor Constantine IV was compelled to recognize the mastership of their khan Asparuch over Moesia.[7] Other

Protobulgarians came from Avaria in Macedonia in 685, under the rule of Kuver, but they were soon assimilated by the local population and by the other participants in this migration.[8]

In Moesia, the Protobulgarians subjected the local Slavic, Greek, and Romance population, but they were assimilated by the Slavs in the ninth century because of their small numbers. Only the name Bulgar was inherited by the new Slavic people. Their state combined the features of the typical Türkic kaganate with some Byzantine elements. The fast sedentarization, mixture with the local population, and closeness with the Byzantine cities led to a different political and cultural evolution than in the Avarian kaganate. The next khan, Tervel (702–718), started building a residence at Pliska, which became a fortress with stone walls (erected by Byzantine craftsmen). The same Tervel extended Bulgaria into Thrace (Zagora) after the wars against the Byzantine Empire in 712–716. On the other hand, this Bulgarian ruler received the title of *caesar*, because he helped the emperor Justinian II to return to Constantinople from exile. Before, this title was granted only to members of the imperial family. In this way began the gradual integration of Bulgaria into the Byzantine commonwealth. The new frontiers were recognized by the treaty conducted in 716.[9] For several decades, Bulgaria remained a weak state, where the rivalries between Slavs and Protobulgarians and between the filo- and the anti-Byzantines aristocrats led to many fights for power. The emperor Constantine V (741–775) thus found a good opportunity to wage war against Bulgaria several times, in the years 756–775. He stopped the Bulgarian expansion for a while, preserving the power balance in the Balkans.[10]

Constantine V was in fact the emperor who started the second stage of the Byzantine *reconquista* with the war against the Macedonian Sclaviniae in 758–759. Macedonia became a distinct Byzantine province sometime between 789 and 802, after a period of unification with the *theme* of Thrace. The new *theme* of Macedonia included the area between the rivers Nestos and Strymon, but after a few decades the region east of Strymon became a separate province, named after this river.[11] Greece was recovered in the same stage of the *reconquista*. In 783, the *logothete* Staurakios subdued several Slavic tribes from central Greece, which were included in a new *theme*, Peloponnesus, with a residence at Corinth. In this way, all of Peloponnesus was recovered.[12] Even before, after the establishment of the Hellas *theme*, some small Slavic rulers had been attracted to the framework of the Byzantine administration. They received the title of *archon*, attested to by several lead seals dated after 700.[13] Slavs from western and central Peloponnesus remained free until a new offensive of Nikephor I (802–811), in 805–806, which represented in fact the end of the *reconquista*[14] and the full establishment of imperial administration over the inland territories peopled by Slavs and ruled by their tribal chiefs. Other *themes* created in the eighth century and at the beginning of the ninth century were Strymon, Cephalonia, Dyrrachion, and Thessaloniki. In this way, many territories occupied by the Slavs in the seventh and eighth centuries were recovered by the Byzantines. The few rebellions of Slavic communities from Greece that occurred in the ninth and tenth centuries had no significant effect.[15]

If Greece was recovered, Macedonia and Thrace were still in danger, because Bulgaria was expanding after the victory achieved by Krum (803–814) against the emperor Nikephor I (802–811) in the battle at Vărbinka gorge in the Balkan range (July 26th, 811). The Byzantine army was slaughtered, and the Bulgarian ruler continued to advance toward Thrace and Macedonia, with the help of the local Slavic communities. The result was the division of Thrace between Bulgaria and the Byzantine Empire, with a frontier established south of Philippopolis (Plovdiv). Bulgaria continued the expansion in 837–842, when a large part of Macedonia entered under its domination.[16] This was not a simple territorial gain, since mastership over the central part of the Balkan Peninsula gave a great strategic advantage to Bulgaria.

Another direction of expansion was the west. After the fall of the Avarian kaganate in the first years of the ninth century, Bulgaria occupied its eastern part, becoming a neighbor of the Frankish Empire. Khan Omurtag (814–831) launched a campaign against the Franks in 827, conquering a new territory that extended up to Belgrade.[17] In this way Bulgaria gained control over one of the most important strategic zones in the Balkan Peninsula, the northern end of the road along the Morava valley.

The Bulgarian state was strengthened by the conversion to Christianity of khan Boris (852–889), who took the name of his godfather, emperor Michael III (842–867). The circumstances and consequences of this act will be analyzed in the following chapter. This fact enabled the integration of Bulgaria into the family of European states. The increasing of contacts with Byzantium, the presence of craftsmen from the empire working at the new capital Preslav, and relationships established with the Western world are some of the outcomes of the christening of Boris-Michael, who ruled Bulgaria between 852 and 889.

The climax of Bulgarian power was the reign of tzar Symeon (893–927). In the first years of his rule, he was confronted with a twofold attack by the Byzantine Empire, a reply to Bulgarian aggression in southern Thrace and Macedonia launched in 894. The emperor Leon VI (886–912) decided to encircle Bulgaria with an offensive in its south combined with a naval operation on the Danube supported by Hungarian warriors summoned from the northern steppe. The conflict of 895–896 ended with the crushing victory of Symeon at Bulgarophygon (in southern Thrace), in the summer of 896. In the first part of his reign, Symeon pursued the goal of extending Bulgaria to the south. When an Arab fleet ravaged Thessaloniki in July 904, he used this opportunity to conquer another part of Macedonia.[18]

The Bulgarian–Byzantine wars continued until 904. The peace was suspended by the new emperor Alexander (912–913), who stopped payments to Bulgaria, granted by the treaty of 896. Symeon started a new war against the Byzantine Empire, because he claimed the imperial title after the death of Alexander, since the new emperor, the child Constantine, was considered illegitimate by Patriarch Nicholas Mystikos (912–925), being the fruit of the fourth illegal marriage of Leon VI. Symeon used this opportunity, advancing to Constantinople in the summer of 913, requesting to be recognized as true emperor. The patriarch accepted only the title of emperor of Bulgarians and the marriage of Symeon's daughter with Constantine VII. By this marriage (not achieved), Symeon would have acquired a leading position in the empire. Even if his plan was only half accomplished, Symeon thus became the first foreign Balkan ruler who claimed imperial power from a Byzantine source. After 913, he entitled himself "tzar and autokrator of all the Bulgarians," according to the Byzantine formula. One of his lead seals bears the title *eirenopoios* ("pacificator"), which suggests that Symeon assumed one of the specific attributes of the Byzantine emperors. Because the empress Zoe (the mother of Constantine VII) did not recognize the concessions made by the patriarch, Symeon launched a new war against Byzantium that led to other conquests in Macedonia, Greece, and Albania, in 914–917. Finally, Bulgaria obtained another crushing victory at Acheloos, near the important harbor Anchialos (August 20th, 917).[19]

After the occupation of these Byzantine territories, Symeon began wars against the Serbs ruled by chiefs such as Peter Gojniković (892–917) and Zacharia Prvoslavljević (920–924), who were Byzantine allies, and against the Croats. But Croatia was a quite powerful kingdom, and Symeon was defeated by its king Tomislav in 926. The great Bulgarian tzar died a short time after this failure, in 927. His heir Peter (927–969) preferred to keep peaceful relations with the Byzantine Empire.[20]

Bulgaria remained a powerful state that shared control over a large part of the Balkan Peninsula with the Byzantine Empire. This status quo favored the integration of Bulgaria into Byzantine civilization but also prepared its future annihilation. After more than two centuries of fights and territorial changes, the political map of the Balkan Peninsula displayed different configurations for its eastern and western parts. The east was covered by two strong power centers, Byzantium and Bulgaria, while the west was divided between the quite powerful kingdom of Croatia and several small polities peopled by different Slavic tribes, whose history will be discussed in the next pages. The dividing line between these two Balkan worlds was nearly the same as the boundary between the former western and eastern Roman Empires and between the Croatian and Serbian territories.

THE SMALL SLAVIC STATES FROM THE CENTRAL AND WESTERN BALKANS

If the Slavs settled in Moesia and Thrace were subjected by Protobulgarians, those from Illyricum remained under Avarian domination until the end of the eighth century. This maintained a certain stability in the northwestern part of the Balkan Peninsula. The ruling class was mainly of Avarian origin, but also included Slavic, Kutrigur, and Gepidic warriors. When the Avarian power collapsed after the Frankish attacks of 791–803, some of these Slavic warlords became leaders in the peripheral areas of the former kaganate (Moravia, Croatia, and Serbia). These chiefs were recorded in the sources with the title *župan*, most probably of Avarian origin, ruling over small areas called *župe*, evolved from the unification of several Slavic clans (*zadruga*) in Croatia and Serbia. The title *župan* or great *župan* survived among the Serbs with the significance of "political ruler" and later, "prince."[21]

Some of these Slavic chiefs entered in alliance with the Franks during the wars against the Avars (for instance, Vojnomir, a Croatian prince from Pannonia who was baptized). After the downfall of the Avarian kaganate, other local rulers tried to establish independent polities. The most important was created in southern Pannonia (between Drava and Sava) by Ljudevit, who rebelled in 819 against the Franks in alliance with the Slovenians from Carniolia and Carinthia. This principality centered at Sisak (the former Roman town Siscia) ended after short time, when Ljudevit was killed in 823. Another small Slavic state appeared on the Dalmatian seashore, at Nin, the residence of *župan* Višeslav who became Christian around 800. For several decades, the Croats remained under Frankish sovereignty, but the creation of the Byzantine province Dalmatia around 870 gave one of their rulers, Domogoj (864–876), the opportunity to obtain independence for his small state. The reign of Croatia reached its climax under the rule of king Tomislav (910–928), who acted in the favorable circumstances of the Hungarian conquest of the Frankish Pannonian march and of the Moravian kingdom. He also closed an alliance with the Byzantine Empire in 923, in order to fight against Bulgaria. Tomislav received the administration of Byzantine Dalmatia, which meant in fact the extension of his realm. In *De Caerimoniis*, a text that describes the ceremonial procedures observed at the Byzantine court by the middle of the tenth century, the *archon* of the Croats was in the first position among the Slavic rulers from the western Balkans. This situation concerns the age of Tomislav, when Croatia also occupied Bosnia, up to the Drina and Neretva Rivers. Tomislav was crowned as king by Pope John X (914–928), most probably in 925. The first residence of the Croatian rulers was Nin, but it was moved to Biograd, on the Dalmatian seashore. Great Croatia shattered after the death of Tomislav. Bosnia was occupied by a Serbian *župa*, but it was recovered by Croatia at the end of the tenth century.[22]

The Serbian *župe* evolved in the ninth–tenth centuries in two regions: present-day central Serbia (Raška) and in Montenegro (also called Dioclea or Zeta). Raška is the depression located on the both sides of the river with the same name, around the city of Novi Pazar. Raška was a good region for the development of a state because of its placement at the intersection of several roads toward Danube and Thessaloniki and its resources (fertile land, iron, lead, silver). The first Serbian state was created by the great *župan* Vlastimir by the middle of the ninth century, in Raška and Dioclea. His heir Mutimir, who by baptism became a Byzantine ally, repelled an attack by Bulgaria around 880. Another small Serbian state emerged in Zachlumia at the end of the ninth century under the rule of Michael Višević, an ally of Bulgaria.[23] Other Serbian rulers, Peter Gojniković and Zacharia Prvoslavljević from Raška, also entered in alliance with the Byzantine Empire because they were threatened by the Bulgarian expansion. The Byzantines tried in 917 to stimulate the Serbs and the Hungarians to attack Bulgaria, but the plan failed and Symeon took the initiative, invading Serbia in 917 and replacing Peter with a faithful prince, Pavel Branović. In 920, Symeon continued the expansion against Zacharia, who expelled Pavel at the request of the Byzantine emperor Romanos Lekapenos (920–944). However, Zacharia regained power with Byzantine aid in 923 and fought against Bulgaria in 925, but he was finally defeated, his state being occupied by Bulgaria. This was the climax of Bulgarian power in the Serbian area; an offensive in Croatia (926) was a disastrous defeat. The unexpected result of the western expansion of Bulgaria was the consolidation of the Byzantine influence in Croatia and in Serbian lands, because these polities needed a strong ally, which was naturally Byzantium.[24]

A new Serbian state ruled by the great *župan* Ceslav Klonimirović (927–960) was formed in Dioclea after the disappearance of the Bulgarian danger. Klonimirović unified several Serbian tribes from Dioclea, Raška, Herzegovina, and central Bosnia, but for a short time, because his state was shattered after a Hungarian attack.[25]

The Slavs settled in the central and western parts of the Balkan Peninsula were not able to create a single state, like the Bulgarians. The main reason is the fragmentation of the geographic environment, not existing in Bulgaria. Another cause was the location between the Bulgarian and Frankish spheres of influence. This fact impeded the unification of the small Serbian and Croatian polities and has also contributed to the future divergent evolution of these peoples.

THE BYZANTINE OFFENSIVE (NINTH–ELEVENTH CENTURIES)

After the restoration of its administration in all of Greece, the Byzantine Empire remained face-to-face with an increasingly stronger enemy: Bulgaria. The Balkan Peninsula became a bipolar space after the extension of Bulgaria into Thrace and Macedonia in the ninth century. In the same century, Byzantine imperial ideology returned to offensive universalism. In the collection of laws *Epanagogè* (883–886), the patriarch Photios states that the duty of the emperor is to recover the lost properties, which meant the reconquest of the former Roman provinces occupied by the barbarians. In turn, the patriarch of Constantinople had the mission of converting the pagans and heretics from the empire and from abroad. In this way, military expansion and the missionarism of the Church were combined in a single doctrine of world domination by Constantinople.[26]

The new offensive policy followed two centuries of defensiveness in a lessened space, threatened by west and by east. Emperor Theophilos (829–841) began a military reform and launched a strong offensive against the Arabs. His policy was further developed by Basil I (867–886), the founder of the Macedonian dynasty. During this dynasty, the Byzantine Empire reached the apex of its political and military power. Basil I recovered many of the lost territories from Asia Minor as well as zones from southern Italy that were conquered by the Arabs. However, the achievement of the western offensive policy was hindered by the existence of Bulgaria. Basil I managed to attract to the Byzantine sphere of influence the small Serbian polities west of Bulgaria, but the fight against this powerful state was the task of his heir, Leon VI (886–912). The confrontation ended with the victory of the Bulgarians, under Symeon. However, the weak policy of Bulgaria's next tzar, Peter (927–969), favored a kind of Byzantine hegemony over Bulgaria. The Byzantine Empire waited for a good opportunity to extend effective domination in this country.

This occasion came in 966. The emperor Nikephor II Phokas (963–969) decided to make retaliations against Bulgaria, because Peter did not hinder the attacks of the Hungarians who crossed his realm toward the Byzantine capital. The emperor requested the cooperation of the Russian prince Svyatoslav, but the prince started his own campaign of conquest in Bulgaria in 968. In Bulgaria, the new tzar Boris II (969–972) closed an alliance with Nikephor, but many Bulgarian aristocrats supported the Russians. In the second Russian offensive (969), the capital Preslav was conquered by Svyatoslav, who decided to advance toward Constantinople. At that time, the new emperor John Tzimiskes (969–976) was at war with the general Bardas Phokas. He was thus forced to accept the peace proposed by Svyatoslav in 970, but he started a counteroffensive in 971. After the occupation of Preslav, the Russians took refuge in Dristra (today, Silistra), but they did not resist the siege. Svyatoslav was compelled to retreat to his own country, while the Byzantine army began taking Bulgaria.[27] John Tzimiskes organized in the Lower Danube the new province of Dristra, later called Paradunavon. Its western limit was on the valley of the Iskăr River. In Thrace the *themes* Berrhoia (around Stara Zagora) and Philippopolis (around Plovdiv), included in the duchy of Adrianople, were created.[28]

The Byzantine domination in Bulgaria was soon threatened by a rebellion initiated in 976 in Macedonia by a local aristocrat, Samuel, and his brothers. The fight for liberation was favored by the civil wars in which the Byzantine emperor Basil II (976–1025) was involved until 989. In the meantime, Samuel had already conquered Thessaly and a large part of Bulgaria, including Preslav (in 986). Samuel continued to rule from Ochrid, a Bulgarian fortress with a well-defended position on the shore of the lake with the same name in western Macedonia. The conquest of the Danubian region was motivated not only by the desire for liberation of all of Bulgaria. The presence of the Byzantine army in northern Dobrudja even after 986 was a serious threat. Dobrudja was not the only recovered Danubian territory. Just after the death of John Tzimiskes a small province was created in the area of the Morava River, attested to by the lead seal of Adralestos Diogenes, imperial *protospatharos* and *strategos* of Morava (the city located at the mouth of this river).[29] This Byzantine penetration into the Middle Danube caused Hungarian duke Geza to create an alliance with Samuel. Geza offered one of his daughters to Gabriel Radomir, the son of Samuel and future tzar around 995, but the marriage was broken after two or three years, when Gabriel Radomir took another wife, a Greek from Larissa. At that time, the province of Morava had already disappeared (perhaps since 986, when the northern offensive of Samuel took place).[30]

The main offensive directions of Samuel were south and west. In 997, he became the master of Dioclea and of the important harbor Dyrrachion, the western end of *Via Egnatia*. He also crowned himself tzar of Bulgaria. During two decades, he reconquered Macedonia and western Thrace (former Bulgarian possessions), and also Thessaly, Epirus, and Albania. The small rulers from Dioclea, Raška, and even Bosnia were his vassals. Basil II failed to attract Croatia and Dioclea to his side. The victories of Basil II against the Arabs in 995–999 and his alliance with the Fatimide caliph Al-Hakim in 1001 allowed the transfer of armies in Europe to the Bulgarian front. The first great Byzantine victory against Samuel was achieved in 997. In 1001, the armies commanded by the generals Theodorokanos and Nikephor Xiphias reconquered Thessaly, Macedonia, Thrace, and the eastern Bulgaria, including Preslav.[31] Next year, through another campaign, conducted by the emperor himself, the important city of Vidin was occupied.[32]

In 1004 the Byzantine army again attacked Macedonia, and important fortresses like Servia and Vodena came under Byzantine control, assuring a powerful strategic position at a small distance from the Bulgarian power center. After this, Basil II planned to leave free a part of Bulgaria (a region around Ochrid and Prespa), but the Bulgarians resumed the war in 1014. A decisive victory of the Byzantine army on July 20th, 1014, in the Kimbalongon gorge on the Strymon River ended the supremacy of Samuel. The tzar died when he found out about the disaster suffered by his army (14,000 prisoners were blinded and sent back). The following four years represented the agony of the Bulgarian empire. The last two tzars, Gabriel Radomir (1014–1015) and John Vladislav (1015–1018), were not able to resist. The Bulgarian state disappeared in 1018 after the conquest of Ochrid, its last capital. In this way the Byzantine *reconquista* of the Balkan Peninsula was achieved.[33]

The *theme* of Bulgaria, which included the entire central part of the Balkan Peninsula, was organized in 1018. The residence was established at Skupion (Skopje), under the command of David Arianites.[34] In order to ensure the pacification of Bulgaria, Basil II attracted several Bulgarian commanders to his side (since 1001), while other leaders, including members of the ruling family, were sent to the eastern provinces after 1018. He thus tried to prevent any revival of the Bulgarian state, but future events would show that these measures had no real effect.[35] For the common people, Basil II accepted keeping taxation in kind and not in money. For the Church, he decided that Ochrid would continue to be an autocephalous archbishopric with jurisdiction over the entire former Bulgarian state, and that this eparchy would be ruled only by Bulgarian clergymen.[36]

During the military operations against Bulgaria, the Byzantine army marched up to Sirmium (Sremska Mitrovica). This city in 1018 or 1019 became the seat of another *theme*, developed perhaps in the framework of the former *theme* of Morava. The *theme* of Sirmium included two other important towns, Belgrade and Branicevo. Its first known commander was Constantine Diogenes, attested to between 1018 and 1027.[37]

In several previous studies[38] the establishment of the province Paradunavon has been dated to the year 1018, following the opinion first expressed by Nicolae Bănescu[39] and supported by other historians like Ion Barnea,[40] Vasilka Tăpkova-Zaimova,[41] and Hans-Joachim Kühn.[42] The other point of view, sustained by Ivan Jordanov,[43] Paul Stephenson,[44] and Ion Bica,[45] argues that the lack of evidence of seals with the title *katepano* (duke) of Paradunavon before the 1050s would mean that the *theme* called Dristra existed with this name until the Pecheneg crisis of 1045, when the Lower Danubian area was reorganized. A recently published seal of Leon Drymis, *anthypatos*, *patrikios*, and *katepano* of Dristra,[46] who was *katepano* of Bulgaria sometime between 1055 and 1065, clarifies the problem, because it shows that the province called Dristra was still in existence at the middle of the eleventh century. Paradunavon was most probably introduced as official name on the occasion of the campaign led by Isaac I Comnenos in 1059 in the Danubian region, to which time can be dated the first *katepano* of Paradunavon, Demetrios Katakalon.[47]

The Byzantine Empire lost the strong position of Dyrrachion in 997, but not for long, because the defeats suffered by Samuel caused the local dignitaries to turn to Basil's side in 1004 or 1005. In this way, the *theme* of Dyrrachion was recovered, but north of it, the ruler of Dioclea, John Vladimir, was forced to become the vassal of Samuel in 998. This change of loyalty from Byzantium to Bulgaria was advantageous, since more lands came under his control.[48] After 1018, in Dioclea or near this territory another province called Serbia was organized, whose limits are not known. For some time, scholars believed that this province was the same as Sirmium.[49] The administration of the *theme* of Serbia was soon granted to the local Slavic rulers, who enjoyed a kind of autonomy. In these remote areas, Byzantine authority was exerted through such local chiefs (*archontes* or *župani*), watched by the *strategoi* installed in the main cities. One such *archon*, Ljudevit, was entitled in 1039 *strategos* of Zachlumia and Serbia. He was in fact the ruler of all the Serbs. Another, Dobronas, was recognized before 1036 as *archon* of the cities Zadar and Salona.[50]

A part of the Dalmatian seashore was conquered by the Venetian doge Pietro II Orseolo in 1000 with the agreement of Byzantium. Only the end of the Bulgarian wars made possible the restoration of Byzantine control in the former *theme* of Dalmatia, but the centrifugal trends of the Slavic communities from the western Balkans, supported by Venice and Hungary, led to the gradual disappearance of Byzantine power in Dalmatia and Croatia. In Croatia, King Krešimir III (997–1030) accepted Byzantine vassalage in 1019. Croatia tried several times between the 1020s and the 1060s to expand into Byzantine Dalmatia. Finally, the emperor Romanos Diogenes (1067–1071) offered this province in 1069 to the Croatian king Peter Krešimir IV (1058–1074). The consolidation of the Croatian kingdom continued with the coronation of Zvonimir by Pope Gregory VII (1073–1085) in 1075, but the succession crisis that followed after his death

(1090) was an opportunity for the Hungarian king Coloman (1095–1116) to crown himself as king of Croatia, Slavonia, and Dalmatia. Croatia was in this way annexed by Hungary in 1102. However, the preservation of significant forms of autonomy allowed the survival of the ethnic and cultural Croatian identity through the Middle Ages. The real rule was exerted by a kind of viceroy called *ban*.[51]

The expansion of Hungary in Croatia and Dalmatia was an important change in the balance of power of the Balkan space that affected the positions of the Byzantine Empire. In the twelfth century, Byzantine–Hungarian relations, sometimes hostile, sometimes peaceful, would be definitive for the Balkan policy of Constantinople, because no other significant power was able to jeopardize Byzantine domination in the peninsula, until the revival of Bulgaria.

PAX BYZANTINA AND CENTRIFUGAL TRENDS IN THE ELEVENTH AND TWELFTH CENTURIES

The successive reconquests achieved during the ninth and tenth centuries by Basil II seemed to open an era of regional stability in the Balkan Peninsula, a *pax Byzantina*, like the ancient *pax Romana*.

After the death of Basil II in 1025, the transition from a long state of war to peace decreased the resources allocated for military purposes, despite the income of the state being increased by an excessive tax policy. This income was provided by a growing urban economy. After three or four centuries of devolution when the ancient towns became small fortresses (*kastra*), whose only real urban function was the bishopric, the cities revived as economic centers. The recovery of the Balkan regions and the pacification of the Eastern Mediterranean space by wars against the Arabs were good opportunities for the development of long-distance trade on sea and along the terrestrial roads where such cities were located. The towns supported the progress of the monetary economy, which offered in turn resources for the conversion to a paid army, after the middle of the eleventh century.[52] The evolution was contemporary with the urban revival in the West, but with three significant differences. The first concerns the place of agriculture in the economy of these cities, preserved in a higher degree than in the western towns.[53] The second was the absence of official autonomy in relations with the imperial power, that is the absence of city councils, and, generally speaking, of a public life.[54] Finally, unlike in the West, rich landowners had their residences in the cities.[55]

Autonomy was a desire of the new class that emerged in the cities: rich people who acquired top positions in society and in the state, whose fortunes came especially from the surrounding estates. These *dynatoi*, "the powerful," or *archontes*, a kind of gentry, were disturbed by the strong control exerted by the state. The emperors issued several laws in the tenth century against the increasing power of these landowners, in order to protect the small properties of the military (*stratiotai*). As long as the army was mainly based on the manpower of the small landholders, it was imperative for the state to limit the pressure exerted by the *dynatoi* against them. Things changed after the death of Basil II. The conversion to a paid army made this concern futile, while the increasing influence of the aristocracy in the exercise of imperial power gave support to the ambitions of the provincial rich men, masters of *oikoi* (aristocratic residences in the towns). Their wealth and power made them a kind of local dynasts in the small and medium cities. This was a premise for unrest. With their *synkastritai* (the citizens) and their soldiers, they were able to defend their interests, which were sometimes the same as the interests of the city. This evolution was manifest in times of disorder, for instance at the end of the 1070s at Adrianople. The power of these local dynasts was not necessarily given by official dignitaries. It was only based on their fortunes and military force.[56] Indeed, these *dynatoi* began to gather private armies that allowed them to control the cities and their surroundings.[57]

The revenues of the state were used more and more for different civilian purposes, some of them useless, including gifts for the favorites of the emperors, but also for potential external enemies. As Michael Angold and Paul Stephenson have shown, Basil II left a "poisoned legacy": a too large and expensive army. For this reason, successive emperors tried to transform their general strategy after the hard Pecheneg inroads of 1036, when it became obvious that a classical *limes* was not useful. They replaced the defensive policy based on warfare with a policy based on trade and gifts for the barbarians ("trading, not raiding").[58] This policy failed. The conversion to a paid army had no significant results, since the Byzantine Empire was not able to repel invasions that occurred on the Danube and in the east. Only the short reign of Isaac I Comnenus (1057–1059), who took power after a military mutiny, attempted reform that aimed for a new militarization of the state, required by the increasing danger. The real recovery would be achieved by a new military regime introduced by Alexios I Comnenus (1081–1118).[59]

Another feature of the eleventh century in the Balkans was the crisis in relations between center and periphery, caused by increasing taxes. The peasants and shepherds were not able to pay more and more for the state when the emperors increased taxes or converted money to levies in kind in order to obtain extra resources for the wars. Rebellions like that of Peter Delian (1040) or Constantine Bodin (1072) were an answer to this fiscal pressure and to the corruption and bad administration,[60] but they were not started by the peasants. The initiative belonged to the local rich landholders, *dynatoi* of Bulgarian and Serbian origin, who were too disturbed by the fiscal pressure. In fact, the opposition against the central power did not have a "national" character, since these movements also involved the Greek-speaking population. The hate of the central power unified people of different ethnic origin and of different social status, under the rule of *dynatoi*, who became the defenders of the local communities against the state.[61]

Basil II established a policy of cooperation with the local aristocrats of Bulgarian and Serbian origin in the Byzantine administration of Bulgaria, Dalmatia, Dioclea, and Raška. They were monitored by Byzantine *strategoi* settled in the main cities. The relations between the *strategoi* and the local *archontes* were based on gifts, stipends, and honors, like the relations between the emperor and the barbarian chieftains. In this way, Byzantine power was exerted over territories included in the empire, but separated by internal frontiers.[62] When these *archontes* became disturbed by the fiscal policy of the center, they initiated the rebellions.

The eleventh-century Balkan rebellions can be classified as:

1. mutinies of generals who wished to usurp imperial power (for instance, Georgios Maniakes in 1042–1043, and Leon Tornikios in 1047);
2. rebellions that wished to usurp imperial power under the form of the restoration of the Bulgarian state (Peter Delian, Tihomir, George Vojtech, Constantine Bodin); and
3. separatist rebellions in small and medium-size territories (Stephen Vojslav, Niculitzas, Tatos and Nestor).

The first type will not be discussed here, because those mutinies were not centrifugal movements (sometimes, they expressed only a rivalry between western and eastern armies).[63] The separatist rebellions were not specific to the Balkans. In the same period, the Byzantine Empire was confronted with similar movements in Apulia (1040), Armenia (1051–1052), and Antioch (the independent principality of Philaret Brachamios, after 1073).[64] The Balkan region was not itself a problem for the empire. The real problem was the crisis in relations between center and periphery, whatever the periphery, a crisis caused by increasing taxes that burdened poor and marginal regions. If elsewhere the autonomist movements expressed only the ambition of the local rulers, in the Balkans the ultimate reason for mutinies was poverty. The conversion from the *stratiotic* army to a paid army after the 1030s required higher incomes,[65] but the peasants and shepherds from underdeveloped regions were not able to pay more and more for the state when the emperors increased taxes or converted the money to levies in kind to obtain extra resources for wars against the Pechenegs or other enemies.[66]

However, the common people did not start the revolts; the local rulers, of Greek Bulgarian, Serbian, Pecheneg, or Vlach origin, did. They planned the movements with autonomy, independence, or imperial power in mind. The aristocrats were the real rulers or beneficiaries of all the "popular" uprisings.[67] The leaders found support among the common people eager to escape from the fiscal pressure of the center. Paul Stephenson has remarked that the self-interest of the local aristocrats was the main factor in the centrifugal uprisings, and in some cases, "the principal mean to galvanize popular support for a secessionist movement was to appeal to the common memory of an independent ruler of the northern Balkans, whose authority resided in the title 'emperor of the Bulgarians.'"[68]

Some of the leaders were aristocrats who acquired the status of *douloi* or *anthropoi* of the emperors. Such chiefs from the peripheral areas bore the title *toparch* in Byzantine sources. A *doulos* was a *toparch* who renounced his territory, a kind of vassal. The *toparch* was a ruler who preserved a position between autonomy and subjection to the imperial power. Basil II was wise to accept partial freedom for these local chiefs. Their unrest meant the tentative recovery of former territory or its independency, and the breaking of the *douleia*.[69] Other leaders were civilian or military dignitaries (Tihomir, Nestor, and Niculitzas). The movement from the *theme* of Bulgaria led by George Vojtech from Skopje was initiated by a group of local landowners affected by actions of Nikephoritzes, the dignitary of Michael VII who tried to apply an innovative but unpopular financial policy.[70] Finally, other rulers involved in rebellions were barbarian chiefs like those who took power in Paradunavon in 1072 (Tatos, Sesthlav, Satza).

The territorial target of the centrifugal movements varied from the independency of a small or medium-sized territory (Thessaly, Paradunavon) to the restoration of Bulgaria as an independent state ruled by a tzar (Peter Delian and Constantine Bodin). In the case of Delian, the legitimacy of the title of tzar was given by claimed descent from Gavril Radomir. According to Michael of Devol (the copyist of the chronicle of Skylitzes), Peter Delian was the son of a Hungarian princess (sister of King Stephen I), the first wife of Gabriel Radomir.[71] Real or not, what matters is that the rebels believed it. He was acclaimed as a tzar at the beginning of the revolt, at Belgrade.[72] It seems that he took also the old Bulgarian title of *khan*.[73] Constantine Bodin was invited by the Bulgarian aristocrats to take for himself the same title of tzar of Bulgarians in the revolt led by George Vojtech.[74]

The first separatist movements rose in the *theme* of Bulgaria, because the emperor Michael IV (1034–1041) cancelled the fiscal and religious

privileges granted by Basil II to the population of the former Bulgarian
state (in 1037 he appointed a Greek as head of the archbishopric of
Ochrid). In the summer of 1040, nobleman Peter Delian proclaimed himself tzar of the Bulgarians. He pretended he was the son of tzar Gabriel
Radomir (1014–1015). This fact is highly possible, but still unproven. It
seems that Hungary was somehow involved in the initiation of the
mutiny (if Peter Delian was the son of Gabriel Radomir, he was at the
same time the nephew of King Stephen I of Hungary).[75]

The troubles started at Belgrade and soon covered the entire *theme* of
Bulgaria. The rebels conquered important cities like Niš and Skopje.
Meanwhile, another leader, Tihomir from the Dyrrachion *theme*, pretended to the same title of tzar, but he was eliminated by Peter Delian,
who conquered the city of Dyrrachion. From Bulgaria, the rebellion extended to the *theme* of Nikopolis, where the local population was also affected by the financial policy of the center. In the autumn, the mutineers
advanced from Skopje to Thessaloniki, following the imperial army that
had retreated to Constantinople. The upheaval was not defeated with a
Byzantine counteroffensive, but as a consequence of the rivalry between
Peter Delian and a truly legitimate heir of the Bulgarian dynasty: Alusian,
the son of the last tzar John Vladislav (1016–1018), who abandoned the
command of a city in Asia Minor to join the rebels. Of course, Alusian
wanted sole leadership, and this led to discord. In the end, after he
blinded Peter Delian, Alusian made peace with Michael IV. The unrest
thus finished in 1041, mainly because its leaders were not united. This
does not decrease its importance, since it has been proven that the fiscal
pressures of the center could undermine the stability of the newly conquered provinces and could revive "national" feelings. It is clear that the
movement aimed for the restoration of the Bulgarian state, but it is likewise true that the participants had mainly economic and social goals.
They were not only Bulgarians, but also Serbs, Greeks, and Aromanians.
It was a general uprising against the tax burden of the poor people from
the Balkan provinces.[76]

In Zeta (Montenegro), the vassalage ties were broken in 1042 by the *župan* Stephen Vojslav (1018–1043). The army commanded by the duke of
Dyrrachion sent against him in 1043 was defeated in the hard, nearly inaccessible rocky region. In this way, the former principality led by John
Vladislav was restored.[77]

When a Hungarian army conquered Sirmium and ravaged the area between Belgrade and Niš in 1071–1072,[78] the population from the *theme* of
Bulgaria found a new opportunity to rebel, trying for a second time to restore their state. This time, the Bulgarians were helped by the Serbian
prince, Mihailo Vojslav (1046–1081), who followed Stephen Vojslav as
ruler of Zeta. In that period there was no rivalry between Bulgarians and

Serbs. The Bulgarian aristocrats led by George Vojtech from Skopje proclaimed as tzar Constantine Bodin, the son of Mihailo, with the name of Peter. The uprising started at Skopje in 1072. The rebels advanced toward Niš and Ochrid, but they were defeated after a few months. Bodin was imprisoned until 1078. The province of Bulgaria was pacified, but Zeta remained a free territory. In his attempt at liberation from the Byzantine hegemony, Mihailo Vojslav was supported by the Norman kingdom of Sicily and by Pope Gregory VII, who crowned him as a king in 1077, in certain circumstances that will be analyzed in the next chapter. After his death, Constantine Bodin, who became king of Zeta (1081–1101), extended the state into northern Albania and Bosnia. His political action was thus determined by the anti-Byzantine trends that found support among the Catholic Serbs and Albanians. Entitled *Rex Slavorum* by Pope Clement III (1084–1100), he had the chance to include in the realm almost all the Serbian lands, but he was finally defeated by Alexios I Comnenos in 1101.[79]

The centrifugal movements presented above had only a rural background. The first rebellion with exclusively urban origin took place in Thessaly in 1066. According to the so-called *Strategikon* written by Kekaumenos between 1075 and 1078, Niculitzas, an aristocrat from Larissa, the main city in Thessaly, forewarned the emperor Constantine X Dukas (1059–1067) in the spring of 1066 that too-high taxes could cause a rebellion in the Hellas *theme*. This emperor tried to compensate for the devaluation of coinage and payments for mercenaries with supplementary taxes. Even with this increased budget, the military expenses were not enough to support defense, which resulted in a disastrous situation on all frontiers. The invasions of the Selgiuk Turks and of the Uzoi (1065) caused large damages, showing how powerless the army was; moreover, the Sicilian kingdom was ready for an offensive in the Greek lands of the empire.[80] This weak defense was an incentive for mutinies. The movement was started by a group of notables of Vlach and Greek origin from Larissa, some of them military. The population of Larissa and from the neighboring area composed by Greeks, Aromanians, and Bulgarians was stricken by the abusive fiscal policy. There is no reason to see in this unrest a movement of Aromanian liberation, as some historians have thought.[81]

Kekaumenos tried to minimize the guilt of Niculitzas, ascribing all the responsibility to the Vlachs and to the local leaders, pretending that Niculitzas accepted the leadership of the mutiny because he thought he would be able to control and stop it. The rebellion started in June 1066 with an offensive against Servia, the powerful fortress that defended the Stena Petras pass between Thessaly and Macedonia. The main leaders were arrested when they tried to continue the conflict, as well as Niculitzas, who remained suspect by the emperor. George Murnu supposed that Niculitzas was not truly loyal.[82] Indeed, we can express doubts about his faithfulness. Another plot against Constantine X was organized by Romanos Diogenes (the future emperor), when he was *dux* of Serdica (Sofia), a short time before the death of Constantine X (May 22nd, 1067). Niculitzas had had friendly relations with Romanos Diogenes since the latter was in office in Serdica.[83] Just after he became emperor, Romanos Diogenes released Niculitzas from prison, appointing him to a high position in the navy.[84] It is difficult to say if this denotes clemency or complicity, and if Romanos Diogenes began his plot when the Thessalian rebellion was still in progress (before September 1066). However, a common action is not excluded, as well as cooperation with Robert Guiscard, the Norman king of Sicily, who launched after a short time a campaign against the Byzantine Empire, namely against Macedonia.[85] *Via Egnatia*, the major road used by Guiscard in his offensive, was the target of an offensive by Thessalian insurgents.

Jadran Ferluga holds that the rebellion of 1066 indicates the progress of feudalization in the Byzantine Balkans.[86] In fact, the most specific feature of this movement was the evolution toward urban autonomy. The conflict resulted from the interaction between a growing monetary economy and the fiscal pressure of the center, unable to cope with the new trends. The conspirators declared they wanted Niculitzas to be their "master" (*authentes*), a word reserved for the emperor. In the same time, the acclamation *polychronos* addressed to Niculitzas by the people of Servia was the expression used when an emperor was proclaimed. They also declared they were *douloi* of Niculitzas. This is the Byzantine expression for "vassal," used in relations between the emperor and his subjects. Therefore, it seems that the rebellion evolved toward the usurpation of imperial power,[87] the instrument by which the rebels tried to reach their goal of urban autonomy.

After a few years, the desire for urban autonomy fired another region, Paradunavon. The financial reforms introduced by Nikephoritzes were perceived as a threat by the people of Paradunavon. In fact, they lost the payments previously sent from the center to secure frontier defense.[88] Sources recorded that the *stratiotai* were dissatisfied because they were excluded from the administration of the *theme*.[89] In these circumstances, the city of Dristra accepted the rule of the Pecheneg chief Tatós, who inherited the autonomy granted to Pechenegs by the treaty signed by Constantine IX in 1053.[90] A seal found at Silistra proves that the Byzantines recognized the autonomy of a territory called Patzinakia, located inside Paradunavon.[91] It follows that Tatós was an ally of the Byzantine Empire who seized the opportunity to stir up a rebellion of the Byzantine population.

The dignitary Nestor, sent by Michael VII as *katepano* of Paradunavon, also came over to the side of the rebels and, moreover, led an attack against Constantinople. Attaliates said that Nestor was a former *doulos* of Constantine X, of "Illyrian" origin. This archaism could indicate a Serb or Vlach, and seems less probably to be equal to "Bulgarian,"[92] as some historians believed.[93] He was perhaps a local aristocrat who had abandoned his possessions to the emperor Constantine X and become an intimate of Michael VII. This could explain the high rank of *vestarchos* held by Nestor. The title *anthropos*, synonymous with *doulos*, is confirmed by the seals that belonged to Nestor.[94] His actions in Paradunavon could be interpreted as an opportunity to acquire an independent territory for himself, during the crisis of 1072. A connection with the mutiny led by Constantine Bodin cannot be excluded. Nestor was forced to share power with Tatós. This dual leadership weakened the mutiny and the offensive against Constantinople.[95] After six years, the coming of Nikephor Botaneiates as new emperor changed the attitude of the rebels; their messengers to Constantinople promised that they would not continue to attack the empire together with the Pechenegs.[96] The initial reason for the Paristrian mutiny ceased to exist, but the Pechenegs remained hostile to Byzantine power. They were also helped by their brothers from the area north of the Danube. A lead seal of Nikephor Basilakes, *dux* of Dyrrachion, found in the Byzantine fortress Nufăru on the Danube,[97] confirms the information that Basilakes sent some messages to the Pechenegs when he rebelled in 1078.[98] Relations between the Paristrian people and the Pechenegs evolved from cooperation against the center to the mastership of the latter. Confronted with the force of these professional warriors, the natives entered under a new domination, a local and barbarian one, that replaced the central Byzantine administration. The centrifugal trends were expressed in this case by the settlement of a barbarian power in Paradunavon.

The Pecheneg mutiny transformed the area between the Danube and the Balkans into an independent territory, a Pecheneg realm, Patzinakia. This situation was recognized by Alexios I by the treaty concluded after the defeat of autumn 1087.[99] The master of this territory was at that time the Pecheneg Tzelgu. This chieftain made an alliance with the former Hungarian king Solomon. In this way a powerful anti-Byzantine coalition was established.[100] The Pechenegs from Paradunavon were already allied with the Bogomils from Veliatova, since 1084, and with Tzachas, the emir of the Selgiuk Turks from Smirna. The victory of Lebounion against the Pechenegs (1091) ended this long crisis.[101]

The Hungarian annexation of Croatia in 1105 changed the whole balance of power in the Balkans. Future Byzantine policy was compelled to take into account this new factor. It is true that Sirmium, the important outpost at the Hungarian front, was recovered around 1078,[102] but Byzantine control was still weak in this contact zone with a potential enemy. John II Comnenus (1118–1143) tried to keep good relations with Hungary, in order to concentrate his forces in the eastern part of the empire. The Byzantine-Hungarian wars of 1127–1129 on the Danube had only a defensive goal.[103] Things changed during the reign of Manuel I Comnenos (1143–1180), who, in his attempt to recover the lost possessions of Basil II, reconquered Dalmatia (1165) and a part of Croatia, after the great victory against Hungary (Zemun, 1167).[104] The wars against Hungary were imminent with the consolidation of the Danubian frontier after 1156. A recent inquiry into Manuel's policy argues that the emperor intended to transform Hungary into a kind of buffer state between Byzantium and the German Empire, and that the relations between him and Frederic I Barbarossa after 1156 could be characterized as a kind of "cold war" (an idea first expressed by Paul Magdalino).[105]

The Byzantine–Hungarian clash involved a region which was in that period the new political center of the Serbian lands: Raška. By the end of the eleventh century, the great *župan* Vukan founded a new state in Raška. He tried to extend in 1093 into some Byzantine territories (Skopje, Tetovo, Vranje), without success.[106] His center was the fortress of Ras, located at Pazarište, ten km west of the present town Novi Pazar, a bishopric see since the eleventh century.[107] The Serbs from this region, ruled by the great *župans* Uroš I (c. 1125–c. 1145)—the father-in-law of the Hungarian king Bela II (1131–1141)—and Uroš II (c. 1145–c. 1160) rebelled in 1127 and 1149–1151 during the Byzantine–Hungarian wars, but failed. The Serbs were especially dangerous because they jeopardized the security of the Belgrade–Niš–Sofia road.[108] The pacification of this remote area of the empire that had close relations with Hungary was a must for Manuel I Comnenos, who finally succeeded in appointing a faithful ruler in 1166, the great *župan* Tihomir (1166). Tihomir divided his polity with his three brothers, Stephen Nemanja, Miroslav, and Stracimir, but the first rebelled against him. The help given by the Byzantine army in 1171 was useless. Stephen Nemanja remained the single ruler, but after he accepted subjection to Manuel. He founded a dynasty that ruled Serbia exactly two centuries, until 1371.[109]

When the powerful emperor Manuel died, the Hungarian king Bela III (1172–1196) found a good opportunity to take back Dalmatia and Sirmium in 1181. Much more, involved in the intrigues at the Byzantine court, he continued attacks against Byzantine territories pretending he was fighting against the usurper Andronikos Comnenos. He thus annexed a large region of Hungary between Belgrade and Sofia after two campaigns fulfilled in 1182–1183, in cooperation with Stephen Nemanja. The same usurpation was taken as a pretext by the Norman king of Sicily William II (1166–1189) for an offensive in the Byzantine Empire that supported the pretender Alexios, a nephew of Manuel. The most important result of this campaign of June–August 1185 was the conquest of Dyrrachion. Other places along *Via Egnatia* were plundered, including Thessaloniki.[110]

The new emperor Isaac II Angelos (1185–1195), who murdered Andronikos, made a peace agreement with Bela III, which included his marriage with Margaret-Maria, the young daughter of the Hungarian king. As dowry, he received exactly that territory that was occupied in 1183–1184. He did not recover Dalmatia and Sirmium.[111] The restoration of Byzantine control over a large section of the Morava corridor was in fact futile, because the empire was already on the fringe of collapse. It is true that Isaac repelled the Norman army, but he faced after a short time a major crisis in the northern part of the Balkan Peninsula. The abusive fiscal policy of Isaac II Angelos, who suddenly increased taxes in 1185–1186 to collect more money for the imperial wedding, was a too-difficult burden for Romanian owners of large sheep flocks from the area of the Balkan Mountains. As in 1066 in Thessaly, the unrest against the central authority was launched by these Romanians, who attracted Bulgarians to the movement. Two of these Romanians, Asan and Theodore (afterward called Peter, after the name of the former Bulgarian tzar and of the rebel Peter Delian), asked the emperor for a *pronoia* and mastership over the so-called toparchy of Moesia, which meant in fact an autonomous status for Bulgaria within the empire.[112] *Pronoia* was a lifetime possession granted by the emperors to aristocrats who where obliged in this way to provide military forces from those estates. Over the long term, this institution contributed to the feudalization of the Byzantine state and stimulated autonomist trends (especially when they became hereditary, in 1258), but during the Comnenian dynasty the results were favorable, because the professional army organized in this way was indeed efficient.[113]

The Romanians and the Bulgarians started the rebellion because Isaac II rejected their claims. The events began near Anchialos (Pomorje) in early 1186. They attacked the fortresses from eastern Bulgaria. The Byzantine Empire was also troubled by a new military mutiny, started by general Alexios Vranas against the emperor Isaac II Angelos. This general, a supporter of the former emperor Andronikos Comnenos, was appointed commander of the army sent against the Romanian and Bulgarian rebels. He tried to take power with the help of inhabitants from the periphery of Constantinople, but the mutiny failed in September 1187. A part of his army passed to Peter in October 1187. If Peter accepted subjection to Byzantium, Asan would take refuge among the Cumans, north of the Danube, to find help from them. In 1188, operations resumed by the Byzantine army, but they did not succeed in defeating the Romanians, Bulgarians, and Cumans. Isaac II was compelled to make a truce in the summer of 1188, which recognized Bulgaria, and the new Romanian and Bulgarian state extended into Paradunavon and a part of Thrace. As in the rebellion of Tatós, nomad warriors from the north had a decisive role in increasing the military capability of this state. The civilian unrest evolved into a separatist movement because the Cumans improved the military force of the rebels, and because the Byzantine army was poorly commanded.[114]

The second stage of the evolution of the state founded by the Asan brothers started with the throning of Asan as tzar of the Bulgarians and Vlachs, in the new capital Tărnovo, at the end of 1188. This means that he considered himself the inheritor of the former Bulgarian tzardom. It seems that Vlachia was then a distinct territory, which could be located in the Timok basin or in northeastern Bulgaria and Dobrudja.[115]

The dissolution of Byzantine domination in the northern Balkans was influenced by Norman attacks and by the third and fourth crusades. In this context the rebels searched for the support of the Western powers. Asan managed to use for his own interests the conflict between Byzantium and the participants at the third crusade, offering his support to the German emperor Frederic I Barbarossa, who with his army entered the Morava valley toward Constantinople in 1189. Asan pretended to be recognized as emperor by Frederic, of course without success. This reveals too the evolution from a simple rebellion to the claim of imperial power.[116]

Unlike the previous Bulgarian rebellions, the events started in 1186 led to the formation of a state that was indeed the heir of the former Bulgarian empire. In 1191–1196, the army composed of Romanians, Bulgarians, and Cumans conquered new territories that roughly covered ninth-century Bulgaria. The state continued to consolidate, despite the internal fights that led in 1196 to the killing of Asan by Ivanko, a Bulgarian chief who afterward became until 1199 the ally of the Byzantine emperor Alexios III Angelos (1195–1203), who gave him a feudal estate at Philippopolis. The new tzar Peter was murdered in 1197, but his younger brother and heir John or Ioanitza (1197–1207) firmly established his authority and gained new victories against Byzantium in 1200–1202. In these circumstances, Alexios III recognized the existence of the Romanian–Bulgarian state in 1202. Another consequence of the new offensive of Ioanitza was the change of loyalties of Ivanko. He passed to the side of Ioanitza in 1200, but after a few months he was captured by Alexios III.[117]

In the same years, an Aromanian polity ruled by the *pronoiar* Dobromir Chrysos from the city of Prosakos (Prosek) emerged in southern Macedonia. First a Byzantine ally, he changed to the side of Ioanitza, most probably in 1194. Alexios III fought against him several times in 1196–1199, but he failed to conquer its residence, although the forces of Dobromir were quite limited. Finally, Dobromir's possessions were occupied by Ioanitza around 1205. A Bulgarian governor was installed at Prosakos.[118] Another rebellion against the central power inflamed Peloponnesus in 1202. An aristocrat called Leon Sguros proclaimed himself independent and master of Nauplion and next of Corinth. From this center he exerted domination over the eastern Peloponnesus until 1208, in cooperation with his relative the *megadux* Michael Stryphnos.[119]

In the last decades of the twelfth century, the small Serbian state from Raška continued expansion toward the south in the favorable circumstances of the conflicts between the Byzantine Empire, Bulgaria, Hungary, and Venice. The rise of the Nemanja dynasty was favored by the downfall of Byzantine power in the Balkans after 1180. At the beginning, the great *župan* of Raška Stephen I Nemanja (1171–1196) was the vassal of Manuel I Comnenos, between 1171 and 1180. The death of Manuel and the rebellion of the Asan brothers stimulated the breaking of ties with Byzantium. Stephen Nemanja had already conducted an alliance with Hungary in 1182–1183, when this kingdom conquered the territory between Belgrade and Sofia. Stephen Nemanja was later defeated by the Byzantines in 1190 in the Morava valley, but the peace treaty had some favorable outcomes for Serbia. Receiving as daughter-in-law the princess Eudoxia, the Serbian great *župan* entered the Byzantine family of princes with the high title of *sebastokrator*. The peace did not last. Stephen I Nemanja resumed fights against the Byzantine Empire, conquering some territory from Kosovo. In this way Serbian penetration toward the central parts of the Balkan Peninsula began. Stephen Nemanja was again defeated by the Byzantine army, but he kept for a time the zones conquered in Kosovo (Peć, Prizren) and in northern Albania and Montenegro (Bar, Shkodër).[120]

All these centrifugal actions started by the Vlach, Bulgarian, Serbian, or Greek local leaders in the last decades of the twelfth century and in the first years of the thirteenth century occurred when Constantinople was no longer able to exert real authority over the provinces. The fights for power between the emperors Alexios III and Isaac II weakened the state and especially provided a pretext for foreign intervention (Alexios Angelos, the son of Isaac II, requested the help of the participants in the fourth crusade for the restoration of his father as emperor in August 1202). The fourth crusade started in 1202 was transformed by Venice as an instrument for its own anti-Byzantine policy. The crusaders put Alexios on the throne as co-emperor with Isaac II (he is known as Alexios IV) in July 1203, but he was replaced by Alexios V, who tried to resist the crusaders, but with no success. On April 12th, 1204, Constantinople was conquered and ravaged by the crusaders.[121]

The division of the Byzantine state was made according to the treaty entitled *Partitio Romaniae*. At Constantinople a new empire, ruled by Baldwin of Flanders, was established. This Latin Empire included Thrace and Asia Minor. Boniface of Montferrat became the master of Thessaloniki and of a part of Macedonia. In Greece, several participants in the crusade received feudal estates, among which the most important became the duchy of Athens, ruled by a Burgundian dynasty until 1311. However,

Venice received the greatest advantage, because it obtained half of Constantinople and many islands and harbors in the Aegean and Adriatic Seas that enabled the development of trade in the Mediterranean and Black Seas.[122]

The collapse of Byzantine authority in the Balkan space that followed after the end of the Comnenian dynasty shows that Pax Byzantina was more a desideratum than a reality. *The centrifugal trends led finally to the appearance of several new states that also had imperial ideals, taken from the single possible model, Byzantium.* This clash between small imperialisms is the origin of the rivalry between Bulgarians, Serbs, and Greeks for hegemony in the Balkans, manifested not only in the Middle Ages, but especially in the nineteenth and twentieth centuries. *All the national Balkan states created in the nineteenth century (Greece, Serbia, Bulgaria, later Albania in 1913) built their political ideologies and mythologies on a medieval background (or even ancient, in Greece).*

THE INHERITORS OF BYZANTINE IMPERIALISM

After 1204, only some territories from Asia Minor remained free: the new Greek empires of Trabzon and Nicaea. The Nicaean Empire founded by Theodore I Lascaris (1206–1222), the son-in-law of Alexios III, recovered quite quickly a part of the territories that were conquered by the Latins. The legitimation of this new empire was ensured by the establishment of its own patriarchate. The wise policy of successive emperors John III Dukas Vatatzes (1222–1254) and Theodore II Lascaris (1254–1258) created the economic and military bases of the reconquest of Constantinople, later achieved by the emperor Michael VIII Paleologos (1259–1282). Theodore II Lascaris created a new army recruited only from among the Greeks, because he thought that he could not rely on an army composed of strangers. It was a completely different army than the previous one, from the eleventh and twelfth centuries, composed by mercenaries. With its efficient army, the Nicaean Empire was able to recover Constantinople on August 15, 1261.[123]

The empire restored by the Nicaean dynasty was no longer a universalist, but a Greek empire. This made possible the acknowledgment of the new empires created by Bulgarians and Serbs in the thirteenth and fourteenth centuries by the Byzantine imperial ideology of their period.[124] Orthodoxy remained definitive for Byzantine political ideology, but a change that denoted a kind of malleability toward the Catholic Church can be observed. Although Constantinople was reconquered, the empire was still weak and it was forced to avoid the hostility of the western states. The recovery of the capital caused the reaction of the Catholic powers, which tried to restore the Latin Empire. The main enemy was the Kingdom of Naples ruled by the Anjou dynasty. At the beginning, King Charles I of Anjou (1266–1285) organized an anti-Byzantine coalition together with Serbia and Bulgaria, after the conquest of Albania in 1271. In these circumstances, the emperor Michael VIII was forced to accept the possible unification of the Church, that meant in fact the subordination of the Byzantine Church under the jurisdiction of Rome. With this purpose the Council of Lyons II was convened in 1274, where the unification of the churches was proclaimed. The fierce opposition of the Byzantine clergy thwarted the actions of Michael VIII, but the political target was reached: the aggression of the Angevine kingdom was stopped.[125] Later, pressed by the Ottoman danger, John VIII Paleologos (1425–1448) tried another compromise, accepting discussions for the reunification of the Church at the Council of Florence (1438–1439).[126] Before Michael VIII, John III Vatatzes also agreed to the unification in 1254, with the condition that Pope Innocentius IV (1243–1254) stop protecting the Latin Empire, but the victories against this enemy made this compromise useless.[127] These facts show that the Byzantine Empire was no longer in the thirteenth–fifteenth centuries the same state based on militant Orthodoxy and universalist ideology as it was before 1204. The empire became a state of Greeks that tried to defend itself by different means, including negotiations with the Catholic powers and with the popes, a fact that was unthinkable before.

There is some proof for the emergence of a Greek "proto-nationalism" in the thirteenth–fifteenth centuries, emphasized not only by the Byzantinists but also by a specialist in political sciences.[128] The revival of the word *Hellenes*, which was previously synonymous with "heathen," is significant. In the thirteenth century, this ethnic name again gained prestige, receiving the meaning of "Byzantine citizen." The so-called Paleologian Renaissance (an amazing cultural flourishing that occurred during the political decline of Byzantium) was in fact a recovery of the values of ancient Hellenism. Among the ideological and political conflict between the Byzantine and the Latin worlds rose a feeling of "national" pride based on Hellenic roots and stimulated by the difficult circumstances. This Greek patriotism appeared in the Empire of Nicaea as a synthesis between Roman universalism and Hellenic culture.[129] In 1246, when the Macedonian city of Melnik was attacked by John III Dukas Vatatzes, someone urged the inhabitants to surrender the fortress, because "our region used to form a part of the Byzantine Empire . . . and we . . . are by race pure Romans [Byzantines]."[130]

In the European part of the former Byzantine Empire, the prince Michael I Dukas Angelos (1204–1215) founded a small state in Epirus just after the dissolution of the empire, which gained after a short time some territories taken from Venice and from different Latin feudals, including

Thessaly. His brother Theodore I Angelos Comnenos Dukas (1215–1228) extended the principality in Albania, Thessaly, and in southern Macedonia during the offensives of 1217–1218 and 1224. In Albania, the decline of central Byzantine authority favored the rise of some *archontes* in the region near Dyrrachion.[131] Progon was the first Albanian ruler recorded between 1190 and 1198, with a residence at Kroia (in Arbanon). He still recognized the Byzantine suzerainty. After 1204, his sons Gjin and Demetrios became independent, following the model of Dobromir Chrysos and Leon Sguros. After the death of Demetrios (1215), his land was occupied by Theodore I Angelos Comnenos Dukas.[132]

The great achievement of Theodore I Angelos Comnenos Dukas was the occupation of Thessaloniki in 1224 and his coronation as emperor of Thessaloniki in 1225 or 1227. The two surviving Greek states were in competition for the position of legitimate successor of the Constantinopolitan empire. At the same time, the emergence of this state transformed the previous bipolar relationship in the Balkans to a tripolar one. The ascension of the new Greek empire of Thessaloniki, that wished in fact for the liberation of Constantinople, was stopped by Bulgaria at the battle of Klokotnica, in the valley of the Maritza River (March 9th, 1230). The Greek empire of Thessaloniki survived only to 1246, when it was conquered by John III Dukas Vatatzes. Epirus, having remained independent after this event, would continue competition with the Empire of Nicaea until 1259, when the victorious campaign of the army commanded by the general John Paleologos against Michael II Dukas of Epirus led to the expansion of the Nicaean Empire over the western part of *Via Egnatia*, including Dyrrachion.[133]

In the years after 1204, the Balkan Peninsula was divided between two major poles of power: the Latin Empire and Bulgaria. The confrontation between them was unavoidable, because Ioanitza also wanted Constantinople. Since 1202, he had asked Pope Innocentius III (1198–1216) to confer upon him the title of emperor of Bulgaria, accepting conversion to Catholicism. The negotiations were complicated by the attitude of Hungary, disturbed in its expansionist policy by the pretensions of Ioanitza, who claimed the Belgrade–Sofia region, the former possession of Hungary. Finally, John I Asan was crowned at Tărnovo in November 8th, 1204 by the envoy of the pope, Cardinal Leon of Santa Croce, but only as king of Bulgaria and Vlachia.[134]

The conflict between the Latin Empire and Bulgaria started soon after the division of the Byzantine Empire. At the beginning, Bulgaria was successful. The Latin emperor Baldwin of Flanders was captured in the battle of Adrianople (April 14th, 1205). With the help of the Cumans and allied with Theodore I Laskaris, the emperor of Nicaea (1204–1222), John I Asan advanced south in Macedonia in 1205–1207. The main target was

Thessaloniki, but this city remained in the hands of Boniface of Montferrat. Only the killing of Ioanitza in October 1207 by plotters led by his nephew Boril did the intent to destroy the Latin Empire of Constantinople end.[135]

After the death of John I Asan, the new tzar Boril (1207–1218) tried to extend Bulgaria into northern Macedonia and Thrace by changing alliances with Epirus, Nicaea, and the Latin Empire. He was also compelled to establish peaceful relations with Hungary when Andrew II (1205–1235) conquered Vidin in 1211.[136] His reign was a fiasco, but the following Bulgarian ruler, John II Asan (1218–1241), made Bulgaria temporarily the greatest power in the Balkans. The expansion of Bulgaria was achieved especially toward the south, where the battle was a great defeat for the Greek Empire of Thessaloniki. Its ruler Theodore II Angelos was defeated and imprisoned. In a commemorative inscription for that victory, John II Asan was entitled "tzar of the Bulgarians and Greeks," a title that reflected his supremacy in the Balkan Peninsula (up to Albania and Thessaly) and his claims over Constantinople.[137]

Bulgaria thus became a great danger for the Latin Empire, and Pope Gregory IX (1227–1241) tried to stop it with the help of its faithful kingdom, Hungary. John II Asan maintained an alliance with Hungary in the first part of his reign, but in 1231–1232 he was attacked by the Hungarian king Andrew II. In 1232, Andrew II conquered two important cities in Bulgaria, Belgrade, and Branicevo. Next, he organized a border area called Banat of Severin, whose mission was fighting against Bulgaria. The conflict caused the abandonment of the Catholic affiliation of the Bulgarian Church and the alliance with the Nicaean emperor John III Dukas Vatatzes, in 1234–1235, directed against the Latin Empire. Constantinople was three times besieged by the two emperors, in 1235–1237, but John II Asan ceased because he was afraid of a Hungarian attack.[138]

The death of John II Asan coincided with a major event in the history of Eastern and Central Europe: the Mongol invasion. Bulgaria was not seriously affected in the first years of the Mongol attacks, but the new wave of 1259–1260 led to its vassalage. In the south, Bulgaria lost Thrace after the offensive of Theodore II Lascaris in 1256. The internal fights for power after 1241 and the successive Byzantine, Latin, and Hungarian attacks between 1254 and 1266 weakened Bulgaria and led to the division of this state into two smaller tzardoms centered at Tărnovo and Vidin. Some of the seashore territories were recovered by Byzantium in 1263. The decline was accentuated after the civil war of 1278–1284. Another independent state, entitled despotate, was formed in the 1280s near Dristra (Silistra). Bulgaria continued to be subjected to the Golden Horde after the extension of the domination of khan Tokta (1291–1312) over the Lower

Danubian khanate ruled by Nogai (1299). Tzar Theodore Svyatoslav Terter (1300–1322) of Tărnovo used his position as vassal of the Mongols to take from Byzantium some zones on the seashore and south of the Balkan Mountains in 1304–1308. Although Michael Šišman (1323–1330) united the state of Vidin with his tzardom, the shattering of Bulgaria continued in the third decade of the fourteenth century with the formation of two more autonomous principalities, in Dobrudja (led by Balica) and in Zagora (led by a certain Voislav).[139]

The decline of Bulgaria after the middle of the thirteenth century was the consequence of the concentric expansion toward it of the Byzantine Empire, the Golden Horde, and Hungary. The real winner of this change of the power balance was Serbia.

THE RISE AND THE BREAKING UP OF GREAT SERBIA

The history of Serbia in the thirteenth–fourteenth centuries shows how *the decline of the Byzantine Empire favored the filling of the power vacuum by a state that usurped the imperial idea.* Serbia annexed former Byzantine territories with a heterogeneous population in Kosovo and Macedonia, moving in several steps its political and religious centers into these regions that did not belong to the ethnogenetic area of the Serbs. After the shattering of this Great Serbia, the center of the surviving state turned back to the north.

The king Stephen II Părvovečani ("The First Crowned"), who reigned between 1196 and 1227, continued the expansion of Serbia with the annexation of Zeta (Montenegro) in 1216 and of another part of Kosovo in 1217 (with the city of Prizren). Zeta was until then the possession of his eldest brother Vukan, who considered himself the inheritor of the former Dioclean dynasty that ruled once in the eleventh century. Vukan established an alliance with the Hungarian king Emeric (1196–1204), because he dreamed of extending his domination over Raška, but finally his brother proved to be stronger. In 1217, Stephen received the royal crown from Pope Honorius III (1216–1227), despite the opposition of the Hungarian king Andrew II. This act signified the acknowledgment of Serbian sovereignty, but it also expressed the general offensive of the Roman Church in the Balkans (see the next chapter). The southern extension led to the movement of the residence of the kings from Ras to Prizren, in Kosovo.[140]

The political development of Serbia was favored by economic growth (the exploitation of the silver mines provided increasing income for the state, including for the recruitment of a professional army) and by the decline of neighboring Bulgaria after the middle of the thirteenth century.

The internal consolidation of the state achieved during the long reign of Stephen I Uroš (1243–1276) was a precondition of the future expansion, even if the next ruler Dragutin (1276–1282) divided the state in 1282. Dragutin continued to master a separate region near the Hungarian kingdom, called Mačva, under Hungarian vassalage, while his younger brother Milutin remained king of Serbia.[141]

The expansion of Serbia into Macedonia started during the reign of Stephen II Uroš Milutin (1282–1321). It has to be observed that this great success, which was decisive for the future evolution of the state, was due to participation in a large anti-Byzantine alliance with George I Terter of Bulgaria (1279–1292), the *sebastokrator* John I Angelos Dukas of Thessaly (1268–1296), and Charles I of Anjou, the king of Sicily (1268–1285). The latter hoped to restore the Latin Empire of Constantinople. But history evolved in another direction, because it was the time of the rise of Serbia. A decisive moment was the conquest of Skopje, dated 1282 (or 1290, according to L. Mavromatis). This city became the new capital of Serbia, located in the region that assured supremacy in the central Balkans, Macedonia. The ethnic situation of this region became more complex with the Serbian penetration. Moreover, the conquest of Dyrrachion in 1295 or 1296 gave Serbia control over the western end of *Via Egnatia*.[142]

The emperor Andronikos II (1282–1328) was forced to make peace in 1299, recognizing as Serbian the territories located north of the Ochrid–Prilep–Štip line. In fact, these regions were bestowed as dowry for the princess Simonis (a five-year-old girl given as wife to Stephen Milutin). Stephen Milutin continued the offensive against Byzantium, joining in 1308 a coalition formed at the initiative of Pope Clement V (1304–1314) in order to support Prince Charles of Valois, pretender to the throne of Constantinople.[143] It can be again observed how Serbia chose the alliance with the Catholic powers to fight against the Byzantine Empire. This trend began with the Serbian rebellions from 1126 and 1149–1151. *All these facts contradict the usual cliché of Serbian Orthodox militancy.* This militancy existed, *but only since the reign of Stephen Dušan, when the Serbian state assumed from Byzantium the imperial idea.* Until the coronation of Stephen Dušan in 1346, Serbia fought several times against the Byzantine Empire, sometimes in cooperation with the Catholic states. Even after the coronation, Stephen Dušan promised to Pope Innocentius VI (1352–1362) in 1354 that he would convert to Catholicism in order to stop a possible Hungarian attack, and hoped that the pope would appoint him the commander of an anti-Ottoman crusade.[144]

The alliance of Stephen II Milutin with Charles of Valois in 1308 was intended to prevent the latter's cooperation with the rival brother Dragutin, who had converted to Catholicism. In 1300, Milutin decided to unify Serbia and launched a war against his brother, which lasted until 1314. Only the death of Dragutin in 1316 made possible the unification of Serbia. This event, as well as the recovery of Dyrrachion in 1315 (the city was taken back by Byzantium in 1299), caused a serious change in the balance of power in the Balkans and provoked the formation of a new Catholic coalition, composed of Charles Robert, king of Hungary (1301–1342), Philip of Taranto (duke of Achaia, 1313–1331), and the *ban* of Bosnia, Mladen Subić. Being defeated, Serbia lost in 1319–1321 two important strategic points, Belgrade and Dyrrachion. The Catholic Albanians, who rebelled against Serbian domination, were also involved in this conflict.[145]

Serbian expansion continued into Macedonia in 1308, when the fortress Štip was conquered. The city was next given back to the Byzantine Empire in 1319, but the surrounding region would be again occupied by Serbian tzar Stephen III Uroš Dečanski (1321–1331) in 1322. The latter formed an alliance with the Byzantine emperor Andronikos II, who was at war with the pretender Andronikos III, his nephew. In this civil war that raged between 1321 and 1328 was also involved the Bulgarian tzar Michael Šišman, allied with Andronikos III against Serbia in 1326 (after he broke vassal relations with Stephen Dečanski). During the offensive in Macedonia, Serbia conquered new strategic points like Prosek and Veles, but the frontier remained unstable, because Andronikos III took the area after a few years, around 1330.[146]

The end of the civil war by the victorious entry of Andronikos III into Constantinople on May 24th, 1328, made possible the decisive confrontation between Bulgaria and Serbia. The alliance between the Byzantine emperor and the Bulgarian tzar still existed, but its target was now the defeat of Serbia, the state that disturbed both powers. After the penetration of the Serbian army into Byzantine territory in 1329, Andronikos III and Michael Šišman decided on a common offensive against Serbia, but they were defeated at Velbužd (today Kjustendil) on July 28th, 1330, by Serbian king Stephen III Dečanski. Michael Šišman died in the battle. *The confrontation of 1330 was a turning point in the history of the power balance in the Balkan Peninsula, because Serbia became the strongest state in the region.*[147]

The greatest expansion of Serbia was achieved during the reign of Tzar Stephen Dušan (1331–1355). In his first years, he was confronted with a Catholic coalition composed of Hungary, the Angevine kingdom of Naples, and Albanian rebels from Zeta. The latter started the mutiny in 1319 against Stephen Dušan when he was the local governor of Zeta and northern Albania, with a residence at Shkodër. In 1332 and 1336, the Catholic Albanian chiefs rebelled again, with the support of Pope John XXII (1316–1334) and of the Kingdom of Naples. Archbishop Guillaume Adam decided in 1332 that northern Albania was a good starting zone for attacks against Serbia, and that the Albanians would be very useful in the fight against Serbia.[148]

In the meantime, Stephen Dušan started a war against Andronikos III, helped by Bulgaria (he married the sister of the Bulgarian tzar Ivan Alexander). In 1334, Serbia reconquered the areas from western Macedonia that were lost in 1330 (Ochrid, Prilep). The new civil war in Byzantium in 1341–1347 between John V Paleologos (1341–1391) and John VI Cantacuzenus (1347–1354) was an opportunity for Stephen Dušan to intervene first on the side of John VI Cantacuzenus, and later, to attack him when he was defeated. The result was the Serbian occupation of the rest of Macedonia in 1343–1348. The fortresses Vodena, Verria, Gynaikokastron, Servia, and Serres were conquered one after another. The occupation of Serres in September 1345 was a turning point, because this town was the most important in Macedonia after Thessaloniki. In these cities were installed garrisons that became kernels of the Serbian colonization of Macedonia. Feudal and church estates were granted to the Serbian noblemen who owned them until the disappearance of the principality of Serres ruled by John Uglieša, in 1371. Stephen Dušan also conquered Thessaly, Epirus, Aetolia, Acarnania, and Albania (in 1343–1348). Thessaly survived for a time as an independent principality, split from Epirus after the death of the despot Michael II Dukas Angelos, in 1268. His son John I Dukas Angelos (1268–1296) continued the leadership of the Epirote dynasty. It seemed that this principality would take the prominent place of Epirus, but the land was divided between local and western aristocrats at the beginning of the fourteenth century. Thessaly thus became easy prey for Serbia.[149]

The great expansion of Serbia (doubled in size from its area before the reign of Stephen Dušan) was facilitated by the military weakness of the Byzantine state and by the hope of the local inhabitants that the new master would stop the calamities caused by the long civil and international wars.[150] Seizure of important Byzantine territories was a good reason for Stephen Dušan to claim the imperial title. He was crowned at Skopje on April 16th, 1346 (Easter), as tzar, not of Serbia, but of the Serbs and *Romaioi* (Byzantines), as several documents remember. *Romania*, that is the Byzantine Empire, was mentioned in the title because Stephen Dušan acquired a part of it. In this way, Serbia usurped the Byzantine model. Several Byzantine political institutions like *despot, caesar,* and *sebastokrator* were rtaken, as well as the symbol of the two-headed eagle.[151] Stephen Dušan considered himself a follower of the Byzantine imperial idea, when the Constantinopolitan empire was in decline. In the previous century, the same overtaking of Byzantine court titles and symbols could be observed in Bulgaria. In fact, it was proven that the final target of Stephen Dušan was the conquest of Constantinople.[152] The analysis of the facts and of the documents issued during his reign shows that Stephen Dušan intended to build his own empire according to the Bulgarian model, but that the ultimate target was the conquest of Constantinople.[153]

Stephen Dušan conquered a large territory that included all of the central part of the Balkan Peninsula. In the north, Serbia reached the Danube, while in the west eastern Bosnia was occupied. Kosovo became the political and spiritual center of the Serbian empire, whose capital was established at Priština. Stephen Dušan ruled directly the southern part of the tzardom (Kosovo and Macedonia), while the northern part was granted to his son Stephen Uroš, who held the same title of tzar of the Serbs and *Romaioi* (1355–1371).[154] Therefore, Great Serbia was not a unitary state. Stephen Dušan was not able to unify this large ethnically and religiously heterogeneous territory. The state was not centralized, because some regions (Thessaly, Epirus, Albania) were ruled by almost independent princes. The empire would have a chance to survive only if Stephen Dušan conquered Constantinople.[155]

The fate of Great Serbia shows that this state was an artificial one. Following the death of the powerful tzar Stephen Dušan in 1355, his empire was shattered. The new tzar, Stephen Uroš (1356–1371), who had ruled in the northern part of the former empire, was not able to preserve the unity. Being the result of some favorable circumstances and of the action of a great political and military leader, Great Serbia was an ephemeral polity in Balkan history. Even so, or maybe because of this, the myth of Great Serbia survived in Serbian national ideology as a support for the nineteenth-century revival, the foreign policy of Serbia, and Serbian hegemony within the Yugoslavian federation. One of the successor states was ruled in eastern Macedonia, at Serres, by the despot John Uglieša, between 1365 and 1371. The Serbian state from Serres was strongly influenced by Byzantium. Many dignitaries were Greeks, while the clergymen were mostly Serbs. The Macedonian state of John Uglieša was more Byzantine than Serbian, in the same way that the empire of Stephen Dušan was an imitation of the Byzantine Empire. The southern part of the empire (western Macedonia and Kosovo) came under the leadership of King Vukašin (1365–1371) who resided at Prilep.[156] Another prince, Symeon Uroš, a stepbrother of Stephen Dušan, was appointed in 1347 governor of Epirus and Acarnania. After the extension of his realm over Thessaly in 1356, his ambitions increased so much that he claimed the title of "emperor of the Serbs, Greeks (*Romaioi*), and Albanians." He reigned at Trikkala until 1371.[157] The son-in-law of Symeon Uroš, Thomas Preljubović, was appointed governor of Epirus in 1367 (he reigned until 1383). His small principality centered at Jannina was constantly attacked by the Albanians.[158]

The real power was exerted in Albania by several local rulers from the families Thopia, Spata, Dushman, and Dukagjin. The rise of an Albanian state had been hindered by the domination of the kingdom of Naples (1271–1284, 1304–1345) and of Serbia, which occupied northern Albania and Dyrrachion in 1295 and for a second time in 1343–1345. Charles I of Anjou created in the conquered regions a *Regnum Albaniae*. This caused the extension of the name Albania beyond the limits of the old Arbanon, from the Mat River up to Kanina and up to the Drin River.[159] Albania remained divided between several power centers after the dissolution of Great Serbia. The despots Gjin Buia Spata and Peter Liosha were recognized by Symeon Uroš in 1359–1360 as rulers in Epirus and Aetolia. Albanian historians consider Gjin (or Ghinu) Buia and Peter Liosha Albanian, but it is sure that at least the Buia family was of Aromanian origin (about the clan of Buioi, see p. 32). Gjin Buia Spata (1360–1400) tried to create an independent state in Epirus, fighting during four decades with Thomas Preljubović and with the Venetian feudals.[160]

The Balšić family from Montenegro took control over northern Albania in 1362. They established their residence at Shkodër. In order to consecrate his independence, George Balšić I (1362–1379) converted to Catholicism in 1369, his state becoming an instrument of Catholic expansion in the Balkan Peninsula. His realm soon expanded southward to the line Vlora–Berat–Kostur, and for few years into Kosovo (in 1372–1378). This was a side effect of the great Ottoman victory at Cernomen (1371) that gave an opportunity for expansion to the neighbors of the defeated Serbia. The state of the Balšić family was on its way to unification of all the Albanian lands, of Montenegro, and of the future Herzegovina, but this evolution was stopped by another Ottoman victory, at Savra, near Berat (September 18th, 1385), which also ended the reign of Balša Balšić II (1379–1385), a king who occupied the small Albanian state of Carol Thopia, including Dyrrachion. Thopia was the ruler who summoned the Turks in the region, to help him. Later, George II Balšić (1385–1403) accepted Ottoman vassalage until 1387, in order to consolidate his position. He took part with the Serbs at the battle of Kosovopolje in 1389. In 1392–1396, Venice became the true master of Albania, because it seized the opportunity to use the discord between small chiefs from southern Albania, opponents of George II Balšić. A powerful Albanian kingdom was a danger for the Venetian possessions along the eastern Adriatic seashore.[161]

Albanian historiography considers the attempt of the Balšić (also called Balsha) family to build a "Great Albania" that included Kosovo a first form of the unitary and centralized Albanian state. In fact, like other medieval polities, it was only the temporary result of some circumstances that allowed the extension of the domination of a noble Albanian family (whose Albanian origin is, however, not certain, since it was argued that it was Serbian or even Aromanian).[162]

The history of Serbia in the fourteenth century demonstrates that *in the medieval Balkans, the unification of states was made by the usurpation and imitation at a smaller scale of the Byzantine Empire*, the single source of legitimate power. For this reason, thirteenth-century Bulgaria and fourteenth-century Serbia cannot be considered "national" states, since they were created on the basis of the imperial aspirations of their aristocracies, and not on an ethnic principle. These aspirations were possible because the imperial power from Constantinople was in decline. The fall of Constantinople in 1204 allowed these Balkan rulers to pretend the inheritance of imperial power. Andrei Pippidi observes that:

> the rise of the Bulgarian and Serbian states did not have the significance of a secession: they were simply competitors to the Byzantine Empire. Samuel or Dušan could never have been what the nationalist mythology has made of them [founders of national states].[163]

By the claim or by the usurpation of imperial power, the Balkan states were completely different in comparison with contemporary Western kingdoms, where the idea of empire was revived by Charlemagne, but not claimed by the kings of France, Spain, or of other states that finally evolved toward centralization based on ethnic background. We have already seen that the Bulgarian tzar Symeon pretended the title of "emperor of the *Romaion*" when Constantinopolitan power was weak. This fact indicates that his aspirations did not concern a "national" Bulgarian state, as some Bulgarian historians believe. A great military commander and state leader, Symeon wished for imperial power, but not a different empire. His ultimate target was to conquer Constantinople and become a Byzantine emperor. He believed that he had the same right to become emperor as did other non-Greek rulers that held the imperial power before him. His Great Bulgaria was not a national state, but a starting base for the ambitious plan of the conquest of the Byzantine Empire, including Constantinople.

The climax of this competition for the imperial title was reached in Serbia, during the reigns of Stephen Dušan and of his heir John Uglieša. The great Byzantine historian Nikephor Gregoras (*Byzantine History*, II, 747) observed that Stephen Dušan ruled "according to the usual way of the Byzantines."

In 1916, Nicolae Iorga remarked that it is not possible to justify the modern political claims of Bulgaria and Serbia with the boundaries of the medieval empires created by Symeon or Stephen Dušan. Our national ideas were not shared by the medieval man, and the states created by the Bulgarian and Serbian sovereigns were only substitutes for the Byzantine Empire.[164] Victor Papacostea has interpreted the meaning of the states created by Bulgarians and Serbs in the Middle Ages in the same way: they were not national states that prefigured the modern ones, but simply more or less successful imitations of the Byzantine model.[165] It was even postulated that a national conscience based on the use of the Slavonic language in church and administration existed in the first Bulgarian tzardom.[166] Of course, a Bulgarian conscience existed, but it was not a modern national conscience. The autocephaly of the Bulgarian patriarchate (recognized by Byzantium in 927) did not express a modern national identity, but the imitation at a smaller scale of the Byzantine imperial model. The same is true for the Bulgarian and Serbian patriarchates created in 1232 and in 1346.

In 1972, Dimitry Obolensky identified some elements of specific forms of national consciousness in medieval Europe, but he also remarked that "the growth of nationalism in Eastern Europe was in some degree arrested by the prevailing belief in the existence of a single Christian community, whose centre was in Constantinople."[167] Romanian historian Ioan-Aurel Pop has published two books that provide convincing proofs for the idea that a kind of ethnic conscience existed in the Middle Ages, a preliminary form of the modern national conscience.[168]

Medieval societies were based on many solidarities that differed from the modern ethnic solidarity, namely religion, social position, and family or clan. States organized on ethnic principles appeared only at the end of the Middle Ages, as a consequence of the centralization made by kings (France and England in the fifteenth–sixteenth centuries), because the "nation" reflected regional identities (like the Aquitans in France) rather than the entire body of speakers of a language.[169] In a medieval Europe where the territories peopled by a certain ethnicity belonged to several seniors (France is the best example), or where the Roman-German Empire was a supra-ethnic state, the idea of a national state made no sense. The idea promoted by some Bulgarian and Serbian historians that their medieval states were created on ethnic criteria is unthinkable.

Ethnic antagonisms were not reasons for wars in the fourteenth century between the competing states that fought for domination in Macedonia (Byzantium, Serbia, and Bulgaria). The reasons were strictly economic. All the rival powers wished to control the trading routes and economic resources, and the wars were a form of redistribution of these resources amongst the feudals.[170]

The "Great Bulgaria" and "Great Serbia" that existed in the Middle Ages cannot be used as support for the territorial claims of the present states of Bulgaria and Serbia (or Yugoslavia). Generally speaking, the medieval frontiers could not legitimate the contemporary frontiers, because the principles of international relations are completely different. A medieval frontier expressed the limits of the mastership of a senior, resulted from a power balance, while a modern frontier is established on geographical, ethnic, demographic, and economical criteria. In the medieval Balkans, the frontiers were only those established by the changing power balance.

The identity of the Balkan Slavic successors of the Byzantine imperial idea was established on religious, not ethnic, criteria. Bulgaria after 1232 and especially Serbia during the reign of Stephen Dušan claimed their identity through Orthodoxy, that is by opposition against Catholicism. In both states Catholic believers were persecuted. In Serbia, the anti-Catholic policy was very punitive. The laws of Stephen Dušan punished with death conversion to Catholicism (see the next chapter). In both cases, hatred of Catholicism was a development of the Byzantine religious and political doctrine, but also a result of hostile relations with the Catholic powers (Hungary, the Angevine kingdom of Naples). The Serbian Orthodox Church was in the fourteenth century a kind of national church, but this came from the identification of ethnicity with religion. The persecution of the Albanians has religious and not ethnic reasons, because those Albanians were Catholics (see chapter 1). Usually, the Orthodox churches protected national identity.

THE OTTOMAN CONQUEST

As with the Serbian expansion during the reign of Stephen Dušan, the penetration of the Ottoman Turks into the Balkan Peninsula was occasioned by the civil war that took place in the Byzantine Empire between 1341 and 1347. Both actions changed radically the power balance in the region. The emperor John VI Cantacuzenus summoned the Ottoman Turks led by the emir Orhan (1326–1362), who ruled in Asia Minor, at Brusa. The Turks had already made some inroads west of the Sea of Marmara since 1326 and even fought in the army of Andronikos III in the campaign of 1337 against the despotate of Epirus. In 1344, Turkish soldiers helped John VI against John V, and next against Stephen Dušan, in 1352. When this emperor lost power in 1354, Orhan found the opportunity to launch his own offensive in Thrace. In this way, the Turks entered Europe for the first time in 1354, when they conquered the city of Gallipoli. In 1362, they occupied Adrianople, the first Ottoman capital in Europe since 1365 and a strong attack base toward Bulgaria and Serbia. At Plovdiv (conquered in 1363) the residence of the *beglerbeglik* of Rumelia, the first European Ottoman province, was established. In a few years, all of southern Bulgaria was occupied. These European conquests were recognized by John V Paleologos in 1363.[171]

A decisive moment of the Ottoman offensive in the Balkans was the battle of Cernomen (on the Maritza River), on September 26, 1371. The Ottoman army defeated the Serbian forces commanded by King Vukašin and by John Uglieša, after another victory against Bulgaria. Both Serbian rulers were killed in the battle. The Serbs were forced to recognize Ottoman suzerainty, while the former state of John Uglieša from Macedonia was occupied by the despot Manuel II Paleologos, the ruler of the Byzantine state from Thessaloniki, the future emperor of Constantinople (1391–1425). The battle of Cernomen allowed the solid implantation of Ottoman power in Europe.[172]

In the following period, the center of Serbia moved constantly to the north, from Kosovo to the Morava basin, Danube, and Sava. In that area the Serbian state survived, after the conquest of Macedonia and Kosovo.[173] The capital was installed at Belgrade in 1403, when the despot Stephen Lazarević (1389–1427) received this fortress from Hungary, in exchange for the vassalage.[174] In 1372 Kosovo came under the domination of the Albanian king George Balšić I until 1378, when the Serbian *knez* Vuk Branković succeeded in establishing his authority over the southern part of this region.[175]

After the death of Stephen Uroš and Vukašin in the same year, 1371, the single heir of the Nemanja dynasty remained Tvrtko I (1353–1391), the king of Bosnia, a descendant of the Serbian king Dragutin. After the division of Great Serbia, Tvrtko I became the most powerful leader in the western part of the Balkan Peninsula. At the beginning, Bosnia was ruled by a kind of dukes called *bani*, vassals of the Hungarian kings, like the Croatian *bani*. The most important Bosnian *bani* were Kulin (1180–1204), Mathew Ninoslav (1232–1250), and Stepan II Kotromanić (1322–1353). The latter extended the state into Croatia and the future Herzegovina and acquired independency, after the defeat of rival feudals in the first years of his reign.[176] After the defeat of the invading Hungarian army in 1363, Tvrtko I was crowned with the crown of Saint Sava as king of Serbia and Bosnia in 1377, even if he was a Catholic (he acquired new lands in western Serbia but also on the Dalmatian seashore).[177] The kingdom of Tvrtko I was an ephemeral creation. Internal fights for power, Hungarian interference, and finally the Ottoman offensive in the Balkan Peninsula caused the fast decline of the Bosnian kingdom.

The victory of Cernomen was followed by the partial conquest of Macedonia, achieved in 1371–1373. In 1383, Serres was also occupied by the commander Evrenos Bey. After a long siege between 1383 and 1387, the despotate of Thessaloniki ruled by Manuel II became a vassalage, being finally occupied in 1391 by Bayazid I.[178] The rest of Macedonia remained under the rule of two Ottoman vassals, the king Marko Kraljević, son of Vukašin, at Prilep (1371–1395), and the prince Constantine Dejanović, in eastern Macedonia (1371–1395). Both would die in the battle of Rovine in Walachia, on October 10, 1395, as participants in the war started by Bayazid

I against prince Mircea (1386–1418). Following their death, the rest of Macedonia entered the *beglerbeglik* of Rumelia, being divided into the *sandjaks* Paša, Kjustendil, Ochrid, Thessaloniki, and Skopje.[179]

After the same battle of Cernomen, the Ottomans occupied most of western Bulgaria (including Sofia, in 1384). The key position acquired in Macedonia made possible the conquest of the entire Balkan Peninsula. In this way, the Ottoman Empire replaced the former state of Stephen Dušan as the hegemonic power in the region. *The battle of Cernomen can be considered a turning point in the balance of forces in the Balkans*, that—as stated by a well-known scholar—led to the "complete dezorganization of the Balkan world."[180] In that moment, the bipolar situation (Serbia versus the Byzantine Empire) was replaced with a unique power center, the Ottoman state, which was then able to unify the Balkan Peninsula under its rule. In the aftermath, the Serbian *knez* Lazar Hrebeljanović, the Bulgarian tzar of Tărnovo John III Šišman (1371–1393), and the Byzantine emperor John V Paleologos became the vassals of Murad I (1359–1389).

The Ottoman expansion was favored by the discord among the Christians. The Great Serbia of Stephen was already shattered, as well as Bulgaria, divided since 1356 into three states (the tzardoms of Vidin and Tărnovo and the despotate from Dobrudja), which had not enough power to resist the Turks. This divided Balkan world was not able to unify and oppose the increasing Ottoman power, and at first nobody guessed how great this danger was. Both Byzantium and Serbia believed that these brave warriors could be used to supplement their own forces in the conflicts between the Christian states. John VI Cantacuzenus had requested an alliance with the Turks in the war against Stephen Dušan. The Serbian tzar tried to close a similar alliance with Orhan in 1351. A Greek historian observes that:

> absorbed in rivalries and wars among themselves, the Christian rulers of southeastern Europe could not rise above personal ambitions and realize that their policies, which would leave the Turks as the unchallenged arbiter, would lead to such a disaster.[181]

An overview of international relations between the Balkan states during the second half of the fourteenth century emphasizes that Byzantium, Bulgaria, and Serbia were not able to resist Ottoman expansion because these states did not cooperate, and that this lack of cooperation expressed the political antagonisms provoked by the self-seeking policies of their rulers.[182] The Balkan Peninsula faced the Ottoman expansion like the Roman one: in a state of deep discord that facilitated the conquest and the unification achieved from outside.

The Ottoman expansion followed a two-stage strategy. In the first, enemies were transformed into vassal states, while the second was the extension of direct control over them. The second stage started during the reign of Bayazid I (1389–1402).[183] This policy was applied because the Ottoman army did not have enough manpower. The sultans therefore needed the troops of their Christian vassals (especially Serbs). Even later, in the first half of the fifteenth century, significant Christian forces fought on the Ottoman side in important battles (the Aromanians from Thessaly at Ankara in 1402 and at the siege of Constantinople in 1453—see p. 91). This means that one of the premises of Ottoman success was the speculation of rivalries between the Christian powers combined with the use of the military fervor of the Balkan aristocracy in large operations that also offered benefits to the Christian feudals. In fact, the continuous anti-Ottoman fight of the Balkan peoples is a nice and useful myth of all the national historiographies from Southeastern Europe, which is not true nor for Serbs, nor for Greeks, nor for Romanians. The periods of confrontation alternated with periods of cooperation.

Nicolae Iorga wrote that the Christian Balkan states were so easily annihilated by the Ottomans because these medieval structures were not able to support themselves in the face of *the unifying force of the Ottoman Empire, which had the same role as centralization in Western kingdoms*. In this view, the battle of Cernomen was a reaction of the Balkan leaders against Ottoman unification.[184] Therefore, like the Roman Empire, *the Ottoman Empire was an instrument of unification of the Balkan space, something that was impossible to achieve from inside*.

The disunity does not concern only relations between the states. Within these states, social cohesion was affected by the way that feudal relations evolved in the fourteenth century. In the Byzantine Empire—the best known in this respect—the privileged cities and the surrounding districts ruled by great landowners were almost independent from the center. Much more than in the eleventh century, these aristocrats were responsible for the centrifugal trends that hindered common action against the external danger. In this period, what remained from the Byzantine Empire was in fact a conglomerate of appanages that tended to independency.[185]

The Ottoman expansion in the Balkan Peninsula was not stopped by the unique victory of the Serbian and Bosnian coalition conducted by the prince Lazar Hrebeljanović (1371–1389) at Pločnik (on the Neretva valley in Bosnia) in 1388.[186] The son of a high dignitary of Stephen Dušan, Lazar Hrebeljanović became ruler of northern Serbia in the aftermath of the battle of 1371. Because Lazar Hrebeljanović did not accept vassalage, the sultan Murad I started the war against Serbia. The allies of Lazar were prince Vuk Branković (from southern Kosovo), Tvrtko I (king of Serbia and Bosnia), the Bulgarian tzar from Vidin John Stracimir (1360–1396), and the Albanian king George II Balšić. After the defeat of 1388, Murad I attacked Serbia in its most important and vulnerable zone, Kosovo. The famous battle of June 15th, 1389, on the Kosovo field (Kosovopolje), near Priština, did not have a clear winner, but it contributed over the long term to the consolidation of Ottoman domination in the Balkan Peninsula, by the extension of suzerainty over the Serbian rulers. The son of Lazar, the *knez* Stephen Lazarević, became a faithful vassal of the new sultan Bayazid I after he received the lands previously mastered by Vuk Branković. He fought with fidelity for his senior in the battle of Ankara, when Bayazid was taken prisoner by Timur Lenk (July 28th, 1402).[187]

The disastrous defeat suffered at Ankara in front of Timur Lenk and the fights between the sons of Bayazid I stopped for a time the Ottoman advance in the Balkan Peninsula. In these circumstances, the Byzantine emperor Manuel II Paleologos offered his support to one of the rival brothers, Suleyman. As a reward, the emperor obtained Thessaloniki and other territories in 1403, as well as liberation from vassalage.[188]

As Ottoman vassals, the Serbian princes (*knezi*) Stephen Lazarević and Marko Kraljević continued after 1389 to master the central and northern parts of Serbia (Raška), Montenegro, and Kosovo—which was a border province after 1394. Just after the battle of Ankara, Stephen Lazarević used the opportunity of the fights for succession in the Ottoman Empire to become in 1402 the vassal of the Hungarian king Sigismund of Luxemburg (1395–1437), who offered him the city of Belgrade, where the capital of Serbia was moved. He also established relationships with Byzantium (the emperor Manuel II Paleologos bestowed upon him the title of despot).[189]

In the north, the Ottoman offensive continued with the conquest of the Bulgarian tzardoms of Tărnovo, in 1393, and of Vidin, in 1396 (after the great victory of Nikopolis of September 28th, 1396, against the crusaders led by Sigismund of Luxemburg). In this way, *the Ottoman state reached the natural limit of the Lower Danube, a necessary requirement for any power which aims to master the Balkan Peninsula.* The wars led by Bayazid I in 1394 and 1395 against Walachia (with the cooperation of the Serbian vassals Stephen Lazarević, Marko Kraljević, and Constantine Dejanović) did not seek the extension of Ottoman domination north of the Danube; it was merely a punishing campaign against Mircea, who in late 1393 launched a surprise attack against the Ottoman camp of Karinovasi (Karnobat, Bulgaria), at the suggestion of some emirs who were in opposition to Bayazid.[190]

At the end of the fourteenth century, the Ottoman Empire advanced toward the southern Balkan Peninsula. Thessaly was conquered in two stages: 1386–1387 and 1392–1397. Bayazid I replaced Manuel Angelos, the last despot of Thessalian Great Vlachia, with the Turkish dignitary Evrenos Bey. The region became a *sandjak* included in the *begleberglik* of Rumelia. The Aromanians from Thessaly were made subjects of the Ottomans. Later, some of them who received estates called *timar* in exchange for military service took part at the battle of Ankara (1402) in the army of Bayazid I and at the conquest of Constantinople (1453).[191]

After the elimination of the other pretenders, the sultan Murad II (1421–1451) resumed an offensive policy in the Balkan Peninsula. The main rival was not a Balkan state, but Venice, which continued to maintain economic and military hegemony in the region. In 1423, Venice occupied Thessaloniki, thus ensuring mastery over one of the most important harbors in the Balkan Peninsula. Against these Venetians fought Murad II, until 1430 when he took back Thessaloniki. The outcome was Ottoman control over the intersection of the major Balkan roads (Morava–Vardar and Via Egnatia). In the same year the conquest of Epirus and Albania was achieved, which meant control of the entire *Via Egnatia*, including the harbor of Dyrrachion (Durrazzo, Durrës).[192] Albania was conquered after the crushing of the prince Gjon Kastrioti (the father of the famous Skanderbeg), master of a region extended from the Mati tableland up to Prizren in Kosovo and up to the mouth of the Ishem River. Gjon Kastrioti was forced to accept vassalage in 1428, and rebelled in 1429, but his land was occupied.[193]

Montenegro had a particular evolution. After the extinction of the Balsha dynasty in 1421, the Serbian *knez* Stephen Crnojević (1421–1465) took power. He established an alliance with Venice, in order to resist the Ottomans. The next ruler, Ivan Crnojević (1465–1490), was forced to recognize Ottoman suzerainty in 1471. Following the death of the prince Djuradj Crnojević (1490–1496), Montenegro was included in the Ottoman Empire, but some forms of resistance and autonomy survived in this territory. The younger son of Ivan, Skenderbei (Stanisa), converted to Islam in 1485, ruled the *sandjak* that was organized in Montenegro in 1514–1528. After 1516, the bishops from Cetinje elected by the Montenegrin people assumed political power. Montenegro remained a semi-independent region, ruled until 1852 by the bishops of Cetinje and by the chiefs of the clans who secured solidarity in the face of Turkish pressure. This semi-independent situation was enabled by its location in a scarcely accessible mountain territory and sometimes by Venetian support.[194]

The Romanian commander of the Hungarian army Iancu of Hunedoara tried to expel the Ottomans from Europe through the campaigns of 1441, 1443–1444, 1448, 1454, and 1456. The final result of these Christian offensives was negative. Although Iancu defended Belgrade in 1456, the Christian forces were not able to stop the consolidation of Ottoman domination in the central and northern Balkan Peninsula, after the victories of Varna (November 10th, 1444) and Kosovopolje (October 17th–19th, 1448). The wars between Hungary and the Ottoman Empire stirred the Greeks to break their chains. The despot of Morea Constantine Paleologos (1428–1448), who would became the last Byzantine emperor, started in

1444 an offensive to liberate central Greece, with the support of Greek and Aromanian rebels from Pindus. The uprisings continued sporadically in Thessaly and western Macedonia until 1449, but fate was decisive. Nothing was possible in the face of the Ottoman superpower. It was easy for Murad II to reconquer these territories in 1446–1447.[195]

The harshest anti-Ottoman fight was led by the Albanian leader Gjergj Kastrioti, also called Skanderbeg (1405–1468), who mastered the mountain region from northern Albania. From that area, he extended into Kosovo and southern Albania. In 1443, Skanderbeg moved against the Ottoman domination, in cooperation with other local chiefs who gathered in March 1444 at Lezhe. Installed in the fortress of Krujë, Skanderbeg won several brilliant victories until his death on January 17, 1468, but this resistance did not hinder the final integration of Albania under Ottoman domination in 1506, after other failed rebellions.[196]

The upheavals of the Balkan populations and the crusades of the 1440s failed to reach their targets. The natural consequence of the successive Ottoman victories was the end of the Byzantine Empire. The events are well-known. After a cleverly conducted siege started on April 18, 1453, Constantinople was conquered by the army of Mehmed II on May 29, 1453. The last Byzantine emperor, Constantine XI Paleologos (1449–1453), was not able to obtain effective support from the Christian powers. Venice, which possessed a very powerful navy, did not participate in the battle.[197]

A turning point in world history, the conquest of the Second Rome by the Ottomans had various consequences. Among them, the most important for our discussion seems to be that *the Ottoman Empire inherited the idea of Roman universalism*. A short time after the conquest, the sultan Mehmed II assumed a prerogative of the Byzantine emperors, appointing as patriarch Gennadios Scholarios, the leader of the group that was against any compromise with Catholicism.[198] Of course, the main purpose was the encouragement of the hate between the Orthodox and the Western Catholic powers. The continuity of the Byzantine imperial idea was fostered by cooperation between Greeks and Turks, initiated during the fourteenth century. The Ottomans were regarded by the Orthodox fundamentalists as allies in the fight against Western Catholicism.[199]

The last stage of the Ottoman conquests in the Balkans took place after the fall of Constantinople. The duchy of Athens fell in 1456, and the despotate of Morea in 1460. In the latter case, the conquest was facilitated by the rebellion of the Albanians and especially by internal fights for power between the brothers Demetrios and Thomas Paleologos. Venetian possessions in Greece were also occupied after the war of 1499–1503.[200]

A short time after the fall of Constantinople, most of Serbia was conquered, in 1454–1455. The despot George (Djuradj) Branković (1427–1456) tried to save the Serbian state by a policy of balance between the Ottoman

Empire and Hungary. He fought beside the sultan Murad II at the battle of Kosovopolje (October, 17–19, 1448), where he captured Iancu of Hunedoara (this caused a war with Hungary). However, this policy failed when George Branković decided to return to the Hungarian side in 1453. After the death of the last despot of Smederevo, Lazar Branković (1456–1458), the sultan Mehmed II has occupied what remained of Serbia. The residence Smederevo (Semendria) was conquered on June 20th, 1459. From the territory of the former Serbian state was created the *sandjak* of Semendria. The Ottoman conquest was facilitated by the feelings of some people who hoped that this would end the internal insecurity and Hungarian danger. However, other Serbs took refuge in southern Hungary and in Banat.[201]

In Bosnia, the long internal fights of the king Stephen Tvrtko II (1404–1409, 1421–1443) with rival noblemen weakened the state that was for a while the strongest in the Balkan Peninsula.[202] Bosnia was conquered by the Ottomans in 1463–1464, after the death of its last king, Stephen Tomašević (1461–1463), in battle. In 1448, a group of forty thousand Bosnians was established in the valley of Neretva under the command of the rebel duke Stjepan Vukčić. The territory received the name Herzegovina (from *herzeg* = "duke"). Herzegovina was conquered by the Ottomans in 1482–1483.[203]

In this way, most of the Balkan Peninsula came under Ottoman domination, except some small zones on the Adriatic seashore owned by Ragusa, the trading city that preserved a privileged position, recognized by the sultans. *The Ottomans thus achieved the first unification of the area after the Romans.* The Byzantine Empire was not able to do this in the ninth–eleventh centuries, because some of the central and western regions peopled by Serbs and Croats remained outside its frontiers. Bulgaria and Serbia failed too in their projects of unification of the Balkan space in the form of successor empires of the Byzantine state. In both cases, the imperial ideal was an illusion, an artificial model, and a fiasco. It is very meaningful that, unlike the Byzantines in the thirteenth–fourteenth centuries, the Ottomans succeeded in securing strategic control over the entire *Via Egnatia*.[204]

Although in previous periods Macedonia was conquered by Bulgaria and Serbia, these states were not able to take all the advantages from control over this key position in the Balkan Peninsula. The rise of the Bulgarian empire of John II Asan was stopped by the Mongol domination, while the Serbian empire was shattered before the establishment of a durable control over the strategic roads intersecting in Macedonia. Instead, this was achieved by the Ottoman Empire, which was in the second half of the sixteenth century the absolute master of Southeastern Europe. The plurality of power centers would disappear for a long time in the Balkan Peninsula.

PAX OTTOMANA

In the fifteenth and sixteenth centuries, the Ottoman Empire ensured in
the Balkans the same stability had in the early Roman period. It was a *Pax
Ottomana* similar with *Pax Romana*. The autocratic regime and the administration shaped according to the Byzantine model, but not corrupted in
this early period, led to an internal security that did not exist in the rest of
Europe. A French traveler wrote in 1528 with admiration that "the country is sure and there are no news about bandits . . . or robbers on the roads.
. . . The emperor does not admit any brigand or thief."[205]

Contrary to the usual historiographic preconceived ideas and to the image of the Turks common in the European mind, the Ottoman domination
was an advantage for most of the Balkan population. This domination
stopped the former endless conflicts between different local rulers. From
social and economic points of view, the Ottoman administration was
more bearable for the peasants. Fernand Braudel believed that its introduction was a real "social revolution" for the Balkan peasants. The fiscal
policy was soft at the beginning. It was forbidden for soldiers to pillage or
commandeer the goods of the civilians. Most of the Greek, Serbian, and
Bulgarian grand owners disappeared and their properties were given to
the *spahis* and to Islamic religious foundations. On the estates possessed
by *spahis* (*timar*), the situation of the peasants was quite good at the beginning, because they were not subjected to the feudal burdens specific to
Western societies. This social situation assured the stability of the Ottoman domination, because the peasantry had no serious reasons to rebel,
while the population of the towns was not yet a middle class able to
launch a national revival.

Only the general decline of the Ottoman state that started in the first
decades of the seventeenth century changed this situation. The *timar* estates were step-by-step replaced by another kind of properties called *ce-
flik*, where the peasants were subjected to serfdom and abuses (in all of
Eastern and Southeastern Europe the rural world was subjected in the
seventeenth–eighteenth centuries to a so-called second serfdom; the
process belonged to the general trends of the European economy and was
not specific to Ottoman society).[206] The decline was more perceptible in
the administration and in the military. The corruption, abusive fiscal policy, and mutinies of some army corps weakened the state when the fight
began against Austrian and Russian expansion into Ottoman territory.

The reduction of the effects of the Ottoman conquest to the ravages that
happened during the wars and in their aftermath is wrong. Besides all the
damages caused by the conflicts—which are incontestable—the long-term
consequences were partially favorable for Christians who entered under
Ottoman domination,[207] not only for urban development (even if this fol-

lowed patterns other than those in the West), but also for the countryside, where the *timar* estates assured a certain prosperity.[208]

A famous specialist in the medieval and modern history of the Balkans holds that the idea of the so-called five centuries of continuous fight against Ottoman tyranny and oppression is a myth created in the period of the national revival of the Balkan states, a typical example of modern nationalist mythology.[209] As long as serious reasons of upheaval did not exist—and they usually did not in the fourteenth–sixteenth centuries— Christian peoples from the Balkans did not fight against the Ottomans. When such events happened, they echoed the wars started by external powers that sought Ottoman territories.

The most privileged were the Albanians and the Aromanians, because Ottoman military power relied greatly on these populations, which often had marginal positions in the Byzantine Empire and in Serbia. The Aromanians were recruited into special military units with fiscal privileges that continued similar forms of organization from Serbia. The heads of the Romanian villages from the former Serbian territories, called *primikeri* and *cnezi*, were recognized by the Ottoman authorities. As *timar* owners, these Romanian chiefs fought in the *spahi* corps of the Ottoman army, although they were Christians. The autonomous forms of organization of the Aromanians improved the defense of the borderlands, especially in the fifteenth century and in the first half of the sixteenth century. Many such Vlach military communities existed in Bosnia and Croatia, where the Ottoman Empire was in contact with its main enemy in the sixteenth century. Some of these communities survived until the middle of the eighteenth century.[210] Many Ottoman commanders and dignitaries were recruited from the converted Albanians, but also, to a lesser extent, from the Greeks, Serbs, and Bulgarians.[211]

In Serbia and Thessaly, the Christian *timariots* were quite numerous in the fifteenth century. In 1455, 36 of the 182 *timariots* from the *vilayet* (district) Trikkala in Thessaly were Christians (Greeks and Aromanians). In Macedonia, the former owners of the *pronoiar* estates became soon *timariots* in order to preserve their wealth and privileged social position. Their military obligations gave them an important role in the Ottoman army, as Christian *spahis*.[212] From the religious point of view, the Ottoman conquest offered to the Orthodox Church a shield against the Catholic expansionism that was more and more active in the fourteenth century in the region. Curiously Islam contributed to the consolidation of the Orthodox Balkan world, because the former tolerated the latter. Of course, the Christians were in an inferior position, but they were not usually persecuted.

The long decline of the Ottoman state in the seventeenth–eighteenth centuries put an end to this stability. From the military point of view, the decline started with defeat in the naval battle of Lepanto against Venice (October 7, 1571). This moment followed after an extraordinary series of victories and after the glorious reign of Suleyman the Magnificent (1521–1566), when the Ottoman state reached the apex of its power. As a matter of fact, at Lepanto began a transition period, which lasted until another great defeat, at Vienna (1683). The empire was already sick, and the failures in the wars were only the signs of the illness that affected the Ottoman society. The deep reason for this decline was increasing economic and technical backwardness in comparison with the Western states. The Ottoman Empire was no longer able to reply to this challenge.[213]

The Balkan population rebelled only when the Ottoman Empire was in a difficult military situation. During the war of 1593–1606 launched by the Catholic League, the Serbs rebelled in Kosovo (at Peć) and in Herzegovina, in 1595 and 1597. They believed they were conducted in battle by Saint Sava, revived to crush the enemies of Christ.[214] In this atmosphere of Messianism and enthusiasm, the Romanian prince Michael the Brave (1593–1601), who fought in the Catholic League, was perceived by the Balkan peoples as a liberator and a reviver of the Byzantine Empire.[215] The Albanians tried several times between 1596 and 1614 to obtain the help of Venice or Spain to support liberation from the Ottoman yoke, but without success. In the same years, namely in 1608, the Serbian patriarch of Peć, Iovan (1592–1614), plotted a rebellion in Herzegovina, Montenegro, and Albania. (As shown in the next chapter, the patriarchate of Peć was a factor in national resistance for the Serbs, after its restoration in 1557.) Only in the last part of the seventeenth century did the general decline of the Ottoman state facilitate large troubles, stimulated by the actions of the great European powers that were interested in occupying the Ottoman territories, Austria and Russia. In 1645, at the beginning of the Ottoman–Venetian war of 1645–1669 for the domination of Crete, the Catholic Albanians passed to the Venetian side, as directed by their priests.[216] The failure of the Ottoman siege of Vienna (July 17–September 12, 1683) represented the start of Austrian counteroffensive toward Southeastern Europe, in cooperation with Venice and Poland. The new political and military context radically changed the power balance in the Balkan Peninsula, signaling the end of Ottoman supremacy.

The Serbs rebelled after the beginning of the offensive of the Holy League (organized in 1684 by Austria, Venice, Poland; Russia joined later). They were helpful at the conquest of Belgrade (September 6, 1688) and in the fast advance to southern Serbia and Kosovo in 1688–1689, when the Austrian army commanded by general Giovanni Norberto Piccollomini conquered the cities of Niš, Peć, Prizren, and Skopje. The Serbian upheaval was planned by a Serbo-Romanian nobleman from Transylvania, George Branković (1645–1711), who asked the help of Austria in the constituting of a large Serbian state that would include Raška, Kosovo, Banat, and Slavonia. Austria used the anti-Ottoman actions of the Serbs according to its interests, while the Ottomans took revenge at the end of 1689, when Kosovo and southern Serbia were subjected to harsh retaliations because of the Serbian betrayal (it should be observed that some Albanians also fought with the Austrian army). The plan to revive the Serbian state failed. In 1690–1691, tens of thousands of Serbs and Albanians took refuge in the north, led by the patriarch of Peć, Arsenije III Čarnojević (1674–1706). They were received by the Habsburg authorities and settled in Banat and in the south of Hungary, while their place in Kosovo was taken by Muslim Albanians moved there by the Ottomans. The war continued, and the victory of the Holy League was finally decided in the battle of Zenta (September 11, 1697).[217]

The anti-Ottoman fight especially had religious support in the sixteenth–seventeenth centuries. The idea of national revival existed only as an expression of the Christian fight against Islam. It is true that the Slavic or Greek brigands (*haiduks* and *klefts*) led a permanent fight against the Ottoman authorities.[218] These romantic heroes could be considered symbols of the anti-Ottoman fight, but unbiased judgment does not allow us to see them as anything but examples of specific Balkan brigandage, attested to since Greek antiquity.[219]

The new power balance in the Balkan Peninsula was consecrated by the Peace Treaty of Karlowitz (Sremski Karlovci), signed on January 26, 1699. The Ottoman Empire lost Croatia, Slavonia, Morea, a part of Dalmatia, and some islands claimed by Venice. The most important outcome is that, for the first time in history, the Ottoman Empire acknowledged the right of European powers to intervene in the Balkan Peninsula. *In this way the "Oriental Problem," the competition for the division of the Ottoman Empire, was opened.*[220]

The Oriental Problem would bring back onto the stage of the theater of history the old Balkan conflict areas, because all the modern national states that appeared in the nineteenth century and in the first two decades of the twentieth century would try to extend their area as much as possible, entering into conflicts for borders and territories with mixed populations. *The use of the principle of nationalities as a support for irredentism was combined with historical arguments based on the medieval domination of a certain territory.*

Unlike the Roman Empire, the Ottoman Empire did not proceed to a uniformization of the Balkan space. There was no Turkization or Islamization similar to Romanization. On the contrary, the Islamization of some segments of Balkan societies accentuated their division. *Pax Ottomana* meant stability without ethnic and religious homogenization. It is nevertheless true that the Orthodox Christians had solidarity, since they belonged to the same community (*millet*), protected by the patriarch of Constantinople (who had also the title of *millet-başa*). For the Ottomans, the ethnic differences between Greeks, Bulgarians, and Serbians had no significance. All of them were "Greek" in the religious meaning, that is Orthodox. The patriarch became thus a kind of substitute for the Byzantine emperor. The disappearance of the Christian elites also contributed to the solidarity of the subjected populations.[221] *This uniformization that resulted from Ottoman political doctrine did not impede the future national revival of the Balkan peoples, but preserved in latency the ethnic and religious differences and antagonisms that rose with extreme violence in the nineteenth century. This was the distant background of the Balkan wars of 1912–1913, of the Balkan campaigns of the two world wars, and of the conflicts carried on in the Yugoslavian space after 1989.*

NOTES

1. M. Whittow, *The Making of Byzantium, 600–1025*, Berkeley, CA, 1996, 77–79; J. F. Haldon, *Byzantium in the Seventh Century. The Transformation of a Culture*, Cambridge, 1997, 41–46; W. Treadgold, *A History of the Byzantine State and Society*, Stanford, CA, 1997, 237–241, 290, 295, 297; F. Curta, *The Making of the Slavs. History and Archaeology of the Lower Danube Region c. 500–700*, Cambridge, 2001, 106–109.

2. W. Treadgold, *Byzantium and Its Army. 284-1081*, Stanford, CA, 1995, 206–207.

3. P. Lemerle, *Les plus anciens recueils des Miracles de Saint Démétrius et la pénétration des Slaves dans les Balkans*, vol. I, *Le texte*, Paris, 1979.

4. G. Ostrogorsky, *Histoire de l'État Byzantin*, Paris, 1956, 147–148, 161–162; S. Antoljak, Die Makedonische Sklavinien, *Macédoine 1970*, 34–36; J. Koder, Zur Frage der Slavischen Siedlungsgebiete im mittelalterlichen Griechenland, BZ, 71, 2 (1978), 316; M. Graebner, The Slavs in Byzantine Empire. Absorption, Semi-Autonomy and the Limits of Byzantinization, BB, 5 (1978), 44–45; Haldon 1997, 56; Treadgold 1997, 333.

5. J. Ferluga, Gli Slavi del Sud ed altri gruppi etnici di fronte a Bisanzio, *Gli Slavi*, 324–325. The origin and the chronology of the thematic organization have been much discussed in the last four decades and we cannot give here an overview of this issue. See for instance R. J. Lilie, *Die zweihundertjährige Reform. Zu den Anfängen der Themenorganisation im 7. und 8. Jahrhundert* (I–II), ByzSl, 45, 1 (1984), 27–39; 2, 190–201 and I. Shahîd, *Heraclius and the Theme System Revisited. The Unfinished Themes of Oriens*, in E. Kountoura-Galaki (ed.), *The Dark Centuries of Byzantium (7th–9th c.)*, Athens, 2001, 15–40.

6. P. Charanis, Observations on the History of Greece during the Early Middle Ages, BS, 11, 1 (1970), 3–5; R. J. Lilie, *"Thrakien" und "Thrakesion." Zur byzantinischen Provinzorganisation am Ende des 7. Jahrhunderts*, JÖB, 26 (1977), 7–47; A. Stavridou-Zafraka, Slav Invasions and the Theme Organization in the Balkan Peninsula, *Vyzantiaká* (Thessaloniki), 12 (1992), 168–169; F. Curta, Barbarians in

Dark-Age Greece: Slavs or Avars? in Ts. Stepanov & V. Vachkova (eds.), *Civitas di-vino-humana. In honorem annorum LX Georgii Bakalov*, Sofia, 2004, 528.

7. Ostrogorsky 1956, 157–158; V. Beševliev, *Die Protobulgarische Periode der Bulgarischen Geschichte*, Amsterdam, 1981, 173–182; V. Gjuzelev, *Chan Asparuch und die Gründung des bulgarischen Reiches, Mitteilungen des Bulgarischen Forschungsinstitutes in Österreich*, 6, 2 (1984), 25–46; Haldon 1997, 67.

8. P. Charanis, *Kouver, the Chronology of His Activities and Their Ethnic Effects in the Regions around Thessalonica*, BS, 11, 2 (1970), 229–247; Angelov 1980, 85–88, 107; Beševliev 1981, 159–170; Popović 1986, 132–133.

9. G. Cankova-Petkova, *Bulgaria and Byzantium during the First Decades after the Foundation of the Bulgarian State*, ByzSl, 24, 1 (1963), 41–53; B. Primov, *Bulgaria in the Eighth Century. A General Outline*, BB, 5 (1978), 8–13; J. Shepard, Slavs and Bulgars, NCMH II, 231.

10. D. Angelov, *Die Entstehung des Bulgarischen Volkes*, Berlin, 1980, 90; Beševliev 1981, 204–228; J. V. A. Fine Jr., *The Early Medieval Balkans. A Critical Survey from the Sixth to the Late Twelfth Century*, Ann Arbor, MI, 1991, 74–78; Treadgold 1997, 363, 366.

11. A. Stavridou-Zafraka, The Development of the Theme Organisation in Macedonia, *Byzantine Macedonia*, 129–130.

12. P. E. Niavis, *The Reign of the Byzantine Emperor Nicephorus I (AD 802–811)*, Athens, 1987, 76–83; W. Treadgold, *The Byzantine Revival, 780–842*, Stanford, CA, 1988, 136–137, 160; H. Ditten, *Ethnische Verschiebungen zwischen der Balkanhalbinsel und Kleinasien vom Ende des 6. bis zum zweiten Hälfte des 9. Jahrhunderts* (BBA, 59), Berlin, 1993, 245–246.

13. N. Oikonomides, *L'archonte slave de l'Hellade au VIIIe siècle*, VV, 55 (80), 1994 (1998), 2, 111–118; F. Curta, L'administration Byzantine dans les Balkans pendant la "grande brèche": Le temoignage des sceaux, *Byzantinistica. Rivista di Studi Bizantini e Slavi*, serie seconda, 6 (2004), 178.

14. Treadgold 1988, 71–73; Treadgold 1997, 427–428; N. Oikonomides, A Note on the Campaign of Staurakios in the Peloponnese (783/4), ZRVI, 38 (1999–2000), 61–66; Curta 2004a, 532–533; Curta 2004b, 169.

15. Ostrogorsky 1956, 221–225; Antoljak 1970, 37–40; Charanis 1970, 6–11; J. Herrin, Aspects of the Process of Hellenization in the Early Middle Ages, *The Annual of the British School of Archaeology at Athens*, 68 (1973), 115–125; J. Ferluga, Quelques problèmes de la politique Byzantine de colonisation au XIe siècle dans les Balkans, BF, 7 (1976), 215–224; P. Koledarov, Ethnical and Political Preconditions for Regional Names in the Central and Eastern part of the Balkan Peninsula, *Carter 1977*, 300–302; Graebner 1978, 47–48; Treadgold 1988, 190; Fine 1991, 79–83; Stavridou-Zafraka 1992, 172–178; Curta 2004b, 169–171.

16. Ostrogorsky 1956, 225; Antoljak 1970, 41–42; Koledarov 1977, 302; Angelov 1980, 93–95; K. Gagova, *Bulgarian-Byzantine Border in Thrace from the 7th to the 10th Century (Bulgaria to the South of the Haemus)*, BHR, 14, 1 (1986), 66–77; Fine 1991, 94–105, 110–111; Shepard 1995, 235–236.

17. H. Bulin, Aux origines des formations étatiques des Slaves du Moyen Danube au IXe siècle, *Europe 1968*, 168–170; Beševliev 1981, 284–286; A. Schwarcz, *Pannonien im 9. Jahrhundert und die Anfänge der direkten Beziehungen zwischen dem*

Ostfränkischen Reich und den Bulgaren, in *Grenze und Differenz im frühen Mittelalter*, ed. by W. Pohl & H. Reimitz (DAW, 287), Wien, 2000, 99–104.

18. Ostrogorsky 1956, 283–284; I. Božilov, *A propos des rapports Bulgaro-Byzantines sous le tzar Symeon (893–912)*, BB, 6 (1980), 73–81; Fine 1991, 137–140; S. Tougher, *The Reign of Leo VI (886–912). Politics and People*, Leiden, 1997, 173–181; J. Shepard, Bulgaria: The other Balkan 'Empire'; Byzantium Expanding, 944–1025, in T. Reuter (ed.), *The New Cambridge Medieval History, vol. III, c. 900–c.1024*, Cambridge, 1999, 570–571.

19. Ostrogorsky 1956, 287–289; M. Pundeff, National Consciousness in Medieval Bulgaria, SOF, 27 (1968), 21–22; I. Dujčev, *Medioevo Bizantino-Slavo*, vol. III, Roma, 1971, 178–190; I. Božilov, *L'ideologie politique du tsar Symeon: Pax Simeonica*, BB, 8 (1986), 73–88; Fine 1991, 142–144, 148–150; Whittow 1996, 286–292; Shepard 1999, 574–576.

20. Ostrogorsky 1956, 292–296; Fine 1991, 157; Shepard 1999, 578–579.

21. For the *župe*, see: I. Božić, La formation de l'Etat Serbe aux IXe–XIe siècles, *Europe 1968*, 144–145; T. Wasilewski, Les župy et les županie des Slaves méridionaux et leur place dans l'organisation des états médiévaux, in *Ier Congrès International d'Archéologie Slave* (Varsovie), 3, 1970, 217–224; D. Dragojlović, La Župa chez les Slaves Balkaniques au Moyen Âge, *Balcanica* (Belgrade), 2 (1971), 85–115; Ph. Malingoudis, Die Institution des Župans als Problem der frühslawischen Geschichte. Einige Bemerkungen, *Cyrillomethodianum* (Thessaloniki), 2 (1972–1973), 61–76; S. Vilfan, Evoluzione statale degli Sloveni e Croati, *Gli Slavi*, 108–111; A. Pleterski, Die altslawische župa—der Staat vor dem Frühstaat, in *Slavonic Countries in the Middle Ages. Profanum and Sacrum*, Poznan, 1998, 79–81.

22. S. Guldescu, *History of Medieval Croatia*, The Hague, 1964, 92–120; Bulin 1968, 159–165; F. Dvornik, *Byzantine Mission among the Slavs. SS Constantine-Cyril and Methodius*, New Brunswick, NJ, 1970, 21–23, 232–237; Dujčev 1971, 197–199; Vilfan 1983, 106; R. Katičić, Die Anfänge des Kroatischen states, in H. Friesinger & F. Daim, *Die Bayern und ihre Nachbarn*, I (DAW, 179), Wien, 1985, 300–307; Fine 1991, 251–265; E. Malamut, Les adresses aux princes des pays Slaves du Sud dans le Livre des cérémonies, II, 48: Interprétation, TM, 13 (2000), 596–602.

23. Ostrogorsky 1956, 263, 295; Božić 1968, 142–143; Dvornik 1970, 47–48; Ferluga 1976, 291–335; J. Kalić, La région de Ras à l'époque Byzantine, in *Géographie historique du monde mediterranéen* (sous la direction de H. Ahrweiler), Paris, 1988, 127–130; Fine 1991, 110, 141.

24. Ostrogorsky 1956, 293–294; Božić 1968, 143; S. Runciman, *The Emperor Romanus Lecapenus and His Reign. A Study of Tenth-Century Byzantium*, Cambridge, 1969, 86–87, 89, 95–96; Dujčev 1971, 192–199; Fine 1991, 148–154, 157.

25. Ostrogorsky 1956, 294–295; Božić 1968, 144; Fine 1991, 159–160; B. I. Bojović, Le passé des territoires, Kosovo-Metohija (XIe–XVIIe siècle), BS, 38, 1 (1997), 34.

26. H. Ahrweiler, *L'idéologie politique de l'Empire Byzantin*, Paris, 1975, 37–60.

27. Ostrogorsky 1956, 317–321; A. D. Stokes, *The Background and Chronology of the Balkan Campaigns of Svyatoslav Igorevich*, SEER, 40, 94 (1962), 44–57; Idem, *The Balkan Campaigns of Svyatoslav Igorevich*, SEER, 95, 466–496; Fine 1991, 181–188; R. Busetto, Giovanni Tzimisce e Svjatoslav di Kiev. Le operazioni militari bizantine nei Balcani (969–971), *Acta Musei Napocensis*, 33, 1996 (1997), II, 9–32; Whittow

1996, 294–298; Treadgold 1997, 503–504, 509; Shepard 1999, 583–584; Stephenson 2000, 47–55.

28. V. Tăpkova-Zaimova, Les frontières occidentales des territoires conquis par Tzimiscès, *Studia Balcanica. 10. Recherches de géographie historique*, Sofia, 1975, 113–115; V. Tăpkova-Zaimova, L'administration byzantine au Bas-Danube (fin du Xe–XIe siècle), ByzSl, 54, 1 (1993), 95–98; A. Madgearu, The Military Organization of Paradunavon, ByzSl, 60, 2 (1999), 421–422.

29. J. Nesbitt & N. Oikonomides, *Catalogue of Byzantine Seals at Dumbarton Oaks and in the Fogg Museum of Art, vol. I: Italy, North of the Balkans, North of the Black Sea*, Washington, DC, 1991, 195–196; S. Pirivatrić, Vizantijske tema Morava i "Moravje" Konstantina VII Porfirogeneta (Le Théme Byzantin de Morava et la "Moravie" de Constantin VII Porphyrogénète), ZRVI, 36 (1997), 173–201; N. Oikonomides, À propos de la première occupation Byzantine de la Bulgarie (971–c. 986), in *Eupsychia. Mélanges offerts à Hélène Ahrweiler* (Byzantina Sorbonensia, 16), II, Paris, 1998, 589.

30. A. Risos, The Vlachs of Larissa in the 10th Century, ByzSl, 51, 2 (1990), 206–207; Fine 1991, 195–196; F. Makk, *Ungarische Aussenpolitik (896–1196)*, Herne, 1999, 27.

31. Ferluga 1976, 228; Fine 1991, 197; Whittow 1996, 369, 381, 386; Treadgold 1997, 522–525; Shepard 1999, 597–599; P. Stephenson, *Byzantium's Balkan Frontier, a Political Study of the Northern Balkans, 900–1204*, Cambridge, 2000, 59–63; P. Stephenson, The Balkan Frontier in the Year 1000, in P. Magdalino (ed.), *Byzantium in the Year 1000* (The Medieval Mediterranean: Peoples, Economies and Cultures, 400–1500, vol. 45), Leiden, 2003, 111–112.

32. Stephenson 2000, 65; G. Nikolov, The Bulgarian Aristocracy in the War against the Byzantine Empire (971–1019), *Byzantium 2001*, 151.

33. G. Ostrogorsky, Une ambassade Serbe auprès de l'empereur Basile II, *Byzantion*, 19 (1949), 187–194; Ostrogorsky 1956, 325–327, 333–338; Ferluga 1976, 227–228, 345–354; Fine 1991, 188–199; Whittow 1996, 387–388; Treadgold 1997, 525–528; Shepard 1999, 599–601; Stephenson 2000, 64–77; Stephenson 2003, 116–121.

34. H. J. Kühn, *Die Byzantinische Armee im 10. und 11. Jahrhundert. Studien zur Organisation der Tagmata*, Wien, 1991, 227–228; Stephenson 2000, 66, 72–74.

35. J. Ferluga, Quelques problèmes de la politique Byzantine de colonisation au XIe siècle dans les Balkans, BF, 7 (1979), 43–48; Nikolov 2001, 143–158.

36. N. Oikonomides, Tax Exemption for the Secular Clergy under Basil II, in J. Chrysostomides (ed.), *Kathegetria. Essays Presented to Joan Hussey for Her 80th Birthday*, Camberley, 1989, 317–326 (Idem, *Social and Economic Life in Byzantium*, Variorum, Ashgate, 2004, I); Fine 1991, 199; Stephenson 2000, 77.

37. Kühn 1991, 233–235; Stephenson 2000, 66, 74, 124.

38. Madgearu 1999, 422; Idem, The Restoration of the Byzantine Rule on the Danube, RESEE, 37–38, 1999–2000, 1–2, 20; Idem, The Church Organization at the Lower Danube, between 971 and 1020, *Études Byzantines et Post-Byzantines* (Iaşi), IV, (2001), 76.

39. N. Bănescu, *Les duchés Byzantins de Paristrion (Paradounavon) et de Bulgarie*, Bucarest, 1946, 54–60.

40. I. Barnea & Şt. Ştefănescu, *Din istoria Dobrogei*, vol. III, Bucureşti, 1971, 76, 93–95.

41. Tăpkova-Zaimova 1993, 98.

42. Kühn 1991, 223–224.

43. I. Jordanov, The Katepanikion of Paradunavon According to the Sphragistic Data, SBS, 8 (2003), 73.

44. Stephenson 2000, 78, 94; Stephenson 2003, 115.

45. I. Bica, *Thema Paristrion (Paradounavon) în istoriografia bizantină şi română*, Piteşti, 2003, 98–107.

46. I. Jordanov, Vizantijski pečati s imeto na Silistra (Dorostolon/Dristras), *Dobrudža* (Varna), 20 (2002), 80–81.

47. Jordanov 2003, 68–69.

48. Ferluga 1976, 228–232; Fine 1991, 193–195, 198; E. Malamut, Concepts et réalités: Recherches sur les termes désignant les Serbes et les pays Serbes dans les sources Byzantines des Xe–XIIe siècles, in *Eupsychia. Mélanges offerts à Hélène Ahrweiler* (Byzantina Sorbonensia, 16), II, Paris, 1998, 441–442; Shepard 1999, 599; Stephenson 2000, 67, 74; Nikolov 2001, 151–152.

49. V. Laurent, Le théme Byzantin de Serbie au XIe siècle, *Revue des Études Byzantines*, 15 (1957), 185–195; T. Wasilewski, Le thème byzantin de Sirmium-Serbie au XIe et XIIe siècles, ZRVI, 8, 2 (1964), 465–472; T. Wasilewski, Stefan Vojislav de Zahumlje, Stefan Dobroslav de Zéta et Byzance au milieu du XIe siècle, ZRVI, 13 (1971), 117–121.

50. M. Angold, *The Byzantine Empire, 1025–1204. A Political History*, London, New York 1984, 17; L. Maksimović, Verwaltungsstrukturen in Byzanz und in den Balkanländern., in A. Hohlweg (ed.), *Byzanz und seine Nachbarn* (Südost-Europa Jahrbuch, 26), München, 1996, 54–56; Malamut 1998, 442–443; Stephenson 2000, 66, 74, 123, 126–129; Stephenson 2003, 122–124.

51. Guldescu 1964, 121–186; Ferluga 1976, 141–149; Fine 1991, 274–278, 283–288; Shepard 1999, 601; Stephenson 2000, 197–202; I. Goldstein, The Disappearance of Byzantine Rule in Dalmatia in the 11th Century, *Byzantium 2001*, 129–139; M. Dimnik, Russia, the Bulgars and the Southern Slavs, 1024–c.1200, NCMH IV, 271–274.

52. Angold 1984a, 62–65; M. Angold, The Shaping of the Medieval Byzantine City, BF, 10 (1985), 7; P. Kazhdan & W. A. Epstein, *Change in Byzantine Culture in the Eleventh and Twelfth Centuries*, Berkeley, CA, 1985, 31–39; K. P. Matschke, Grundzüge des byzantinischen Städtewesens vom 11. bis 15. Jahrhundert, in K. P. Matschke (ed.), *Die Byzantinische Stadt im Rahmen der allgemeinen Stadtentwicklung. Referate und Diskussionen diskussionen der Byzantinischen Fachkonferenz im Leipzig 9. bis 11. Januar 1990*, Leipzig, 1995, 27–40; J. Ferluga, Die Byzantinischen Provinzstädte im 11. Jahrhundert, in J. Jarnut & P. Johanek (eds.), *Die Frühgeschichte der europäischen Stadt im 11. Jahrhundert* (Veröffentlichungen des Instituts für vergleichende Städtgeschichte in Münster, 43), Köln, 1998, 363–366. For the transformation of the Byzantine economy and society, see P. Lemerle, *Cinq études sur le XIe siècle byzantin*, Paris, 1977, 251–312.

53. Ferluga 1998, 363, 373–374; Matschke 1995, 30–32.

54. Matschke 1995, 42.

55. M. Angold, Archons and Dynasts: Local Aristocracies and the Cities of the Later Byzantine Empire, in M. Angold (ed.), *The Byzantine Aristocracy, IX to XIII Centuries* (BAR International Series, 221), Oxford, 1984, 238; C. Bouras, Aspects of the Byzantine City, Eight–Fifteenth Centuries, in A. E. Laiou (ed.), *The Economic History of Byzantium from the Seventh through the Fifteenth Century*, Washington, DC, 2002, vol. II, 523.

56. G. Ostrogorsky, Observations on the Aristocracy in Byzantium, DOP, 25 (1971), 6–9, 13–14; H. Ahrweiler, Recherches sur la Société Byzantine au XIe siècle: Nouvelles Hiérarchies et Nouvelles Solidarités, TM, 6 (1976), 117–118; Angold 1984a, 68–70; Angold 1984b, 237–238; Angold 1985, 16–22; Kazhdan & Epstein 1985, 46–56; Matschke 1995, 41–56.

57. However, according to K. Inoue, *A Provincial Aristocratic Oikos in Eleventh-Century Byzantium*, GRBS, 30, 4 (1989), 551–559, and J. C. Cheynet, L'aristocratie Byzantine (VIIIe–XIIIe siècle), *Journal des Savants*, 1–2 (2000), 310–316, these private forces were usually weak.

58. Angold 1984a, 1–11; Stephenson 2000, 80–81, 114.

59. For the military reforms and economic changes see Lemerle 1977, 251–312; N. Oikonomides, *L'évolution de l'organisation administrative de l'Empire Byzantin au XIe siècle (1025–1118)*, TM, 6 (1976), 141–147; J. C. Cheynet, La politique militaire Byzantine de Basile II à Alexis Comnène, ZRVI (1991), 64–73; M. Angold, *The Byzantine Empire, 1025–1118*, NCMH IV, 224–231, 247–248.

60. For this relation between corruption and unrest see A. G. C. Savvides, Internal Strife and Unrest in Later Byzantium, XIth–XIIIth Centuries (A.D. 1025–1261). The Case of Urban and Provincial Insurrections (Causes and Effects), *Symmeikta. Ethnikon Idryma Ereynon. Kentron Vyzantinon Ereynon* (Athens), 7, (1987), 263; J. C. Cheynet, Points de vue sur l'efficacité administrative entre les Xe–XIe siècles, BF, 19 (1993), 11–13.

61. Angold 1985, 20–22; Ahrweiler 1976, 118–120.

62. Stephenson 2000, 123–130.

63. W. E. Kaegi Jr., Regionalism in the Balkan Armies of the Byzantine Empire, in *Actes du IIe Congrès International des Études du Sud-Est Européen* (Athènes), 2 (1972), 397–405.

64. J. Hoffmann, *Rudimente von Territorialstaaten im byzantinischen Reich. Untersuchungen über Unabhängigkeitsbestrebungen und ihr Verhältnis zu Kaiser und Reich* (Miscellanea Byzantina Monacensia, 17), München, 1974, 5–12, 78–80, 113; J. Ferluga, Aufstände im byzantinischen Reich zwischen den Jahren 1025 und 1081. Versuch einer Typologie. *Rivista di Studi Bizantini e Slavi* (Bologna), 5 (1985), 151, 153; J. C. Cheynet, *Pouvoir et contestations à Byzance (963–1210)*, Paris, 1990, 48, 63, 82, 397–399.

65. Lemerle 1977, 268–271; Cheynet 1991, 66; J. Haldon, *Warfare, State and Society in the Byzantine World, 565–1204*, London, 1999, 92–93.

66. Stephenson 2000, 82–89, 135–136 has shown that payments for the Pechenegs caused a supplementary burden for the people of the *theme* of Bulgaria, who rebelled in 1040.

67. Cheynet 1990, 14. Savvides 1987, 239, 259 remarks too that all the separatist movements and military mutinies were initiated by aristocrats or landowners.

68. Stephenson 2000, 143–144.

69. P. Lemerle, Prolégomènes à une édition critique et commentée des "Conseils et Récits de Kékaumenos," *Académie Royale de Belgique. Classe des lettres. Mémoires. Collection in-8°, deuxième série*, 54 (1960), 80–81; Ostrogorsky 1971, 12–14; Ferluga 1976, 242; Cheynet 1990, 287–288; Stephenson 2000, 123–129.

70. Ferluga 1976, 393; Ferluga 1985, 157–158; Fine 1991, 213. For the policy of Nikephoritzes, see Angold 1984a, 98–101; Stephenson 2000, 99–100.

71. Ferluga 1976, 341; R. Iljovski, L'alliance Byzantino-Hongroise au début du XIe siècle contre Samuel et ses successeurs. Essai de détermination chronologique, ZRVI, 29–30 (1991), 98–99; Makk 1999, 36.

72. Ferluga 1976, 385; Fine 1991, 204.

73. S. Dimitrov, The Bulgarian Apocryphal Chronicle and Bulgarian Ethnic History, EB, 29, 4 (1993), 99.

74. A. Sacerdoţeanu, Mouvements politiques et sociaux de la Péninsule Balkanique dans la seconde moitié du XIe siècle, *Balcania*, 2–3 (1939–1940), 89–91; Ferluga 1976, 393–395; Fine 1991, 213–214.

75. H. Dimitrov, Die Magyaren in Makedonien (X—XII. Jh.), BHR, 23 (1995), 3, 7, 12; Makk 1999, 47.

76. Ferluga 1976, 383–389; G. Cankova-Petkova, De nouveau sur Kékaumenos, BHR, 1, 3 (1973), 72–74; Ferluga 1985, 140–147; Fine 1991, 203–206; A. Miltenova & M. Kajmakamova, The Uprising of Petăr Deljan (1040–1041) in a New Old Bulgarian Source, BB, 8 (1986), 227–240; Cheynet 1990, 50, 388–389; Treadgold 1997, 588; Stephenson 2000, 130–133.

77. Ostrogorsky 1956, 349; Wasilewski 1971, 113–117; Ferluga 1976, 233–235, 239, 371–375; Ferluga 1985, 148; Fine 1991, 206; Malamut 1998, 442; Stephenson 2000, 133–135; Dimnik 2003, 267.

78. Wasilewski 1964, 480–481; M. Popović, Les forteresses du système defensif Byzantin en Serbie au XIe-XIIe siècle, *Starinar*, NS, 42 (1991), 170, 173; Makk 1999, 64, 66.

79. Sacerdoţeanu 1939–1940, 89–91; R. L. Wolff, The "Second Bulgarian Empire." Its Origin and History to 1204, *Speculum*, 24 (1949), 179–180; Ostrogorsky 1956, 368; Božić 1968, 144; Dvornik 1970, 254–258; Ferluga 1976, 81–84; M. Tadin, Les "Arbanitai" des chroniques byzantines (XIe–XIIe s.), CIEB XV, vol. IV (1980), 323; Cheynet 1990, 389; N. Budak, Die südslawischen Ethnogenesen an der östlichen Adriaküste im frühen Mittelalter, in *Typen der Ethnogenese unter besonderer Berücksichtigung der Bayern*, I (DAW, 201), Wien, 1990, 129; Fine 1991, 213–215; Stephenson 2000, 141–150; Dimnik 2003, 268.

80. Ostrogorsky 1956, 364–365; P. Diaconu, *Les Petchénègues au Bas-Danube*, Bucarest, 1970, 79–80; Angold 1984a, 55; Treadgold 1997, 600–601. For the financial and military policy of Constantine X, see especially Lemerle 1977, 270–271.

81. G. Murnu, *Studii istorice privitoare la trecutul românilor de peste Dunăre*, Bucureşti, 1984, 114–115; G. G. Litavrin, Vostannie Bolgar i Vlakhov v Fessalijij v 1066, VV, 11 (1956), 123–134.

82. Murnu 1984, 112.

83. Bănescu 1946, 81–83; Diaconu 1970, 93–96; Kühn 1991, 242.

84. M. Gyóni, L'oeuvre de Kekauménos, source de l'histoire roumaine, RHC, 23, n.s., vol. 3 (1945), 122; Lemerle 1960, 49.

85. F. Chalandon, *Essai sur le règne d'Aléxis Ier Comnène*, Paris, 1900, 60, 85–86; Murnu 1984, 115. See also Sacerdoțeanu 1939–1940, 97.

86. Ferluga 1976, 392.

87. Lemerle 1960, 47, footnote 6; Cheynet 1990, 72, 288. For *douloi*, see also Ferluga 1976, 407.

88. Stephenson 2000, 98–100.

89. Scylitzes Continuatus, *Chronographia*, ed. E. Th. Tsolakis, Thessaloniki, 1968, 166.

90. Stephenson 2000, 93.

91. I. Jordanov, Sceau d'archonte de PATZINAKIA du XIe siècle, EB, 28, 2 (1992), 79–82.

92. See Diaconu 1970, 103–104. Angold 1984a, 98 also suggests that Nestor was perhaps a Vlach.

93. V. Tăpkova-Zaimova, La population du Bas-Danube et le pouvoir Byzantin (XIe–XIIe s.), CIEB XV (Athènes), vol. IV, (1980), 334; Tăpkova-Zaimova 1993, 99.

94. N. Oikonomides, *A Collection of Dated Byzantine Seals*, Washington, DC, 1986, 93–94, nr. 95; I. Jordanov, Neizdadeni vizantijski olovni pečati ot Silistra (IV), INMV, 28 (43) (1992), 238–239, nr. 14–15.

95. See the remarks of E. Stănescu, La crise du Bas-Danube Byzantin au cours de la séconde moitié du XIesiècle, ZRVI, 9 (1966), 57–59.

96. Stănescu 1966, 59–60.

97. I. Barnea, Sceaux Byzantins inédits de Dobroudja, SBS, 3 (1993), 61–65.

98. Ioannes Zonaras, *Chronicon*, XVIII. 19. 17.

99. Stephenson 2000, 102.

100. Stănescu 1966, 62–63.

101. Stănescu 1966, 49–73; Barnea & Ştefănescu 1971, 136–153; N. Ş. Tanaşoca, *Les Mixobarbares et les formations politiques paristriennes du XIe siècle*, RRH, 12, 1 (1973), 61–82; Angold 1984a, 109–111; Cheynet 1990, 390–392; Treadgold 1997, 617; Madgearu 2003, 52–53.

102. B. Ferjančić, A Byzantine Seal from Sirmium, ZRVI, 1 (1982), 46–52.

103. Fine 1991, 234–235; Makk 1999, 109–110; Stephenson 2000, 206–210.

104. Ostrogorsky 1956, 404; A. B. Urbansky, *Byzantium and the Danube Frontier. A Study of the Relations between Byzantium, Hungary and the Balkans during the Period of the Comneni*, New York, 1968, 43, 47–50, 71–72; Ferluga 1976, 148, 194–199, 204–205; Angold 1984a, 176–177; Fine 1991, 234–242; Makk 1999, 121–128; Stephenson 2000, 239–274.

105. Stephenson 2000, 239–274. See also Ferluga 1976, 193–213; Fine 1991, 236–242.

106. Fine 1991, 225–226; Dimnik 2003, 268.

107. Kalić 1988, 134–140; M. Popović, The Early Byzantine Basilica at Ras, *Starinar*, NS, 48 (1997), 91.

108. Angold 1984a, 174.

109. Ostrogorsky 1956, 412; Kalić 1988, 131–132; Fine 1991, 234–245; J. V. A. Fine Jr., *The Late Medieval Balkans. A Critical Survey from the Late Twelfth Century to the Ottoman Conquest*, Ann Arbor, MI, 1994, 3–6; Dimnik 2003, 269–270.

110. F. Makk, *The Árpáds and the Comneni. Political Relations between Hungary and Byzantium in the 12th Century*, Budapest, 1989, 115–117; Fine 1994, 6–7; Treadgold 1997, 652–654; Stephenson 2000, 281–288.

111. Makk 1989, 120; J. Schmitt, Die Balkanpolitik der Arpaden in den Jahren 1180–1241, *Ungarn-Jahrbuch. Zeitschrift für die Kunde Ungarns und verwandte Gebiete* (München), 17 (1989), 27; Fine 1994, 9–10; Treadgold 1997, 657; Stephenson 2000, 282–283.

112. Wolff 1949, 181–183; Angold 1984a, 272–274; Fine 1994, 9–11.

113. For *pronoia*, see Ostrogorsky 1956, 392–393; Idem, *Pour l'histoire de la féodalité Byzantine*, Bruxelles, 1954, 9–53; Idem, Die Pronoia unter den Komnenen, ZRVI, 12 (1970), 41–54; H. Ahrweiler, La 'pronoia' à Byzance, in *Structures féodales et feodalisme dans l'occident mediterranéen (Xe–XIIIe siècles)* (Collection de l'Ecole Française de Rome, 44), Rome, 1980, 681–689.

114. Wolff 1949, 180–184; Ostrogorsky 1956, 426–429; R. Guilland, Byzance et les Balkans, sous le règne d'Isaac II Ange (1185–1195), in *Actes du XIIe Congrès International d'Études Byzantines*, 2, Belgrade, 1964, 125–137; G. Cankova-Petkova, La libération de la Bulgarie de la domination Byzantine, BB, 5 (1978), 95–121; Cheynet 1990, 436–438; Fine 1994, 12–17; Stephenson 2000, 288–294.

115. N. Ş. Tanaşoca, Din nou despre geneza şi caracterul statului Asăneştilor, RdI, 34 (1981), 7, 1305–1307; E. Stănescu, Premisele răscoalei Asăneştilor. Lumea românească sud-dunăreană în veacurile X–XII, *Răscoala 1989*, 11–15; S. Iosipescu, Românii şi cea de-a treia cruciadă, *Revista Istorică*, 5 (1994), 3–4, 254–255; S. Brezeanu, *Romanitatea orientală în evul mediu. De la cetăţenii romani la naţiunea medievală*, Bucureşti, 1999, 172–194; N. Ş. Tanaşoca, Aperçus of the History of Balkan Romanity, in R. Theodorescu & L. Conley Barrows (Eds.), *Politics and Culture in Southeastern Europe*, Bucharest, 2001, 120–125.

116. Wolff 1949, 184; Fine 1994, 24; Stephenson 2000, 294–300.

117. Wolff 1949, 187–189; Ostrogorsky 1956, 430–434; Angold 1984a, 274–275; Fine 1994, 26–32; Treadgold 1997, 658–662; Stephenson 2000, 300–314. For Ivanko, see especially Hoffmann 1974, 51–55, 92–95, 115–116, 123, 138.

118. A. J. B. Wace & M. S. Thompson, *The Nomads of the Balkans. An Account of Life and Customs among the Vlachs of Northern Pindus*, London 1914, 261–262; Hoffmann 1974, 47–50, 90–92, 114–115, 122, 130, 138; Fine 1994, 29–30, 32–33, 86–87, 95.

119. Hoffmann 1974, 56–60, 95–96, 123, 130; N. Oikonomides, La décomposition de l'Empire Byzantin à la veille de 1204 et les origines de l'Empire de Nicée: À propos de la "Partitio Romaniae," CIEB XV, vol. I, 3–28 (Idem, *Byzantium from the Ninth Century to the Fourth Crusade: Studies, Texts, Monuments.* Hampshire, Variorum, 1992, XX), 1976, 17–18; Angold 1984a, 278; Angold 1984b, 243; A. Ilieva, The Phenomenon Leo Sgouros, EB, 26, 3 (1990), 31–51; Fine 1994, 37, 64; Treadgold 1997, 710, 712, 715.

120. Ostrogorsky 1956, 431; Tadin 1980, 323, 327–330; B. I. Bojović, Historiographie dynastique et idéologie politique en Serbie au Bas Moyen Âge. Essai de synthèse de l'idéologie de l'Etat médiéval Serbe, SOF, 51 (1992), 31; Fine 1994, 7–8, 26; Bojović 1997, 36; Ducellier 1999, 779; Malcolm 1999, 43–44; L. Maksimović & G. Subotić, La Serbie entre Byzance et l'Occident, in *XXe Congrès International des Études Byzantines. Pré-actes, I. Séances plénières*, Paris, 2001, 242–243; L. Maksimović, L'Empire de Stefan Dusan: Genèse et caractère, TM, 14 (2002), 416.

121. Ostrogorsky 1956, 437–440; Angold 1984a, 291–295; Fine 1994, 61–63; Treadgold 1997, 663–666.

122. R. L. Wolff, Romania, The Latin Empire of Constantinople, *Speculum*, 23 (1948), 1–34; Ostrogorsky 1956, 445–448; Oikonomides 1976, 3–28; Treadgold 1997, 709.

123. Ostrogorsky 1956, 450–458, 463–474; S. G. Xydis, Medieval Origins of Modern Greek Nationalism, BS, 9, 1 (1968), 12–18; D. M. Nicol, *The Last Centuries of Byzantium, 1261–1453*, Cambridge, 1993, 21–36; Treadgold 1997, 730–734; M. Angold, Byzantium in Exile, NCMH V, 543–562.

124. N. Iorga, *Histoire des États Balkaniques jusqu'a 1924*, Paris, 1925, 2–3.

125. Ostrogorsky 1956, 479–489; B. Gjuzelev, *Das Papstum und Bulgarien im Mittelalter (9.-14. Jh.)*, BHR, 5, 1 (1977), 50–51; J. M. Hussey, *The Orthodox Church in the Byzantine Empire*, Oxford, 1986, 225–242; B. G. Spiridonakis, *Grecs, ocidentaux et Turcs de 1054 à 1453, quatre siècles de relations internationals*, Thessalonique, 1990, 141; Nicol 1993, 53–57; Fine 1994, 184–187; Treadgold 1997, 740–745; Angold 1999, 565–567; H. Chadwick, *East and West: The Making of a Rift in the Church. From Apostolic Times until the Council of Florence*, Oxford, 2003, 248–253.

126. Ostrogorsky 1956, 583–585; Hussey 1986, 272–282; Nicol 1993, 355–359; Treadgold 1997, 794–795; Chadwick 2003, 246–257.

127. Ostrogorsky 1956, 465; Hussey 1986, 217–218; Chadwick 2003, 238–243.

128. Xydis 1968, 1–20.

129. I. N. Moles, Nationalism and Byzantine Greece, GRBS, 10 (1969), 1, 95–107; J. Irmscher, Nikäa als "Zentrum des griechischen Patriotismus," RESEE, 8 (1970), 1, 33–47; A. E. Vacalopoulos, *Origins of the Greek Nation: The Byzantine Period, 1204–1461*, New Brunswick, NJ, 1970, 28–30, 37–39; M. Angold, Byzantine "Nationalism" and the Nicaean Empire, BMGS, 1 (1975), 50–52, 64–66; Spiridonakis 1990, 131–138; Angold 1999, 561; C. Carras, Greek Identity: A Long View, *Balkan Identities*, 306–307.

130. Georgios Akropolites, *Historiae*, I, 76. See A. E. Vacalopoulos, *History of Macedonia, 1354–1833*, Thessaloniki, 1973, 19; Angold 1975, 63.

131. A. Ducellier, Les Albanais du XIe au XIIIe siècle: Nomades ou sédentaires? BF, 7 (1979), 28.

132. D. M. Nicol, Refugees, Mixed Population and Local Patriotism in Epiros and Western Macedonia after the Fourth Crusade, CIEB XV, vol. I, 3–33 (Idem, *Studies in Late Byzantine History and Prosopography*, London, Variorum Reprints, 1986, IV), 1976, 24–25; Tadin 1980, 322; S. Pollo & A. Puto, *The History of Albania from Its Origins to the Present Day*, London, 1981, 43–44; A. Ducellier, Genesis and Failure of the Albanian State in the Fourteenth and Fifteenth Century, in A. Pipa & S. Repishti (eds.), *Studies on Kosova*, Boulder, New York 1984, 7; K. Frashëri, The Territories of the Albanians in the XVth Century, *Albanians 1985*, 212–213; Fine 1994, 51, 112; A. Ducellier, Albania, Serbia and Bulgaria, NCMH V, 780, 786, 791.

133. Ostrogorsky 1956, 454–460, 464; G. Prinzing, *Die Bedeutung Bulgariens und Serbiens in den Jahren 1204–1219 in Zusammenhang mit der Entstehung und Entwicklung der Byzantinischen Teilstaaten nach der Einname Konstantinopels infolge des 4. Kreuzzuges*, München, 1972, 114–115; A. Ducellier, *La façade maritime de l'Albanie au Moyen Âge. Durazzo et Valona du XIe au XVe siècle*, Thessalonique, 1981, 161–163, 166; D. M. Nicol, *The despotate of Epiros (1267–1479). A contribution to the history of*

Greece in the Middle Ages. Cambridge, 1984, 2–5; Nicol 1993, 20, 24–32; Fine 1994, 65–69, 112–114, 119–128, 157–165; F. Bredenkamp, *The Byzantine Empire of Thessaloniki, 1224–1242*, Thessaloniki, 1996; Treadgold 1997, 718–722; Savvides 1998, 409; Angold 1999, 548, 555.

134. Wolff 1949, 190–197; B. Primov, The Papacy, the Fourth Crusade and Bulgaria, BB, 1 (1962), 183–211; J. R. Sweeney, Innocent III, Hungary and the Bulgarian Coronation: A Study in Medieval Papal Diplomacy, *Church History*, 42, 3 (1973), 320–334; Gjuzelev 1977, 42–43; Schmitt 1989, 33–35; Fine 1994, 55–56; Brezeanu 1999, 180–183; Ducellier 1999, 782.

135. Wolff 1949, 201–202; Ostrogorsky 1956, 449, 451; Prinzing 1972, 25–92; I. Božilov, La "Chronique de Morée" et l'histoire de Bulgarie au début du XIIIe siècle (1204–1207), BHR, 5, 2 (1977), 37–57; Ş. Papacostea, *Românii în secolul al XIII-lea. Între cruciată şi imperiul mongol*, Bucureşti, 1993, 19–20; Fine 1994, 81–87; Treadgold 1997, 713–715; Ducellier 1999, 783.

136. Prinzing 1972, 100–138; Schmitt 1989, 38–40; Fine 1994, 91–105.

137. Ostrogorsky 1956, 460–461; Gjuzelev 1977, 44–45; Papacostea 1993, 39; Fine 1994, 106, 124–126; Ducellier 1999, 787–788.

138. Gjuzelev 1977, 46–49; Schmitt 1989, 46; Papacostea 1993, 39–48; Fine 1994, 128–133; Treadgold 1997, 723–724; Ducellier 1999, 788–789.

139. Papacostea 1993, 116–125; Fine 1994, 154–156, 170–184, 195–199, 224–230; V. Ciocîltan, *Mongolii şi Marea Neagră în secolele XIII–XIV. Contribuţia Cinghizhanizilor la transformarea bazinului pontic în placă turnantă a comerţului Euro-Asiatic*, Bucureşti, 1998, 230–256. For the despotate of Silistra, see P. Diaconu, À propos des soi-disant monnaies de Jakob Sviatoslav, *Dobrudža* (Varna), 12, 1995 (1998), 242–256.

140. N. Iorga, *Études Byzantines*, I, Bucarest, 1939, 127–128; Schmitt 1989, 30–32; Bojović 1992, 32; A. Ducellier, Have the Albanians Occupied Kosova? *Kosova 1993*, 64; Fine 1994, 41–50, 106–108; Ducellier 1999, 784–785.

141. L. Mavromatis, *La fondation de l'Empire Serbe. Le Kralj Milutin*, Thessalonique, 1978, 15–28; Nicol 1993, 118; Fine 1994, 199–204, 217–219.

142. Ostrogorsky 1956, 488, 511; Mavromatis 1978, 29–35, 54; N. Iorga, *Sârbi, Bulgari şi români în Peninsula Balcanică în evul mediu* [1915], in Ş. Papacostea (ed.), *Studii asupra evului mediu românesc*, Bucureşti (1984), 57; G. Soulis, *The Serbs and Byzantium during the Reign of Tsar Stephen Dushan (1331–1355) and His Successors*, Washington, DC (1984), 1; Nicol 1984, 67; Nicol 1993, 119; Fine 1994, 219; Malcolm 1999, 47; Ducellier 1999, 795.

143. Iorga 1939, 150–152; Ostrogorsky 1956, 511–512, 517; G. Ostrogorsky, Problèmes des relations Byzantino-Serbes au XIVe siècle, In *Proceedings of the XIIIth International Congress of Byzantine Studies* (Oxford, September 5–10, 1966), London, Oxford, 1967, 41; Mavromatis 1978, 37–56; Nicol 1993, 119–120; M. Živojinović, La frontière Serbo-Byzantine dans les premières décennies du XIVe siècle, *Byzantium and Serbia*, 1996, 58–59. The project of an anti-Byzantine "crusade" of 1308 was the reason for the report written by Andreas Hungarus mentioned in the previous chapter in relation to the problem of the origin of the Aromanians.

144. Soulis 1984, 53–55; P. Xhufi, Albanian Heretics in the Serbian Medieval Kingdom, *Kosova 1993*, 51.

145. Mavromatis 1978, 22–28, 54–67; Xhufi 1993, 51; Fine 1994, 221, 256–263.

146. Ostrogorsky 1956, 522–527; Nicol 1993, 151–161; Fine 1994, 250–252; Treadgold 1997, 755–759; Živojinović 1996, 64–65.

147. Ostrogorsky 1956, 523–527; Mavromatis 1978, 75–81; R. Iljovski, *Makedonien im dritten Jahrzehnt des 14. Jahrhunderts, Macédoine 1981*, 69–84; Soulis 1984, 2; Fine 1994, 269–274.

148. Mavromatis 1978, 72; Pollo & Puto 1981, 48; Soulis 1984, 3; Xhufi 1993, 51; Fine 1994, 286–290.

149. Soulis 1984, 108; Fine 1994, 169–170, 235–237, 320; A. G. C. Savvides, Splintered Medieval Hellenism: The Semi-Autonomous State of Thessaly (A.D. 1213/ 1222 to 1454/1470) and Its Place in History, *Byzantion*, 68, 2 (1998), 409–414.

150. Ostrogorsky 1956, 538–539, 544; Ostrogorsky 1967, 42; Vacalopoulos 1973, 13–14; Mavromatis 1978, 82–83; Soulis 1984, 6–27, 35–39; Nicol 1984, 128–131; Fine 1994, 292–307, 320–321; Treadgold 1997, 761–770; M. Bartusis, The Settlement of Serbs in Macedonia in the Era of Dušan's Conquests, in H. Ahrweiler & A. E. Laiou (eds.), *Studies on the Internal Diaspora of the Byzantine Empire*, Washington, DC, 1998, 153; Savvides 1998, 414.

151. Ostrogorsky 1956, 544; Soulis 1984, 27–32, 60–67; Bojović 1992, 38; Fine 1994, 309–319; N. Oikonomides, *Emperor of the Romans—Emperor of the Romania*, in *Byzantium and Serbia*, (1996b), 121–128; S. Ćirković, Between Kingdom and Empire: Dušan's State (1346–1355) Reconsidered, *Byzantium and Serbia*, 116; Maksimović 2002, 422–427.

152. T. Teoteoi, Civilizaţia statului Asăneştilor între Roma şi Bizanţ, *Răscoala 1989*, 83–87; Ćirković 1996, 118; Oikonomides 1996b, 126–128.

153. Ćirković 1996, 110–120; Oikonomides 1996b, 128; Maksimović 2002, 428.

154. Ostrogorsky 1956, 546; Ostrogorsky 1967, 42; Soulis 1984, 87; Oikonomides 1996b, 121.

155. Iorga 1925, 15–16; Nicol 1984, 131–134.

156. Ostrogorsky 1967, 44–55; Vacalopoulos 1973, 14, 21–26; Soulis 1984, 91–98; Fine 1994, 353, 362–366.

157. Vacalopoulos 1970, 114; Soulis 1984, 87, 114–117; Fine 1994, 320, 347–352; Oikonomides 1996b, 121; Savvides 1998, 414–415.

158. Vacalopoulos 1970, 112–113; Soulis 1984, 116, 120–126; Fine 1994, 351–354.

159. Ducellier 1981, 144–151, 161–166, 238, 258–261, 357–358; Pollo & Puto 1981, 45–50; Soulis 1984, 135–138; Nicol 1984, 15, 68; Frashëri 1985, 212–213; Ducellier 1999, 793–794.

160. I. Caragiani, *Studii istorice asupra românilor din Peninsula Balcanică*, Bucureşti, 1929, 6–18; M. Ruffini, Ghinu Buia Spata şi luptele aromânilor pentru cuceriea Ianinei (1360–1400) in "Historia Basilissae Mariae atque Thomas et Esau, Despoton Joanninae," *Studii*, 15, 5 (1962), 1127–1154; K. Bozhori, À propos de l'extension du nom Arbanon à l'époque Byzantine, CIEB XIV, vol. II (1975), 311; G. Schirò, La genealogia degli Spata tra il XIV e XV sec. e due Bua sconosciuti, *Rivista di Studi Bizantini e Neoellenici*, NS, 8–9 (1971–1972), 67–85; Soulis 1984, 125–132; Nicol 1984, 139–156; B. Ferjancić, Les Albanais dans les sources Byzantines, in *Les Illyriens 1988*, 318; Fine 1994, 350–355.

161. Ducellier 1981, 471–492; Pollo & Puto 1981, 51–57; Ducellier 1984, 9–12; Soulis 1984, 138–145; Frashëri 1985, 219; S. Pulaha, On the Presence of Albanians in Kosova during the 14th–17th Centuries, *Kosova 1993*, 34; B. Pranvera, Kosova

under the Albanian Feudal State of the Balshes, *Kosova 1993*, 55–62; Fine 1994, 358–362, 371–372, 383–384, 390–392, 414–422; Malcolm 1999, 59.

162. Iorga 1939, 42; S. Dragomir, *Vlahii din nordul Peninsulei Balcanice în evul mediu*, Bucureşti, 1959, 111; I. Božić, *Istorija Crnoje Gore*, Belgrade, 1969, 29 (Pranvera 1993, 55); M. Cazacu, Les Valaques dans les Balkans occidentaux (Serbie, Croatie, Albanie, etc.). La Pax ottomanica (XVème–XVIIème siècles), *Les Aroumains*, 83.

163. A. Pippidi, Changes of Emphasis, Greek Christendom, Westernization, South-Eastern Europe, and Neo-Mittel Europa, *Balkanologie*, 3, 2 (1999), 99.

164. N. Iorga, *Ilusii şi drepturi naţionale în Balcani. Lecţie de deschidere la Institutul de Studii Sud-Ost Europene*, Vălenii de Munte, 1916, 11–15.

165. V. Papacostea, La Péninsule Balkanique et le problème des études compares, *Balcania*, 6 (1943), XVI.

166. Pundeff 1968, 1–27. See also Angelov 1980, 141–143.

167. D. Obolensky, Nationalism in Eastern Europe in the Middle Ages, *Transactions of the Royal Historical Society*, Fifth Series, 22 (1972), 13.

168. I. A. Pop, *Geneza medievală a naţiunilor moderne (secolele XIII–XVI)*, Bucureşti, 1998.

169. K. F. Werner, Les nations et le sentiment national dans l'Europe médiévale, *Revue Historique* (Paris), 94 année, tome 244, 496 (Octobre–Décembre 1970), 285–304; P. J. Geary, *The Myth of Nations: The Medieval Origins of Europe*, Princeton, NJ, 2002, 120–155.

170. A. Laiou, In the Medieval Balkans: Economic Pressures and Conflicts in the Fourteenth Century, in S. Vryonis Jr. (ed.), *Byzantine Studies in Honor of Milton V. Anastos*, Malibu, CA, 1985, 137–162.

171. Ostrogorsky 1956, 530, 539, 541, 551, 558–559; D, Angelov, Certains aspects de la conquête des peuples balkaniques par les Turcs, ByzSl, 17, 2 (1956), 233; L. S. Stavrianos, *The Balkans since 1453*, New York, 1959, 40–43; Vacalopoulos 1973, 27–28; S. Runciman, *The Fall of Constantinople, 1453*, Cambridge, 1990, 34–36; G. Castellan, *Histoire des Balkans (XIVe–XXe siècle)*, Paris, 1991, 56–67; Fine 1994, 292, 378; Treadgold 1997, 774–775, 779.

172. Ostrogorsky 1967, 55; Vacalopoulos 1970, 77; Vacalopoulos 1973, 28; Soulis 1984, 98–102, 155–157; Runciman 1990, 37; Castellan 1991, 63; Fine 1994, 379–382; R. Mihaljčić, Les batailles de la Maritza et de Kosovo. Les dernières décennies de la rivalité Serbo-Byzantine, *Byzantium and Serbia*, 101–102; Treadgold 1997, 780; M. Bartusis, The Settlement of Serbs in Macedonia in the Era of Dušan's Conquests, in H. Ahrweiler & A. E. Laiou (eds.), *Studies on the Internal Diaspora of the Byzantine Empire*, Washington, DC, 1998, 157.

173. R. Samardžić, Migrations in Serbian History (the Era of Foreign Rule), *Migrations 1989*, 83.

174. S. Čirković, Le Kosovo-Metohija au Moyen Âge, *Kosovo 1990*, 36; Fine 1994, 501–502. Belgrade was given to Serbia in 1284, as a part of the inheritance of Milutin from his mother Helena, the queen of Hungary. In 1319, the Hungarian king Charles Robert of Anjou again took Belgrade during the war against Stephen III Milutin. See Mavromatis 1978, 21–22, 67.

175. Čirković 1990, 34–35; Fine 1994, 382–383, 389.

176. Guldescu 1964, 245–251; J. V. A. Fine Jr., *The Bosnian Church. A New Interpretation*, New York, 1975, 170–173; Fine 1994, 17–21, 143–148, 275–284; N. Malcolm, *Storia di Bosnia dalle origini ai giorni nostril*, Milano, 2000, 37–43.

177. Ostrogorsky 1956, 566; Guldescu 1964, 253–255; Fine 1975, 189–192, 197–198; Fine 1994, 368–370, 392–395; Malcolm 2000, 44–46.

178. Vacalopoulos 1973, 41–51, 59–67; Soulis 1984, 155–157; Fine 1994, 407, 427; Treadgold 1997, 782.

179. Ostrogorsky 1956, 562; Angelov 1956, 233; Stavrianos 1959, 44; Vacalopoulos 1973, 28–29, 48–49; P. F. Sugar, *Southeastern Europe under Ottoman Rule, 1354–1804*, Seattle, WA, 1977, 20; A. Stojanovski, La division administrative-territoriale de la Macédoine sous l'Empire Ottoman jusqu'à la fin du XVIIe siècle, *Macédoine 1981*, 87–97; Soulis 1984, 102–107; Runciman 1990, 37; Fine 1994, 380–382, 424.

180. Ducellier 1981, 488. See also Malcolm 1999, 58.

181. Soulis 1984, 52.

182. J. W. Barker, *The Question of Ethnic Antagonisms among the Balkan States of the Fourteenth Century*, in T. S. Miller & J. Nesbitt (eds.), *Peace and War in Byzantium. Essays in Honor of George T. Dennis S.J.*, Washington, DC, 1995, 165–174.

183. H. Inalcik, Ottoman Methods of Conquest, *Studia Islamica*, 2 (1954), 103.

184. Iorga 1925, 1, 17.

185. L. Maksimović, *The Byzantine Provincial Administration under the Palaiologoi*, Amsterdam, 1988, 15, 25–26, 264–266.

186. Sugar 1977, 21; Soulis 1984, 106; Runciman 1990, 38; Fine 1994, 409.

187. Ostrogorsky 1956, 566–567; Stavrianos 1959, 44–45; Runciman 1990, 38–39; Čirković 1990, 35; Castellan 1991, 65–66; Fine 1994, 409–410, 426–427, 499–500; Mihaljčić 1996, 103–105; Malcolm 1999, 61–80.

188. Ostrogorsky 1956, 579; Vacalopoulos 1970, 85; Vacalopoulos 1973, 74; Runciman 1990, 41–43; Castellan 1991, 73–74; Fine 1994, 503–508; Treadgold 1997, 789.

189. Fine 1994, 500–502, 509.

190. Iorga 1925, 18–19; Ostrogorsky 1956, 572–574; Angelov 1956, 234; Stavrianos 1959, 46–48; Fine 1994, 423–424.

191. N. Beldiceanu, *Les Roumains à la bataille d'Ankara*, SOF, 14 (1955), 2, 441–450; Ostrogorsky 1956, 572–574; R. I. Lawless, The Economy and Landscapes of Thessaly during Ottoman Rule, *Carter 1977*, 507; Sugar 1977, 22; T. J. Winnifrith, *The Vlachs, the History of a Balkan People*, London, 1987, 128–129; Cazacu 1989, 86; Fine 1994, 427–428; Savvides 1998, 415–416.

192. Ostrogorsky 1956, 581–582; Stavrianos 1959, 51–53; Vacalopoulos 1970, 145–149; Vacalopoulos 1973, 90–98; Runciman 1990, 46–47; Castellan 1991, 78–79.

193. Pollo & Puto 1981, 65–66; Ducellier 1993, 65.

194. Angelov 1956, 234–235; Stavrianos 1959, 63, 237; G. Arnakis, The Role of Religion in the Development of Balkan Nationalism, *Balkans 1963*, 129; Soulis 1984, 141–142; Castellan 1991, 177.

195. Ostrogorsky 1956, 586–588; Stavrianos 1959, 53–62; Vacalopoulos 1973, 113–117; Runciman 1991, 50–52; Castellan 1991, 81–84; Nicol 1993, 362–367; Fine 1994, 548–550, 562; Treadgold 1997, 796–797.

196. Stavrianos 1959, 64; Pollo & Puto 1981, 71–88; Ducellier 1984, 14–16; Nicol 1993, 361–362, 393; Malcolm 1999, 88–91.

197. Ostrogorsky 1956, 591–593; Stavrianos 1959, 55–59; Runciman 1990, 73–144; Castellan 1991, 85–91; Nicol 1993, 375–390; Treadgold 1997, 797–800.

198. Stavrianos 1959, 90; Runciman 1990, 145–159; Treadgold 1997, 800.

199. Spiridonakis 1990, 210–223.

200. Ostrogorsky 1956, 593; Stavrianos 1959, 64, 67–70; Vacalopoulos 1970, 207–213; Runciman 1990, 171–172; Castellan 1991, 93; Nicol 1993, 396–401; Fine 1994, 564–567; Treadgold 1997, 802.

201. N. Beldiceanu, La région de Timok-Morava dans les documents de Mehmed II et de Selim I, *Revue des Études Roumaines*, 3–4 (1957), 112; Runciman 1990, 182; Castellan 1991, 92; Nicol 1993, 366, 393; Fine 1994, 529–530, 554–556, 568–574; Bojović 1997, 49; Malcolm 1999, 92.

202. Guldescu 1964, 261–263; Fine 1994, 454–481; Malcolm 2000, 46–49.

203. Stavrianos 1959, 62–63; Guldescu 1964, 258–263; G. W. Hoffman, The Evolution of the Ethnographic Map of Yugoslavia, *Carter 1977*, 467; Fine 1994, 532–534, 577–586; Castellan 1991, 94; Malcolm 2000, 48–49.

204. N. Oikonomides, The Medieval Via Egnatia, in E. Zachariadou (ed.), *The Egnatia under Ottoman Rule (1380–1699). Halcyon Days in Crete II: A Symposium Held in Rethymnon (9–11 January 1994)* Rethymnon 1996 (N. Oikonomides, *Social and Economic Life in Byzantium*, Variorum, Ashgate, 2004, XXIII), 12–13, 16.

205. F. Braudel, *La Méditerranée et le monde Méditerranéen a l'époque de Philippe II*, 2 vol., Paris, 1966, II, 15.

206. Stavrianos 1959, 40, 100, 112–115, 138–142; Hoffman 1977, 474; Lawless 1977, 509; Braudel 1966, II, 11, 14.

207. Angelov 1956, 261, 274–275 has expressed this extreme point of view of a catastrophe caused by the Ottoman conquest.

208. M. Vasić, *Der Islamisierungsprozess auf der Balkanhalbinsel* ("Zur Kunde Südosteuropas," II/14), Graz, 1985, 12.

209. Stavrianos 1959, 96–97, 112–115. See also Malcolm 1999, 93–94.

210. A. Tanaşoca, Autonomia vlahilor din Imperiul Otoman în secolele XV–XVII, RdI, 34, 8 (1981), 1518–1528.

211. Iorga 1925, 32; Vasić 1985, 8.

212. Inalcik 1954, 113–114; Vacalopoulos 1970, 152–156; Vacalopoulos 1973, 100–101; Lawless 1977, 510.

213. See the thorough analysis made by Stavrianos 1959, 117–136.

214. T. Stoianovich, *A Study in Balkan Civilization*, New York, 1967, 145.

215. Stavrianos 1959, 160–161, 340–344.

216. J. Cvijić, *La Péninsule Balkanique. Géographie humaine*, Paris, 1918, 130–131; G. Stadtmüller, Die Islamisierung bei den Albanern, *Jahrbücher für Geschichte Osteuropas*, 3, 4 (1955), 415; S. Skendi, Religion in Albania during the Ottoman Rule, SOF, 15 (1956), 317; Pollo & Puto 1981, 89; Malcolm 1999, 120–121; F. Duka, *Some Features of Relations between Albania and the West during the XVIth–XVIIth Centuries*, AIESEEB, 31 (2001), 33–37.

217. Skendi 1956, 317; Stavrianos 1959, 171–175; Hoffman 1977, 476; H. Islami, Anthropogeographic Research in Kosova. An Aperçu on the Work "Kosovo" by Academician Atanasije Urosevic, *Albanians* 1985, 480–483; R. Tričković, Au-devant

des plus dures épreuves: Le XVIIe siècle, *Kosovo* 1990, 97–107; Castellan 1991, 195–198; Bojović 1997, 59; Malcolm 1999, 139–162.

218. For *klefts*, see Vacalopoulos 1973, 197–198, 203–207, 272–279.

219. Stavrianos 1959, 144. For ancient examples, see M. Bartusis, Brigandage in the Late Byzantine Empire, *Byzantion*, 51 (1981), 386–409; C. Farkas, Räubehorden in Thrakien. Eine unbeachtete Quelle zur Geschichte der Zeit des Kaisers Maurikios, BZ, 86–87, 2 (1993–1994), 462–470.

220. Stavrianos 1959, 175–177; Castellan 1991, 198.

221. Stavrianos 1959, 114; Castellan 1991, 119; M. Andonova–Hristova, Modèles historiques de coexistence pacifique entre Musulmans et Chrétiens Orthodoxes pendant les periodes Byzantine et Post-Byzantine, ByzSl, 61 (2003), 247–248.

Chapter 3

The Religious Aspects

A Spanish Byzantinist remarked that religion was one factor in the present Balkan conflicts, acting in combination with ethnic, political, and economic causes.[1] Indeed, the coexistence of three religions (Orthodoxy, Catholicism, and Islam) in the Balkan space favored and increased the potential for conflict in the area. The spheres of influence of Rome and Constantinople had intersected here since the early Middle Ages. Adopting the organizational structures of the late Roman state (the *diocesis* was first an administrative unit introduced by the reforms of Diocletian), the Church became a new field for tensions between the regions of the Roman world. For instance, the Monophysitic heresy expressed the fanatic and fundamentalist mentality of the population of the eastern provinces. On the other hand, the fall of the patriarchates of Alexandria and Antioch under Muslim domination led to a bipolar organization of the Church. In this way a competition for supremacy between the two main centers, Rome and Constantinople, began, first in the Mediterranean basin and next in all of Europe.

The attempt of Heraklios (610–641) to make a compromise between Orthodoxy and the revived Monophysitic heresy failed. The new doctrine imposed by him in 638, Monothelism, provoked the hostility of Rome.[2] For several decades, relations between Rome and Constantinople were strained because of this issue, but also because of the centrifugal attitude of the Italian possessions of the Byzantine Empire. This quarrel culminated

115

with the arrest of Pope Martin I (649–653), who was sent to exile at Cherson in Crimea, because he opposed the religious policy of Constans II (641–668), an adept of Monothelism.[3]

THE CONFRONTATION BETWEEN ROME AND CONSTANTINOPLE IN THE BALKANS

The iconoclastic crisis that fueled the divergent evolution of the two halves of the Mediterranean space increased in the eighth century. The Byzantine emperors who ruled between 717 and 787 and 814 and 843 forbade the worship of icons and started persecuting monks and laymen who continued to practice the old faith. In fact, iconoclasm was a kind of fundamentalism, which originated in oriental mentalities, as well as Monophysism, but with a pragmatic side, because the anticlerical policy of the iconoclast emperors aimed at strengthening the Byzantine state and economy, by taking over large human and material resources from the control of the Church.[4] Of course, the popes condemned the decisions of the iconoclast councils organized in the Byzantine Empire in 754 and 815 and the actions of the emperors who persecuted Orthodoxy, not only for dogmatic reasons, but also because the emperor Leon III took southern Italy and Sicily from Roman jurisdiction in 732. Some church historians believe that Illyricum was annexed by the patriarchate of Constantinople in the same circumstances, but this is not certain. It is possible that this happened in 754, after the end of Byzantine administration in Italy (the conquest of the exarchate of Ravenna by the Langobards in 751).[5] However, we should emphasize that jurisdiction over a large part of the Balkan Peninsula (eastern Illyricum as a church diocese included Epirus, Macedonia, Dardania, Dacia, Moesia) was a major reason for the dispute between Rome and Constantinople, and, as a Yugoslavian historian remarked,

> this controversy was the background of several conflicts that poisoned not only the historical evolution of the relationships between West and East, but especially the relations between the Balkan Slavs, causing fragmentation, discord and national intolerance.[6]

This dispute took place as a new power center was rising in the West: the Frankish kingdom. The expansion of Francia began after the majordomo Pippin the Short took power in 751. In 732, the Franks won a great victory at Poitiers, where they stopped the advance of the Arabs toward the north. After the middle of the eighth century, they started an offensive policy in northern Italy, the region mastered by the Langobard kingdom.

In this way, the Franks became the natural allies of the popes, because the Langobards hindered the consolidation of papal political authority in the peninsula. Rome thus gained a powerful protector that made Byzantine support useless, and that gave the popes the chance to follow an independent policy.[7]

The rise of a new universalist empire in the west (with the coronation of Charlemagne at Rome in 800) increased the fracture between Byzantium and the Latin world, even if iconoclasm was temporarily abandoned (between 787 and 814). The rivalry was political and ideological. Rome was the source of legitimation for the Western Roman Empire and this led to new tensions between the poles of Christianity. On the other hand, the new empire supported the missionary activity of Rome, by the more or less forced Christianization of the conquered populations (Saxons, Avars, and Slavs). One of the consequences was the achievement of the conversion of populations from the western part of the Balkan Peninsula.

The Christianization of the Croats was mainly the result of Frankish expansion toward the east, in Dalmatia and Pannonia, after the defeat of the Avars. In the first decades of the ninth century, the Roman Church organization was restored in these regions in the framework of the bishopric of Nin that covered Croatia, southern Dalmatia (Trebinia and Zachlumia), and Bosnia. Between 805 and 811, the patriarchate of Aquilea baptized the Pannonian Croats ruled by Vojnomir. Later, the Dalmatian Croats were also Christianized, during the reign of Prince Branimir, who was baptized and recognized as king by Pope John VIII (872–882) in 879. These new Christians increased the number of those who survived in the Dalmatian cities (other Croats became Christians after some missions fulfilled in the seventh–eighth centuries). In 852, Prince Trpimir (845–864) founded the first monastery (Benedictine) in Croatia, near Split.[8] By the creation of these new eparchies, Rome came back in western Illyricum.

The revival of the offensive policy of the Byzantine state that coincided with the end of iconoclasm led to the development of missionary activity in Central Europe and in the Balkans, as an expression of the restoration of the universalist ideology. The emperor Michael III (842–867) understood that the Church could support the interests of the Byzantine state in the confrontation with the rival power center that appeared in the West. The Frankish and Byzantine spheres of influence intersected in the Middle Danubian region and in the northwestern Balkan Peninsula. Confronted in 863 with Frankish aggression, the Moravian ruler Rastislav asked for a Byzantine Christian mission, to support him against the Franks and Bulgarians. The emperor sent the Saints Constantine and Methodius, who became the apostles of the Slavs, but Moravia soon exited the Byzantine sphere of influence because of the reaction of the German bishops. Also in Pannonia, Rome revived in 870 the bishopric of

Sirmium (Sremska Mitrovica). If the Byzantine Church was not able to keep under its control such remote regions, the Slavonic liturgy created by Cyril and Methodius was adopted by other Slavic speakers, including those from Croatia, where this ritual survived until the twelfth century, in spite of the opposition of the Latin clergy.[9]

However, the great victory of the Byzantine Church in the Balkan Peninsula was the conversion of the Bulgarians. Their ruler, Khan Boris, started preparations in 863 for Christianization with an envoy to the Frankish king Charles I the Bald (840–877), his ally since 862. This was not acceptable to the Byzantine emperor Michael III, who launched a war against Bulgaria. In these circumstances, in 864, Boris was forced to break the alliance, accept being baptized at Constantinople with the name of his imperial godfather Michael, and put the new Church under Byzantine jurisdiction. However, his real aim was to gain autocephaly for the Bulgarian Church. With this purpose, Michael tried to establish a relationship with Rome. The envoys sent to Rome, Martinus and Ursus (of probable Romanian origin),[10] were received by Pope Nicholas I (858–867), who decided to take the Bulgarian people under his jurisdiction. He had a good reason for that, since a part of Bulgaria belonged to Illyricum, that is to the Roman sphere of influence, before the annexation of Illyricum to the Constantinopolitan see. In 866, many Latin priests who continued the Christianization arrived in Bulgaria.[11] After difficult negotiations, the Bulgarian Church remained under the jurisdiction of Constantinople, but the problem would continue to inflame relations between Rome and Constantinople, when these had already been strained by the reciprocal excommunication of Pope Nicholas I and Patriarch Photios (858–867). The dispute between the heads of the Church concerned not only theological issues, but also the claims of Rome over the lost territories in Illyricum. Pope Nicholas I led an offensive policy in this respect, trying to restore as much as possible jurisdiction over Illyricum, lost in the previous century.[12]

The same claims over Bulgaria were expressed by Constantinople. The new patriarch Ignatios (867–877) granted the rank of archbishopric to the Bulgarian Church at the council held at Constantinople in 869–870, despite the opposition of Pope Hadrian II (867–872). Popes Nicholas I and Hadrian did not intend to appoint a priest, even a Latin one, as archbishop of Bulgaria, that is in a church of metropolis type. As in the western part of the Balkan Peninsula, they planned the establishment of several bishoprics dependent directly upon Rome. This plan failed at the council of 870.[13]

The quarrel was resumed at the next council in 879–880, when Photios, appointed patriarch for a second time (877–886), rejected the pretensions of Pope John VIII (872–882), who requested again jurisdiction over the Bulgarian Church. An important role in the consolidation of Byzantine Christianity in Bulgaria was played by the disciples of Saints Cyril and

Methodius, especially by Saint Clement of Ochrid, who introduced in 893 Old Slavonic as a liturgical language in the Bulgarian Church, at the proposal of the former tzar Michael, who returned from the monastery to stop the pagan reaction of the Bulgarian aristocracy during the reign of Vladimir (889–893). The school from Ochrid led by St. Clement based itself in medieval Bulgarian culture, and favored the development of a "national" Church in Bulgaria.[14]

The new Bulgarian ruler Symeon (893–927) was in his first years an adept of the Roman religion. Pope Formosus (891–896), who as a bishop was sent twenty-five years earlier to Bulgaria by Pope Nicholas I, imposed in Bulgaria a Latin clergy instead of the Greek one. The Roman orientation of Symeon was natural in that moment, because he was at war with the Byzantine emperor Leon VI (886–912). His ultimate target was the independence of the Church, the old dream of Boris. With this aim he established in 918 an autocephalous patriarchate, after the great victory against the Byzantine army of August 20, 917. This patriarchate was later recognized by Constantinople, in 927, when the peace was concluded, after the death of Symeon. During the reign of Tzar Peter (927–969), a Byzantine faithful ally for most of his reign, the Bulgarian patriarchate, although autocephalous, remained a Byzantine satellite, even if Peter was crowned by Pope John X (with the crown that has been sent for Symeon). The Byzantine emperor preserved his right to appoint the Bulgarian patriarch, as it was stated at the council of 879–880, because this did not contradict the principle of autocephaly.[15]

The wars of John Tzimiskes changed the position of the Bulgarian Church and caused another dispute between Rome and Constantinople. In 971, the autocephalous Bulgarian patriarchate was replaced by John Tzimiskes with the metropolis of Preslav, subordinated to the patriarchate of Constantinople. This was not only a consecration of the new political situation, but also a reaction to the hostile position of the popes, who accepted the protection of the German Empire by the *Privilegium Ottonis* in 962, an outrage for the Byzantine emperor. The abolition of the Bulgarian Church was thus a retaliation not only against the Bulgarians, but also against Rome.[16]

In these circumstances, the ephemeral restoration of the Bulgarian state made by Samuel added a new factor in the quarrel between Rome and Constantinople. The new tzar sought his legitimacy on the Roman side, while Pope John XV (985–996) was eager to see the regions mastered by Samuel out of Byzantine jurisdiction. The pope thus recognized the autocephaly of the new Bulgarian patriarchate established at Ochrid in 980, and the imperial title of Samuel.[17]

The autocephaly of the Ochrid see was also recognized by Basil II after the conquest of 1018, but the patriarchate was replaced with an archbishopric.

Basil II tried to maintain stability in the conquered regions by the confirmation of the properties owned by the Bulgarian Church during the reign of Samuel and by naming a Bulgarian monk as archbishop of Ochrid. He also tried to reach a compromise with Rome: Patriarch Eustakios (1019–1025) proposed in 1024 to Pope John XIX (1024–1032) a division of jurisdiction that implied that all the Byzantine possessions would belong to Constantinople, while the rest of Europe would remain to the popes'.[18] The plan failed, and the archbishopric of Ochrid remained a contentious issue. Its first Greek head, Leon (in office between 1037 and 1056), was one of the most fierce enemies of the Roman Church, and one of the actors in the events that led to the Great Schism of 1054.[19]

Often considered a turning point in world history, the new reciprocal excommunication of the pope and patriarch in 1054 was in fact one of the moments—indeed an important one—in the long process of separation between the two Churches. More dramatic consequences for the increasing hate between the Greeks and the Western Catholics had the attitude of the latter in the fourth crusade and in the period when the weakened Byzantium needed their help.[20]

By the appointment of a Greek bishop as head of the Bulgarian Church, the emperor Michael IV (1034–1041) put an end to the wise policy of Basil II. This fact was an incentive for the upheaval started by Peter Delian.[21] According to some eleventh-century Bulgarian texts ("The Vision of Daniil" and "The Legend of Daniil"), Peter Delian had established a relationship with the Roman Church.[22] This fact is not confirmed by other sources, but it seems possible, since the pretender was supported by Hungary, because he was the son of the former tzar Gavril Radomir and of a Hungarian princess. Another reason for this Roman orientation is the former affiliation of Samuel. For Rome, Peter Delian was perhaps a new Samuel, whose rebellion was able to recover what was lost in 1018. On the other hand, the imperial title claimed by Peter Delian required legitimation from Rome.

The losing of the "national" character of the archbishopric of Ochrid impeded the coagulation of Bulgarian ethnic solidarity in the next period. The Bulgarian state was restored after the rebellion of the Asan brothers, and the new religious center coincided with the new political center: Tărnovo. The Bulgarian patriarchate of Tărnovo was established in 1232, when John II Asan closed an alliance with the Empire of Nicaea. The patriarchate existed until the Ottoman conquest of 1393 (in 1402, the Bulgarian territories came under the jurisdiction of the patriarchate of Constantinople).[23]

Although there are some unclear data about a primary conversion during the reign of Heraklios, it seems that the Christian religion was adopted by the Serbs around 870, after the establishment of the Byzantine *theme* of Dalmatia[24] and after the emergence of their first polities. Prince Mutimir (son of Vlastimir) was baptized during the reign of Basil I (867–886). He remained in the Constantinopolitan sphere when Pope John VIII (872–882) invited him in 873 to recognize the jurisdiction of the bishopric of Sirmium. The eastern orientation of the Serbs became more manifest when the Bulgarian tzar Symeon conquered a large part of their land, establishing a bishopric at Ras. After the fall of Bulgaria, Raška entered the Byzantine archbishopric of Ochrid. In this way the integration of the Serbian population from Raška into the Byzantine Church was consolidated.[25] However, the victory of Byzantine Christianity in Serbian lands was not yet complete. A noted Slavicist stated that:

> If Rome had been able to offer the Serbians what SS. Cyril and Methodius had invented for the Slavic nations, it is possible that Serbia would have developed in a Western religious and cultural atmosphere.[26]

The Serbs from Zeta (Montenegro) kept stronger links with Latin Christendom even after the Great Schism of 1054. After 1054, Rome continued to extend and to consolidate its sphere of influence in the Balkan Peninsula. One of the popes who acted tenaciously for the increase of the power and authority of the Catholic Church was Gregory VII (1073–1085). "The Gregorian Reform" started by him had among other targets the preeminence of the popes over all secular rulers. One side of this policy was directed against the Orthodox hegemony in the Balkans. Gregory VII bestowed the royal title to the rulers of Croatia (Dimiter Zvonimir, in 1076) and Zeta (Mihailo Vojslav, in 1077), in order to keep them in the Roman sphere of influence and to support their anti-Byzantine policy (in that period the Byzantine power was in decline in the West, after the retreat from Italy in 1077). The territory of the kingdom of Zeta was under the jurisdiction of the Latin bishopric of Antivari (Bar, Tivar) created in 1066, which became an archbishopric in 1077 the same time as the coronation of the king Mihailo Vojslav. This religious center was an outpost of Catholicism in the western and central Balkan Peninsula, in competition with the Orthodox metropolis of Dyrrachion (subordinated to the Constantinopolitan patriarchate).[27] Later, the great *župan* Stephen Nemanja was baptized as Catholic, when he lived in Zeta. He became Orthodox only when he extended his leadership over the Serbs from Raška.[28] Therefore, Zeta was a territory subjected to a quite strong Catholic influence.

Sometimes, the political interests of Serbia required orientation toward Catholicism, or, anyway, a certain detachment from Constantinople. Serbia tried, like Bulgaria in the ninth century, to gain Church independency. The *župan* of Serbia Stephen Părvovečani (1196–1227) was crowned in 1217 by Pope Honorius III (1216–1227) as king of Serbia, Bosnia, and

Dalmatia. Before this, he asked the help of the Hungarian king Emeric (1196–1204) in the fight against his brother Vukan, promising that he would convert to Catholicism.[29] The result was the expansion of Catholic hegemony in the Balkan Peninsula (begun with the establishment of the Latin Empire of Constantinople and continued with the integration of Bulgaria into the Catholic alliance). This period was defined by a constant policy of Catholic offensives in the east, mandated by Innocentius III and Honorius III, which included the establishment of the Teutonic Order in Transylvania and the Christianization of the Cumans.[30] In order to acquire legitimacy and to find support for the acknowledgment of the imperial title, John I Asan put the Bulgarian Church under the jurisdiction of Rome, in 1204, but Pope Innocentius III decided to bestow upon him only the title of king of Bulgaria and Vlachia. During the reign of John I Asan, Catholicism was consolidated in Bulgaria,[31] but the conflict with Hungary that started in 1232 (for hegemony on the Danube) broke the links with Rome. The emperor of Bulgaria established an alliance with the Nicaean emperor John III Dukas Vatatzes.

One of the consequences of the breakdown of Byzantine authority in the Balkan Peninsula after 1204 was the decline of the archbishopric of Ochrid, a Byzantine creation that included Serbia in its territory. This situation, which was no more supported by political relations, was unacceptable for King Stephen II Părvovečani, who desired his own church. In 1221, he crowned himself for a second time with the same crown, but according to the Orthodox ritual, after the establishment of an Orthodox autocephalous archbishopric of Žiča, in 1219 (the monastery of Žiča is located near the present Kraljevo). The new see was supported by the Byzantine patriarchate from Nicaea, which aimed to counterbalance the archbishopric of Ochrid, recognized as autocephalous by the rival Greek Epirote state in 1217. Sava, the youngest son of Stephen Nemanja, became the archbishop and later the main Serbian saint. The archbishopric was moved from Žiča to Peć in 1253.[32]

At the Council of Lyons (1274) that was summoned for the reunification of the Christian Church, the Byzantine envoy protested the existence of the Serbian archbishopric, because this infringed the privileges of Justiniana Prima (Ochrid). The quarrels for jurisdiction over Serbia continued one more century. When Serbia conquered Ochrid in 1334, the archbishopric of this city became the second Serbian religious center after Peć. In April 1346, the Serbian archbishopric of Ochrid was transformed into a patriarchate (the first patriarch was Ioanikios), becoming completely independent from Constantinople. This action of Stephen Dušan provoked again the anger of the patriarch of Constantinople, who anathematized the Serbian Church and the tzar. In his turn, Stephen Dušan expelled the Greek hierarchs from his country.[33] John II Asan acted in the same way, replacing the Greek and Latin priests with Bulgarians in the territories con-quered in Thessaly and Albania after the battle of Klokotnica (1230).[34] This shows that Orthodoxy acquired "national" features in Bulgaria and Ser-bia in the thirteenth and fourteenth centuries. It has been remarked that Orthodoxy preserved and improved national identities in Southeastern Europe.[35] Only in 1368 did the despot John Uglieša accept the reestablish-ment of Constantinopolitan jurisdiction over the patriarchate of Ochrid. Later, in 1376, under the rule of Lazar, Constantinople recognized the in-dependence of the Serbian Church as a support for the state. In 1459, the patriarchate of Peć was abolished and its territory was included in the Greek archbishopric of Ochrid, as a consequence of the policy promoted by Sultan Mehmed II, who clearly favored the Greek Church.[36]

It can be concluded that the Balkan Peninsula became after the ninth century a field of religious dispute between Rome and Constantinople, which meant in fact a division between two spheres of influence. The dividing line between Catholicism and Orthodoxy did not appear suddenly. Its position was determined by the changing political circumstances of the eleventh–fourteenth centuries. The great Bulgarian medievalist Ivan Dujčev held that the Serbian and Croatian lands were a transition area between the Byzantine and the Latin Church.[37] It is interesting that in 1072 a Latin and a Byzantine bishopric existed in the same town, Sirmium.[38] As a matter of fact, *the final and complete option for Orthodoxy of the Serbs was decided only by the middle of the fourteenth century, when Stephen Dušan assumed an impe-rial mission with a Byzantine pattern.* Before this, Serbian rulers like Mihailo Vojslav, Stephen Părvovečani, and Stephen Milutin had no reserves to search for support in the Catholic world in their conflicts with the Byzan-tine Empire. Their state was closer to the West than to Byzantium. The re-ligious cleavage between Serbs and Croats appeared step-by-step, as a result of the regional balance of power. This religious and cultural cleav-age caused confrontations between Serbs and Croats. Byzantinist Henri Grégoire made a paradoxical but true statement: the Serbs are Orthodox Croats, and the Croats are Catholic Serbs.[39]

The Latin and Byzantine spheres of influence intersected in Bosnia. This region was always a border and transition area. The frontier between the two halves of the Late Roman Empire also crossed by Bosnia. The limit between them was the Drina River, which is the eastern boundary of Bosnia.[40] In the early Middle Ages, the region was at the crossroads of Byzantine and Latin influences. Archaeological finds and surviving mon-uments show that Bosnia was subject to a significant Byzantine influence, even if the Church was affiliated with Rome.[41] For this reason, the opin-ions of some Croatian historians,[42] who exclude any Serbian and Ortho-dox presence in Bosnia before the Ottoman conquest that caused massive Serbian immigrations, are exaggerated.

In fact, the highly mixed population of Bosnia and its geographical position at the crossroads of Western and Eastern political and cultural influences were good starting points for both Serbian and Croatian propaganda in the dispute over the historical rights over this province. For instance, during World War II, rights over Bosnia were claimed by monographs and collections of studies published at Belgrade, Sarajevo, and Zagreb. In the volume *Poviest hrvatskih zemalja Bosne i Hercegovine od najstarijih vremena do godine 1463* (History of the Croatian Lands of Bosnia and Herzegovina since the oldest times to 1463), published in Sarajevo in 1942, it is claimed that Bosnia was always an organic part of Croatia.[43] After World War II, Croatian historians like Stanko Guldescu believed that Bosnia was a Croatian territory, where the Serbs came only during the reign of Ceslav Klonimirović (927–960), who annexed Bosnia to his kingdom.[44]

The particular position of Bosnia between West and East determined a certain specificity of Bosniac Christianity in the thirteenth–fourteenth centuries. Willing to be independent from Catholic Hungary and Orthodox Serbia, clergymen from Bosnia decided to organize themselves in a separate church, sometime between 1234 and 1252. The independent Bosniac Church preserved the Catholic rites and was thus not heretical, but at the same time it was not able to suppress the spreading of a dualist heresy. This heresy, called Patarine, had some analogies with Bogomilism from Byzantium and Bulgaria, but it has been observed that the major influences came from Western dualist heresies (Cathars and Albigens). The conversion of a significant part of the Bosniac population caused the severe reaction of the Catholic Church. The heresy was a cause of disorder, because it stimulated opposition against religious and secular authorities. Finally, many of these heretics would choose to convert to Islam, after the Ottoman conquest of Bosnia.[45]

The Bogomil and Patarine heresies were variants of the dualist faiths that were widespread in eastern Byzantium. Many Paulician dualists were deported in the eighth–ninth centuries from Asia Minor to Thrace and Macedonia.[46] Here, they gained more adepts, and their faith was developed in new forms by the Bogomils, a sect that appeared in the tenth century in Bulgaria. The alleged social and political protesting character of the medieval heresies, and particularly of Bogomilism, has been much discussed by the historians.[47] They emphasize the relationship between heresy and social marginality, but extreme viewpoints of Marxist inspiration have exaggerated the social reasons for the heresies, seen as expressions of the class struggle.[48] Bogomilism contributed to a certain extent to the destabilization of the Byzantine authority in Bulgaria and Macedonia. Some anti-Byzantine unrest was caused and fueled by the Bogomils. For instance, in 1078–1080, the Bogomil Dobromir rebelled at Mesembria (Nesebăr), as did Leka, in the region of Serdica (Sofia). In 1086, another Bo-gomil chief called Traulos established an alliance with the Pechenegs from Dobrudja.[49]

Another area of intersection between Catholicism and Orthodoxy was Albania. The conversion of some Albanians to Catholicism took place in the twelfth–fourteenth centuries. The Albanian Catholics lived on the seashore, in northern Albania, but also in Montenegro and Kosovo. Catholic parishes are attested to at Shkoder, Gjakova, Prizren, Kotorr, and Breskova and in other places. They were affiliated with the *diocesis Arba-nenis*, which belonged to the archbishopric of Antivari. The first known bishop was Lazarus *episcopus Arbanensis* (1166). An important role in the conversion to Catholicism was played by the Venetian domination ex-erted in Albania between 1204 and 1213. Later, the Angevine occupation (1271–1284, 1305–1345) would consolidate the Catholic Church in Alba-nia. The more intensive conversion in the northern part of Albania accen-tuated the differences between this area and southern Albania, which re-mained for the most part Orthodox. Catholicism survived after the conquest of Albania by Serbia (1343–1345), and was even strengthened when Prince George Balšić I converted in 1369, after he acquired inde-pendence from Serbia for his small state located in northern Albania and Montenegro.[50]

The Catholic Albanians that became subjects of the Serbian state suf-fered religious persecutions in the fourteenth century.[51] The law code issued by Stephen Dušan in 1349 was extremely severe as concerns the people who were not Orthodox. This intolerance is not specific to the Orthodox churches, and foreshadows contemporary ethnic cleans-ing actions:

> In regard to the Latin heresy . . . if anyone does not heed the call to be con-verted and return to the true faith, he will be condemned to death as stipu-lated in the book of Holy Fathers. The King, as a true believer, must eradicate from his state any trace of heresy. . . . The heretical clergy of an alien com-munion, who try to make proselytes, will be captured and sent to the mines or be expelled. The heretical churches will be re-consecrated and entrusted to clergy of the true faith. . . . The protopopes of cathedral churches must con-vert the Latins in every town or village. Every Christian must be converted to the true faith as the apostles and the Holy Fathers say. . . . In case a Latin cleric is found trying to convert a Christian to the Latin faith, he will be pun-ished with death. . . . In case it is found that a half-believer has been married in secret to an Orthodox wife, he must be baptized according to the Ortho-dox rite; if he refuses to be baptized, his wife, children and home will be taken from him, he will be reduced to poverty and banished. . . . If a heretic is found who lives among Christians, he will be branded on the face and will be expelled; he who hides him will suffer the same punishment.

This policy of compulsory conversion to Orthodoxy was combined with the Serbization of Albanian names.[52]

The persecutions initiated by Stephen Dušan against the Catholic Albanians had no ethnic reasons, as some Albanian historians tendentiously stated.[53] The reasons were only religious. As a matter of fact, most Catholics in Serbia were Albanian. In other instances, the Orthodox Albanians were favored by Stephen Dušan, in order to create quarrels between them and the Greeks. He granted estates taken from the Byzantines to some Albanian noblemen.[54]

The harassment of the Catholics in Serbia was recorded by Guillaume Adam (archbishop of Antivari between 1324 and 1341), who planned the organization of a new crusade. In a report sent in 1332 to the king of France, Philip VI Valois, he wrote about people from Macedonia:

> these people, both Latin and Albanian, are under the unbearable and very grave yoke of the prince of the Slavs, whom they despise and hate heartily because they are burdened with heavy taxes, their clergymen are treated scornfully, their bishops and priests are often bound in chains, their noblemen expropriated.[55]

This means that Guillaume Adam assured the French king that the crusaders would find strong support in Macedonia, but also that the persecuted people were all the Catholics, regardless of their ethnicity.

When the Albanian state ruled by the Balšić Catholic family conquered Kosovo, it started the reverse action, the persecution of the Serbian Orthodox Church. The patriarchate was moved from Peć to Prizren in 1371, in order to be easily controlled, and the Bulgarian Efrem was appointed patriarch. Later, in 1380, the new patriarch, Spyridon, moved to Raška, at Žiča, in the territory mastered by the Serbian prince Lazar. The Serbian patriarchate came back to Peć only in 1397.[56]

Most of the Albanian Catholics converted to Islam in the fifteenth century, and especially in the second half of the sixteenth century. Unlike the Orthodox believers, who cooperated with the Ottomans, the Catholics were a danger because they were potential allies of the Western powers. For this reason, the Ottomans launched a persecution after the Ottoman–Venetian war of 1645–1669, when Albanian Catholics were involved in the fights.[57] The Roman Church was no more able to exert a strong control over these Albanian parishes, although they continued to exist and although the pope's messengers continued to go there. More and more isolated, many of the Albanian Catholics chose to convert to that religion that gave them a privileged status. In fact, Catholicism became a tolerated and not official religion in Albania and Montenegro since 1403, when prince George Balšić III converted to Orthodoxy. The Albanian Catholics were persecuted by the Orthodox Serbs even during the Ottoman domination. The Catholic archbishop of Shkup (Skopje), Andrew Bogdani (appointed in 1656), reported in 1664 that the Albanians were more harassed by the Orthodox patriarchate of Peć than by the Turks. It seems that the Ottoman authorities stimulated the extension of the jurisdiction of this patriarchate over the Catholics.[58]

THE SPREADING OF ISLAM IN THE BALKANS: A NEW DIFFERENTIATION

The Ottoman conquest of the Balkan Peninsula was followed after a short time by the conversion to the Muslim religion of some of the local inhabitants. The penetration of the new religion was enabled by the quarrels among the Catholic and Orthodox peoples, or among the Catholics and heretics. A major role in the conversion of the Christians was played by the "colonizing derviches," who made intensive propaganda for Islam.[59]

The Muslim religion was a kind of shield against Catholicism and Orthodoxy for the Bosniac ethnic identity.[60] In fact, the Bosnians are the sole Muslims in the world for whom religion is the same as ethnic identity.[61] During the twenty-five years that passed between the conquest of Bosnia (1463) and the census made by the Ottomans in 1488–1489, Bosnians passed in large number to Islam. Their numbers were then 18.4 percent. According to the census organized by the Ottoman administration between 1520 and 1530, 46 percent of the taxpayers from the Bosniac *kaza* were Muslims; the city of Sarajevo was completely Muslim.[62] In Bosnia the most intensive Islamization of the natives took place. The immigration of Christian Serbs from Slavonia, brought to Bosnia as frontier troops, would decrease the proportion of the Muslims in the first half of the fifteenth century, but the increase trend was resumed after a while.[63] It also seems that some of the Bulgarian Bogomils became Muslims. A Bulgarian ethnologist observed survival of Bogomilism in the practices of the Islamic sect of Aliani, in Bulgaria.[64]

Paradoxically, the Ottomans became the protectors of the Orthodoxy endangered by the Catholic offensive. On the eve of the conquest of Constantinople, the hate of the Byzantines against the Latins was so great that they thought that the great enemy was the pope, not the Ottoman Empire. For instance, Militza, the widow of the Serbian prince Lazar, told Bayazid that the Serbs were the natural allies of the Turks against Catholic Hungary.[65]

Mehmed II fostered this hate against the Latins, creating a privileged situation for the Orthodox Church. Just after the conquest of Constantinople, he appointed as patriarch the monk Gennadios, the leader of the fundamentalist group that rejected any concessions to Catholicism. During the Ottoman domination, the patriarch of Constantinople had a greater religious and secular authority than in the Byzantine period, since he was no longer subjected to imperial interference and because he was the spiritual ruler of a larger number of believers (the Bulgarian and Serbian national churches were abolished and their members were included in the community called *millet* led by the patriarch of Constantinople). The national and cultural identity of the Greeks survived through the Church, although the same Church was in the eighteenth century in opposition with the movements of national revival inspired by the Enlightenment.[66]

The Serbian Orthodox patriarchate from Peć was another support of the spiritual resistance of the Serbs during the Ottoman domination. The patriarchate was founded again in 1557 and existed until 1766. It is interesting that its restoration was made by a pasha of Serbian origin (born in eastern Bosnia), Mehmed Sokolović, who became later a great vizir, between 1565 and 1579. He also extended the jurisdiction of this patriarchate over all the territories peopled by Serbs within the Ottoman Empire, regardless of the previous political boundaries. In this case, Serbian ethnic solidarity functioned despite the religious differences. Mehmed Sokolović had a personal interest, because his brother Makarie was appointed patriarch. The patriarchate of Peć was abolished in 1766, but for political and not religious reasons, since it became a support of Panslavism, the instrument of Russian expansion in Southeastern Europe. Even before, the patriarchate of Peć was involved in hostile actions during the Austrian offensive at the end of the seventeenth century. The autocephalous archbishopric of Ochrid was abolished in a similar situation in 1767.[67]

During the conquest period, the Turks were regarded by some of the Balkan Orthodox Christians (Greeks and Serbs) as their defenders against Catholicism. By their specific tolerance, the Turks made possible a particular Christian–Islamic symbiosis in the Balkan world. There were no forced conversions of the local communities to Islam, because this was forbidden by Islamic dogmas and also contrary to the specific Turkish tolerance. On the other hand, the Ottoman administration preferred that the subjected population remain Christian, because only Christians paid capitation (*harach*). The conversions were individual and in most cases willing, because they were motivated by the economic and social advantages of affiliation with Islam. It is nevertheless true that an important role in the conversion was played by the recruitment of Christian boys from the Balkan regions for the Janissary corps. This children tribute (*devşirmé*) that was in operation until 1638 contributed to the increasing of Balkan Muslims, but it cannot be considered a forced conversion of the communities. In some cases, the families accepted the recruitment of the children, because this enabled their social promotion. The massive and willing conversion was specific especially for the religious minorities that were persecuted before the Ottoman domination (the Albanian Catholics and the Bosniac Bogomils), but not restricted to them.[68]

After the fights against the Ottomans in the fifteenth century, Albanians began to convert to Islam. The census of 1520–1530 recorded only 4.5 percent and 5.5 percent of the population respectively as Muslims in the *kazas* of Skutari and Elbasan from present-day Albania.[69] In 1577 it was mentioned that northern and central Albania were still Catholic regions, although the offensive of the Serbian patriarchate of Peć against the Catholics had already started, and although the Catholic archbishopric of Antivari was conquered by the Ottomans in 1571. Around 1600, only 3 percent–4 percent of Albanians were Muslims.[70] Things changed in the seventeenth century, when most of the Albanians converted to Islam. Venice lost Antivari in 1571, the city that was the resistance point of Catholicism in Albania. The archbishopric resumed activity in 1579, but in difficult conditions that did not allow real support of the more and more reduced parishes.[71] The reports of Catholic priests who inspected Albania and Kosovo recorded that changes occurred in the seventeenth century. For instance, at Prizren in 1624 there lived 12,000 Muslims, 200 Catholics, and 600 Orthodox. It seems that the number of Catholics decreased in the first half of the seventeenth century from 350,000 to 50,000. The rest became Muslims. The Islamization continued in the second half of the century.[72]

In Kosovo, conversion to Islam made significant progress in the sixteenth–seventeenth centuries among the Catholic and Orthodox Albanians (in Peć, Prizren, Prishtina, and in the neighboring villages). The Serbs remained Christians, because their church organization that resisted the Ottoman domination provided them a support against the temptation of apostasy. Unlike them, the Albanians did not have such religious and ethnic cohesion.[73] The decisive moment in the Islamization process of Kosovo was the war of 1690–1691, when the Albanians replaced the Serbian refugees. The Catholic Albanians who came to Kosovo from northern Albania were compelled to convert to Islam.[74] Therefore, *the present ethnic and religious situation of Kosovo is mainly the result of events fulfilled at the end of the seventeenth century.* Unlike in Bosnia, where the Islamization was fast and willing, *in Kosovo Islam became majoritarian not only by the conversion of the Catholic Albanians, but also by violence, as a consequence of the persecution of the Serbs who rebelled in 1688.*

The preservation of economic and social privileges was a strong reason for conversion,[75] but there were in this respect some cultural differences between Serbs and Albanians. The former better resisted this temptation, because they had a strong Orthodox Church, while the Catholic Albanians remained quite isolated. However, the advantages given by conversion to Islam explain the spread of this new religion among the Balkan populations (Albanians, Serbs, Bosnians, and to a lesser extent Bulgarians and Greeks).

Islamization was made from top to bottom. The first converted were the local feudals who preserved in this way their properties and privileges, in the new institutional forms introduced by the Ottoman Empire. The conversion of the ruling class (landowners and military commanders) was very intensive since the fifteenth century. The second level was represented by the city dwellers. More open to changes and more willing for social promotion, they started to convert to Islam at the end of the fifteenth century. In the first two decades of the next century, conversions were already numerous. The cities thus became centers of irradiation of the Muslim religion (especially those located on the strategic roads Thessaloniki–Belgrade and Thessaloniki–Dyrrachion).[76]

A case study made for the city of Serres in Macedonia shows that in 1478 the Muslim population outnumbered the Christian one (653 families versus 354 Christian families of different ethnies). The same situation is encountered in strategic areas like Skopje and Bitolia (Monastir). Although these cities were colonized by Turks after the conquest, a large part of the Muslims were converted Christians. In the same town Serres, in 1568, 308 of the 829 Muslim families descended from Christians. The general trend in Macedonia in the sixteenth century was the constant decrease of Christians in the towns. The Muslims thus became the majority in the most important cities (Thessaloniki, Tetovo, Kavala).[77] The situation was the same in other great Balkan towns. According to the census of 1520–1530, Sofia was 66 percent Muslim, Larissa 90 percent, Bitolia and Skopje 75 percent, Silistra 72 percent, and in Sarajevo all the inhabitants were Muslims.[78]

The countryside remained the most conservative. In the villages, except those from Bosnia, Islam was spread especially by populations arrived from other regions rather than by the conversion of the natives. Villages from Albania and Kosovo were converted later and slower. It seems that the massive Islamization of the Balkan Peninsula increased after 1480 and reached its climax under the reign of Suleyman the Magnificent (1520–1566). In this way, several Balkan regions became predominately Islamic in the seventeenth and eighteenth centuries (Bosnia, Macedonia, Albania, a part of Bulgaria, Thessaly).[79]

However, the Islamization of the countryside had some particularities. Several Christian and even pagan elements survived in the popular religion of the Balkan Muslims. This syncretism made easier the adaptation of the new believers to Islam. The Bektashi derviches promoted a kind of Christian–Islamic syncretism, especially in Albania. It is curious, but the

Balkan countryside Muslims preserved in many cases Christian baptism, icons, and the cult of Saints George and Elias. Some of them participated in Christian religious services, while some Christians did the same in the mosques. Both religions preserved a lot of rituals specific for the popular faith (the worship of icons and of saints), which exemplified a remarkable tolerance at the level of the common people. Sometimes, only the father of the family converted to Islam, while the wife and the children remained Christians.[80] Even more surprisingly, the members of a Muslim group from Macedonia, Grecophone but most probably of Aromanian origin, called Vallahades, considered themselves to be Muslims and Christians at the same time.[81]

The facts presented in this chapter show that the confrontation between religions had a role in the genesis of conflict areas in the Balkan Peninsula. The present religious diversity is the result of a long evolution that started in the ninth century and was not linear. At the beginning there was no clear-cut limit between the Catholic and the Orthodox worlds. The frontier between the two European civilizations appeared step-by-step in the center of the space peopled by Serbs and Croats. The expansion of Catholicism in the eleventh–fourteenth centuries was stopped by the Ottoman conquest, which removed Bosnia and part of Albania from the Catholic sphere of influence. The tolerant Ottoman regime protected the Orthodox identity of the Serbs and Greeks. On the other hand, conversion to Islam was a source of stability in the fifteenth–sixteenth centuries. The Christian–Muslim syncretism that defined the popular religion was in its turn a source of tolerance. Only after the emergence of national states in the nineteenth and twentieth centuries did the presence of Muslims in these Balkan countries cause internal tensions and interethnic conflicts. It is no secret that the war in Bosnia and the Serbian–Albanian conflict in Kosovo had religious dimensions. *Knowledge of the historical evolution of the present religious configuration of the Balkan Peninsula could help us to understand the deep causes of the recent bloody conflicts that occurred in the former Yugoslavia.*

NOTES

1. P. Bádenas de la Pena, La composante religieuse dans les conflits balkaniques, AIESEEB, 30 (2000), 151.

2. J. M. Hussey, *The Orthodox Church in the Byzantine Empire*, Oxford, 1986, 10–19; J. F. Haldon, *Byzantium in the Seventh Century. The Transformation of a Culture*, Cambridge, 1997, 56–57, 297–304; H. Chadwick, *East and West: The Making of a Rift in the Church. From Apostolic Times until the Council of Florence*, Oxford, 2003, 59–63. Monothelism recognized the double nature of Christ (divine and human), but sustained that there is a single will in His person.

3. G. Ostrogorsky, *Histoire de l'État Byzantin*, Paris, 1956, 149–151; M. Rouche, La crise de l'Europe au cours de la deuxième moitié du VIIe siècle et la naissance des régionalismes, *Annales. Economies–Sociétés–Civilisations*, 41, 2 (1986), 348–350; Hussey 1986, 19–24; C. A. Frazee, The Balkans between Rome and Constantinople in the Early Middle Ages, 600–900 AD, BS, 34, 2 (1993), 215; Haldon 1997, 305–313.

4. For iconoclasm, see especially: Hussey 1986, 30–68; J. Herrin, *The Formation of Christendom*, Princeton, NJ, 1989, 307–389, 466–469; L. Brubaker & J. Haldon, *Byzantium in the Iconoclast Era (ca. 680–850): The Sources. An Annotated Survey* (Birmingham Byzantine and Ottoman Monographs, 7), Aldershot, 2001; P. Karlin-Hayter, *Iconoclasm*, in C. Mango (ed.), *The Oxford History of Byzantium*, Oxford, 2002, 153–162; P. Brown, *The Rise of Western Christendom. Triumph and Diversity, A.D. 200–1000*, Oxford, 2003, 387–404.

5. Ostrogorsky 1956, 184–194; H.-D. Döpmann, Zum Streit zwischen Rom und Byzanz um die Christianisierung Bulgariens, *Palaeobulgarica*, 5, 1 (1981), 62; Frazee 1993, 219–221; M. McCormick, *Byzantium and the West, 700–900*, in R. McKitterick (ed.), *The New Cambridge Medieval History, II, c.700–c.900*, Cambridge, 1995, 363–365; Chadwick 2003, 71–76.

6. M. Ljubinković, Les Slaves des régions centrales des Balkans et Byzance, *Berichte 1973*, vol. 2, 927.

7. Ostrogorsky 1956, 199–200; Frazee 1993, 222–223; M. McCormick, *Byzantium and the West, 700–900*, in NCMH II, 364–366; M. Whittow, *The Making of Byzantium, 600–1025*, Berkeley, CA, 1996, 304.

8. I. Božić, La formation de l'Etat serbe aux IXe–XIe siècles, *Europe 1968*, 138–139; F. Dvornik, *Byzantine Mission among the Slavs. SS Constantine-Cyril and Methodius*, New Brunswick, NJ, 1970, 5–27; S. Vilfan, La cristianizzazione delle campagne presso gli Slavi del sud occidentali: Organizzazione, resistenze, fondo sociale, in Cristianizzazione ed organizzazione ecclesiastica delle campagne nell'alto medioevo: Espansione e resistenze (Settimane, 28), Spoleto, 1982, II, 904–907; R. Katičić, Die Anfänge des Kroatischen Staates, in H. Friesinger & F. Daim (eds.), *Die Bayern und ihre Nachbarn*, I (DAW, 179), Wien, 1985, 311; Frazee 1993, 214, 223. For the Christian lexic of Latin origin of the Serbo-Croatian language (borrowed from the West), see H. Mihăescu, *La romanité dans le Sud-Est de l'Europe*, Bucureşti, 1993, 435–448.

9. H. Bulin, Aux origines des formations étatiques des Slaves du Moyen Danube au IXe siècle, *Europe 1968*, 188–193; Dvornik 1970, 105–193, 231, 233–236, 242–243; Hussey 1996, 94–99; P. Schreiner, Die Byzantinische Missionierung als politische Aufgabe. Das Beispiel der Slaven, ByzSl, 56 (1995), 525–533.

10. S. Brezeanu, *Romanitatea orientală în evul mediu. De la cetăţenii romani la naţiunea medievală*, Bucureşti, 1999, 66–73.

11. Ostrogorsky 1956, 257–259; B. Gjuzelev, Das Papstum und Bulgarien im Mittelalter (9.-14. Jh.), BHR, 5, 1 (1977), 37–38; Döpmann 1981, 63–68; J. V. A. Fine Jr., *The Early Medieval Balkans. A Critical Survey from the Sixth to the Late Twelfth Century*, Ann Arbor, MI, 1991, 113–124; Frazee 1993, 224–225; J. Shepard, Slavs and Bulgars, NCMH II, 239–243; L. Simeonova, *Diplomacy of the Letter and the Cross: Photios, Bulgaria and the Papacy, 860s–880s*, Amsterdam, 1998, 78–81, 166–197, 223–248; Chadwick 2003, 169–181.

12. For the so-called Photian Schism, see F. Dvornik, *The Photian Schism. History and Legend*, Cambridge, 1970; Hussey 1986, 72–86; Chadwick 2003, 124–181.

13. S. Nikolov, The Latin Bishops and the Balkan Bishoprics, in M. B. Davis & M. Sebök (eds.), *Annual of Medieval Studies at the Central European University, Budapest, 1994–1995*, Budapest, 1996, 204–215.

14. Ostrogorsky 1956, 258–259, 262; U. Swoboda, L'origine de l'organisation de l'Église en Bulgarie et ses rapports avec le Patriarcat de Constantinople (870–919), BB, 2 (1966), 67–81; M. Pundeff, National Consciousness in Medieval Bulgaria, SOF, 27 (1968), 11–18, 23–26; Dvornik 1970, 245–253; Gjuzelev 1977, 39–40; D. Angelov, *Die Entstehung des Bulgarischen Volkes*, Berlin, 1980, 115–124; Fine 1991, 124–128; L. Simeonova, Bulgaria, Constantinople and Rome during the Second Patriarchate of Photios (877–886), EB, 32 (1996), 3–4, 127–141; Simeonova 1998, 260–270, 314–330, 367.

15. Ljubinković 1973, 941–942; Gjuzelev 1977, 40.

16. Ljubinković 1973, 948–951.

17. Ljubinković 1973, 953–968.

18. Ljubinković 1973, 961–962.

19. Ostrogorsky 1956, 349; M. Angold, *The Byzantine Empire, 1025–1204. A Political History*, London, New York, 1984a, 28–31; Hussey 1986, 132; Fine 1991, 204, 219.

20. Hussey 1986, 132–136; Chadwick 2003, 206–218.

21. B. Granić, Kirchengeschichtliche Glossen zu den vom Kaiser Basileios II dem Autokephalen Erzbistum von Ahrida verliehenen Privilegien, *Byzantion*, 12, 2 (1937), 395–415; J. Ferluga, *Byzantium on the Balkans. Studies on the Byzantine Administration and the Southern Slavs from the VIIth to the XIIth Centuries*, Amsterdam, 1976, 381; M. De Vos, *Un demi-siècle de l'histoire de la Macédoine (975–1025)* (Thèse de doctorat du IIIe cycle, Institut National des Langues et Civilizations Orientales), Paris, 1977, 116–118; Fine 1991, 203–204.

22. Gjuzelev 1977, 41.

23. Ostrogorsky 1956, 461; A. Tarnanidis, Byzantine–Bulgarian Ecclesiastical Relations during the Reign of Ioannis Vatatzis and Ivan Asan II, up to the Year 1235, *Cyrillomethodianum*, 3 (1975), 28–52; Ş. Papacostea, *Românii în secolul al XIII–lea. Între cruciată și imperiul mongol*, București, 1993, 43.

24. For this event see Ferluga 1976, 141–151.

25. D. S. Radojičić, La date de la conversion des Serbes, *Byzantion*, 22, 1952 (1953), 253–256; Ostrogorsky 1956, 263–264; Dvornik 1970, 36–38, 254; Fine 1991, 159–160; L. Maksimović, The Christianization of the Serbs and the Croats, in A. E. Tachiaos (ed.), *The Legacy of Saints Cyril and Methodius to Kiev and Moscow. Proceedings of the International Congress on the Millennium of the Conversion of Rus' to Christianity* (Thessaloniki, November 26–28, 1988), Thessaloniki, 1992, 167–184.

26. Dvornik 1970, 258.

27. N. Iorga, *Études Byzantines*, I, Bucarest, 1939, 94; Ostrogorsky 1956, 368; Dvornik 1970, 256; I. Dujčev, *Medioevo Bizantino-Slavo*, vol. III, Roma, 1971, 214; Fine 1991, 215; L. Maksimović & Subotić, La Serbie entre Byzance et l'Occident, in *XXe Congrès International des Études Byzantines. Pré-actes, I. Séances plénières*, Paris, 2001, 242; M. Dimnik, Russia, the Bulgars and the Southern Slavs, 1024–c.1200, NCMH IV, 267–268.

28. Dvornik 1970, 254–257; Dujčev 1971, 215; Maksimović & Subotić 2001, 243.

29. Iorga 1939, 127–128; Dvornik 1970, 258; B. I. Bojović, Historiographie dynastique et idéologie politique en serbie au Bas Moyen Âge. Essai de synthèse de l'idéologie de l'Etat médiéval serbe, SOF, 51 (1992), 32; A. Ducellier, Have the Albanians Occupied Kosova? *Kosova 1993*, 64; Maksimović & Subotić 2001, 243.

30. Papacostea 1993, 28–38; Z. I. Kosztolnyik, *Hungary in the Thirteenth Century,* Boulder, CO, 1996, 93–97.

31. See previous chapter, footnote 134.

32. Ostrogorsky 1956, 453; G. Prinzing, *Die Bedeutung Bulgariens und Serbiens in den Jahren 1204–1219 in Zusammenhang mit der Entstehung und Entwicklung der byzantinischen Teilstaaten nach der Einname Konstantinopels infolge des 4. Kreuzzuges.* München, 1972, 169–172; Hussey 1986, 211; Bojović 1992, 33; J. V. A. Fine Jr., *The Late Medieval Balkans. A Critical Survey from the Late Twelfth Century to the Ottoman Conquest,* Ann Arbor, MI, 1994, 116–119; A. Ducellier, Albania, Serbia and Bulgaria, NCMH V, 784.

33. G. Arnakis, The Role of Religion in the Development of Balkan Nationalism, *Balkans 1963,* 127–128; S. Dimevski, The Archbishopric of Ohrid, in *From the Past of the Macedonian People,* Skopje, 1969, 64; G. Soulis, *The Serbs and Byzantium during the Reign of Tsar Stephen Dushan (1331–1355) and His Successors,* Washington, DC, 1984, 31–32; Bojović 1992, 43; Fine 1994, 310; B. I. Bojović, Le passé des territoires, Kosovo-Metohija (XIe–XVIIe siècle), BS, 38, 1 (1997), 37; Maksimović & Subotić 2001, 244.

34. T. Teoteoi, Civilizaţia statului Asăneştilor între Roma şi Bizanţ, *Răscoala 1989,* 72.

35. W. Bracewell & A. Drace-Francis, South–Eastern Europe—History, Concepts, Boundaries, *Balkanologie,* 3, 2 (1999), 55.

36. N. J. Pantazopoulos, *Church and Law in the Balkan Peninsula during the Ottoman Rule,* Thessaloniki, 1967, 29–30; Dimevski 1969, 65; Soulis 1984, 105; G. Castellan, *Histoire des Balkans (XIVe–XXe siècle),* Paris, 1991, 119; Bojović 1992, 41.

37. Dujčev 1971, 214.

38. T. Wasilewski, Le thème byzantin de Sirmium–Serbie au XIe et XIIe siècles, ZRVI, 8 (1964), 2, 476.

39. H. Grégoire, L'origine et le nom des Croates et des Serbes, *Byzantion,* 17 (1945), 91.

40. For this line see I. Weiler, Zur Frage der Grenzziehung zwischen Ost–und Westteil des des römischen Reiches in der Spätantike, in R. Bratož (ed.), *Westillyricum und Norditalien in der Spätrömische Zeit* ("Situla. Dissertationes Musei Nationalis Labacensis," 34), Ljubljana, 1996, 123–143. G. W. Hoffman, The Evolution of the Ethnographic Map of Yugoslavia, *Carter 1977,* 472 remarked too that Bosnia was a region of intersection between civilizations.

41. N. Miletić, Reflets de l'influence byzantine dans les trouvailles paleoslaves en Bosnie–Herzégovine, CIAS III, vol. II, 287–306.

42. Quoted by S. Guldescu, *History of Medieval Croatia,* The Hague, 1964, 263–266.

43. L. Hadrovics, Les problèmes de la Bosnie médiévale, RHC, 23, n.s., 3 (1945), 217–222.

44. Guldescu 1964, 242.

The Religious Aspects   135

45. L. S. Stavrianos, *The Balkans since 1453*, New York, 1959, 235; D. Dragojlović, Bogomilisme et mouvements hérétiques dualistes du Moyen Âge, *Balcanica*, 4, (1973), 121–143; M. Loos, *L' "église bosnienne" dans le contexte du mouvement hérétique européen*, (Ibidem), 145–161; Hoffman 1977, 473; J. V. A. Fine Jr., *The Bosnian Church. A New Interpretation*, New York, 1975, 148–157; Fine 1994, 146–147.

46. H. Ditten, *Ethnische Verschiebungen zwischen der Balkanhalbinsel und Kleinasien vom Ende des 6. bis zum zweiten Hälfte des 9. Jahrhunderts* (BBA, 59), Berlin, 1993, 203–205.

47. J. V. A. Fine Jr., The Size and the Signification of the Bulgarian Bogomil Movement, *East European Quarterly*, 11, 4 (1977), 385–412 has demonstrated that the heresy was not a support for social and political movements. See also P. Bádenas de la Peña, La resistencia Búlgara y la penetración del Bogomilismo en Bizancio, *Erytheia. Revista de Estudios Bizantinos y Neogriegos*, 23 (2002), 147–150, who emphasizes that, unlike Paulicianism, Bogomilism was a nonviolent movement.

48. For Bogomilism see especially Fine 1991, 171–179; Stoyanov, *The Hidden Tradition in Europe: The Secret History of Medieval Christian Heresy*, London, New York, 1994; D. Obolensky, *The Bogomils. A Study in Balkan Neo–Manichaeism*, Cambridge, 2004.

49. Iorga 1939, 31; A. Sacerdoțeanu, Mouvements politiques et sociaux de la Péninsule Balkanique dans la seconde moitié du XIe siècle, *Balcania*, 2–3 (1940), 89, 98–99; R. L. Wolff, The "Second Bulgarian Empire." Its Origin and History to 1204, *Speculum*, 24 (1949), 180; J. C. Cheynet, *Pouvoir et contestations à Byzance (963–1210)*, Paris, 1990, 85, 94, 392; P. Stephenson, *Byzantium's Balkan Frontier, a Political Study of the Northern Balkans, 900–1204*, Cambridge, 2000, 101.

50. A. Ducellier, *La façade maritime de l'Albanie au Moyen Âge. Durazzo et Valona du XIe au XVe siècle*, Thessalonique, 1981, 108, 204–210, 427, 553–559; S. Pollo & A. Puto, *The History of Albania from Its Origins to the Present Day*, London, 1981, 60; A. Ducellier, Genesis and Failure of the Albanian State in the Fourteenth and Fifteenth Century, in A. Pipa & S. Repishti (eds.), *Studies on Kosova*, Boulder, New York, 1984, 8; K. Frashëri, The Territories of the Albanians in the XVth Century, *Albanians 1985*, 212–213; S. Čirković, Les Albanais à la lumière des sources historiques des Slaves du Sud, *Les Illyriens 1988*, 351; P. Xhufi, Albanian Heretics in the Serbian Medieval Kingdom, *Kosova 1993*, 49; B. Pranvera, Kosova under the Albanian Feudal State of the Balshes, *Kosova 1993*, 56; G. Schramm, *Anfänge des albanischen Christentums. Die frühe Bekehrung der Bessen und ihre langen Folgen*, Freiburg im Briesgau, 1994, 173.

51. Xhufi 1993, 48–54.

52. Xhufi 1993, 48–50. See also S. Pulaha, On the Presence of Albanians in Kosova during the 14th–17th Centuries, *Kosova 1993*, 37.

53. Xhufi 1993, 49–50.

54. Soulis 1984, 135–136.

55. Ducellier 1993, 64; Xhufi 1993, 48.

56. Pranvera 1993, 58–59.

57. G. Stadtmüller, Die Islamisierung bei den Albanern, *Jahrbücher für Geschichte Osteuropas*, 3, 4 (1955), 415; M. Vasić, *Der Islamisierungsprozess auf der Balkanhalbinsel* ("Zur Kunde Südosteuropas", II/14), Graz, 1985, 6–7.

58. S. S. Juka, *The Albanians in Yugoslavia in Light of Historical Documents*, New York (online version at www.alb-net.com/juka2.htm), 1984, 22.

59. M. Balivet, Aux origines de l'Islamisation des Balkans Ottomans, *Revue des mondes musulmans et de la Méditerranée*, 66 (Octobre 1993), 12–14.

60. Stavrianos 1959, 62–63; Carter 1977, 442, 473; Vasić 1985, 6–7; A. Pippidi, De la Kosovo la Sarajevo, *Sud-Estul şi contextual European. Buletin*, 1 (1994), 20.

61. Bádenas de la Pena 2000, 159.

62. S. Vryonis Jr., Religious Changes and Patterns in the Balkans, 14th–16th Centuries, *Aspects 1972*, 163–164; P. F. Sugar, *Southeastern Europe under Ottoman Rule, 1354–1804*, Seattle, WA, 1977, 54; Balivet 1993, 13.

63. R. Samardžić, Migrations in Serbian History (the Era of Foreign Rule), *Migrations 1989*, 85.

64. R. Lipčev, Bogomilski elementi, motivi i siujeti v svetogleda i običaino-obrednata sistema na bălgarskite Aliani, *Dobrudža* (Varna), 6 (1989), 26–37.

65. Stavrianos 1959, 31; Arnakis 1963, 126–127; B. G. Spiridonakis, *Grecs, ocidentaux et Turcs de 1054 à 1453, quatre siècles de relations internationals*, Thessalonique, 1990, 239–240.

66. Stavrianos 1959, 90, 103–104, 150–153; A. Argyriou, Peuples Orthodoxes wet Musulmans dans les Balkans, *Contacts. Revue Française de l'Orthodoxie*, 46, nr. (1994), 249–251; M. Andonova–Hristova, Modèles historiques de coexistence pacifique entre Musulmans et Chrétiens Orthodoxes pendant les periodes byzantine et post-byzantine, ByzSl, 61 (2003), 250–253.

67. J. Cvijić, *La Péninsule Balkanique. Géographie humaine*, Paris. 1918, 166, 353; Stavrianos 1959, 104–105; Arnakis 1963, 123, 128; Dimevski 1969, 67–68; Sugar 1977, 58; Vasić 1985, 9; O. Zirojević, Les premiers siècles de la domination étrangère, *Kosovo 1990*, 78–79; R. Tričković, Au-devant des plus dures épreuves: Le XVIIe siècle, *Kosovo 1990*, 128; Castellan 1991, 243; Bojović 1997, 37, 58.

68. Stavrianos 1959, 89–90, 105–107; Arnakis 1963, 120–121; Vasić 1985, 9; Spiridonakis 1990, 189–190, 221–222, 252–255.

69. Vryonis 1972, 168.

70. Stadtmüller 1955, 408–410.

71. Stadtmüller 1955, 411–412.

72. Stadtmüller 1955, 413–418; S. Skendi, Religion in Albania during the Ottoman Rule, SOF, 15 (1956), 316–318; Pulaha 1993, 39.

73. Pulaha 1993, 38–40; S. Pulaha, *L'autochtoneité des Albanais en Kosove et le prétendu exode des Serbes à la fin du XVIIe siècle*, Tirana, 1985, 52–55.

74. Stadtmüller 1955, 421; Skendi 1956, 317.

75. Arnakis 1963, 122; G. Palikruševa, Islamisation de la région Reka dans le nord-est de la Macédoine, *Macédoine 1970*, 141–142; Vryonis 1972, 167; Vasić 1985, 2–4, 8; Balivet 1993, 16–17; Argyriou 1994, 248; P. Xhufi, Religione e sentimento religioso in Albania durante il Medioevo, AIESEEB, 26–27 (1996–1997), 45.

76. H. Inalcik, Ottoman Methods of Conquest, *Studia Islamica*, 2 (1954), 116–117; Palikruševa 1970, 137; Vryonis 1972, 164; Vasić 1985, 4–5, 8–9.

77. M. Sokolovski, Le Vilaete de Serrès au XVe siècle, *Macédoine 1981*, 110.

78. Vryonis 1972, 163; Balivet 1993, 13.

79. Vasić 1985, 5–6.

80. Stadtmüller 1955, 406; Arnakis 1963, 124–125; Vryonis 1972, 151–152, 155–162, 170–176; Vasić 1985, 4; Balivet 1993, 13–15, 17–18; Xhufi 1996–1997, 44; N. Malcolm, *Kosovo. A Short History*, New York, 1999, 129–135; N. Malcolm. *Storia di Bosnia dalle origini ai giorni nostril*, Milano, 2000, 93–96. In general, for the conversion of the Balkan population, see F. Babinger, *Der Islam in Südosteuropa*, Völker 1959, 211–217.

81. Wace & Thompson 1914, 29–30; Balivet 1993, 18.

Part II

THE PRESENT. HISTORICAL PROPAGANDA AND BALKAN NATIONALIST IDEOLOGIES

Chapter 4

Theories of Ethnogenesis with Political Implications

THE GREEKS

The oldest historiographic dispute on the origin of a Balkan people concerns the modern Greeks. In fact, the history of the theories about ethnogenesis reflects and follows the history of the national revival of the Balkan peoples. As the Greeks were the first in this respect, with the "Megale Idea" (the restoration of the Byzantine Empire) and the revolution started by the Hetaireia, it was natural that their origin also became an issue in the first decades of the nineteenth century.

A book published in the period of the revival of the Greek national state caused a huge dispute, with implications going much beyond the historical research. German author Jakob Philipp Fallmerayer (1790–1861) sustained in *Geschichte der Halbinsel Morea während des Mittelalters* (History of Peloponnesus in the Middle Ages), Stuttgart, Tübingen, 1830, that modern Greeks did not descend from the ancient ones. He stated that the old Hellenic population disappeared in the early medieval Dark Age and that the present Greeks are the heirs of the Slavs that settled there in the seventh century and of the Albanians and Aromanians who migrated to Greece in the tenth–fifteenth centuries.[1] Similar ideas were formulated some time before by archaeologist William Martin Leake (*Researches on Greece*, London, 1814), but without the same impact upon public opinion. Fallmerayer's theory was a reaction to the exaggerations of the filohellenism supported by Western elites during the period of the national liberation of Greece from the Ottoman yoke. In Greece, his ideas were perceived as insulting and dangerous for national interests and were denied by historians, starting with Emmanuel Vivilakis (1840). The great historian Constantine Paparrigopoulos (1815–1891) contested with fierceness and strong arguments the German writer's theories, in a study from 1843 and next in his great synthesis of Greek history published in 1853. Other Greek historians expressed opposite exaggerations. For instance, in 1880, Constantine Sathas sustained that no Slavs lived in Greece and that the Slavs recorded in the Byzantine sources were in fact Albanians, considered by him to be a race of Hellenic stock.[2]

Fallmerayer's book was published in the period of a major Russian offensive in the Balkans, started after the Peace Treaty of Adrianople (1829), which meant not only the independence of Greece, but also the increasing influence of Russia in the Black Sea area and a new step toward the ultimate target, penetration to the Mediterranean Sea. Fallmerayer believed that his theory could reveal the danger that the Orthodox Greeks would become an instrument of Panslavist policy, because, being Slavs in his opinion, they would be easily included in the large Slavic family protected by the Russian tzar. Fallmerayer held that Greece could not be a bulwark against the more and more dangerous Panslavism and that only the Ottoman Empire was able to accomplish this task. Yet, his theory caused concern among the Greeks just because it was perceived as support for Russian expansion, and rightly so. Combating Fallmerayer meant in fact supporting the Greek national policy, which was based on the idea of continuity between the ancient and the modern Greeks.[3]

Fallmerayer's theory was always considered false and biased by Greek historians. It was denied by great specialists in the history of the early Middle Ages like Peter Charanis and Phaedon Malingoudis, but also by other historians who studied the national policy of modern Greece.[4] Unfortunately, some Greek authors reacted with opposite exaggerations, denying the contribution of the alien populations to the medieval Greek ethnogenesis, or affirming that the Aromanians were of Greek origin.

Four decades ago, Byzantinist Romilly Jenkins revived Fallmerayer's ideas, using new arguments, including archaeological material.[5] Of course, Greek historians reacted immediately. Peter Charanis believed that the American Byzantinist gave wrong interpretations to the data he invoked, emphasizing that the final assimilation of the Slavs shows that the Greeks were still numerous in their homeland.[6]

The theory formulated by Fallmerayer was also an instrument for the expansionist policy of Nazi Germany. A book by German philologist Max Vasmer about "The Slavs in Greece,"[7] published during the German occupation of Greece, demonstrated that the Slavization of mainland Greece was very strong in the seventh–eighth centuries. Of course, Vasmer wrote his book some time before the occupation, but, published, this work was very suitable with a political agenda. The partial inclusion of the Greeks in the world of the "sub-human" Slavic race provided ideological support for the interests of Germany (but also for Bulgaria, which occupied a region in Greek Macedonia).[8] These ideas were expressed, for instance, in Georg Stadtmüller's study of Peloponnesus (*Der Peloponnes. Landschaft, Geschichte, Kunststatten*, Athens, 1944), destinated to the German troops of occupation. Although he did not postulate the disappearance of the ancient Greeks as Fallmerayer did, Stadtmüller felt that the Slavic component in the ethnogenesis of the modern Greeks was very significant.[9] Similar implications can be ascribed to a theory expressed by another distinguished German linguist, Ernst Gamillscheg, who sustained in 1940 that the Slavic element had a very important place in the Romanian ethnogenesis. He was then, not surprisingly, director of the German Institute from Bucharest, a propagandistic organization.[10] His study includes some valuable ideas, but these do not keep us from observing, as for Vasmer's book, the political significance of such theories expressed by a representative of the Nazi regime.

Different studies (mentioned in chapter 1) confirm the existence of a quite large population in the Greek territories that was previously depopulated by invasions, plague, and earthquakes, but they also have demonstrated that the natives resisted in the protected zones and in some cities under Byzantine control. The assimilation of the Slavs was possible after the reconquest fulfilled in the eighth–ninth centuries.[11] The comparison of the linguistic and archaeological evidence demonstrates that no Greek–Slavic symbiosis existed in Greece and Macedonia in the seventh–eighth centuries. As long as the Slavs remained heathens, mixed marriages with the native Christians were not possible. Conversion to Christianity started only after the campaign of General Staurakios in 787. Only the forced integration of the underdeveloped Slavic tribal communities into Byzantine social, political, and religious structures allowed this symbiosis. Christianization was the decisive factor of the assimilation of the Slavs into Greece.

The Byzantines defined themselves as a people by their affiliation with Christendom. The barbarians settled in the empire and converted to Christianity became Byzantines just by this act. There were no ethnic discriminations, although specific ethnic features survived in language, customs, and anthroponomy. Christianization had as a final result the assimilation of those non-Greek populations which were not advanced civilizations or which were not living in relative isolation. The Armenians were not assimilated because they had their own flourishing culture, while the Aromanians and the Albanians preserved their ethnicities because they lived especially in the highlands, in closed communities. On the contrary, the Slavs from Greek lands were finally assimilated. This fact could be explained by conversion to Christianity, especially by the missionary activity of monks from the rural monasteries. There was no deliberate action of Hellenization except this Christian mission. On the other hand, colonization with people from Asia Minor had an important role in the assimilation of the Slavs in Peloponnesus, because it increased the proportion of the Grecophones who survived in some cities in the area covered by the Slavic newcomers.[12] The Christianization and Hellenization of the Slavs was achieved mainly in the ninth century. This process was called *graikoo* by Leon VI (886–912).[13]

In conclusion, Fallmerayer's theory is not completely wrong, because some of the present Greeks indeed descend from Slavs who were assimilated in the eighth–tenth centuries. But recognizing this does not mean denying the ethnic and cultural continuity between the ancient, medieval, and modern Greeks. Almost all the European peoples are the result of manifold mixtures. The present Greek people indeed have Slavs among their ancestors, but what matters is the survival of the Hellenic culture throughout the dark centuries of the early Middle Ages, which enabled the assimilation of the Slavs, Albanians, and Aromanians.

Greek scientist Peter Charanis affirms that:

> It may be correct to say that the Greek race did not survive in all its purity, if indeed one may speak of racial purity even among the ancient Greeks, but it is not correct to say that the Hellenic race in Europe is completely exterminated. Besides, it is not really a question of race, but of culture, and of the survival of the Greek culture, as that culture, of course, evolved throughout the centuries, there can be absolutely no question. In this evolution, the Classical tradition, the Roman domination, and Christianity were the principal forces; the settlement of Slavs in Greece was of no decisive significance.[14]

THE ALBANIANS

The origin of the Albanian people is one of the most disputed problems of Southeast European history. At first glance, it seems to be only a scientific problem, but the international relations of Albania transformed this issue into a controversy with political consequences. If the historians and linguists sustain the autochthonous origin of the Albanians in Albania and in Kosovo, then this conclusion is assumed by Albanian propaganda to support Albanian rights over all the regions where they are living now. If the historical and linguistic data do not support an ancient presence of the Albanians in Kosovo, then this point of view is embraced by the official

Serbian historiography. Both Albanians and Serbs have used theories about the Albanian ethnogenesis as weapons in their political propaganda. Since the establishment of the Communist regime in Albania, archaeologists were obliged to follow a nationalist agenda whose main purpose was to provide historical justification for the isolationist policy of Albania and especially for the permanent dispute with Yugoslavia.[15]

The obsession with autochthony led to some extreme ideas, like that of the Pelasgic origin of the Albanians, which would mean that this people has to be considered the forefather not only of the Balkan peoples, but also of the Europeans. This theory was developed by a French author of Albanian origin in a recent book that sustains the existence of three stages of Albanian ethnic identity along the last four millennia: Pelasgians, Illyrians, and Albanians. In his view, the Albanians are the most ancient European people. They lived without interruption in Albania and Kosovo.[16] We shall see below that Pelasgian origin was also claimed for the Macedonian Slavs and for the Aromanians by some dilettanti. However, the Albanians were the first in this contest for the oldest origin. A political proclamation from 1888 stated that:

> The Albanians are descendants of the Pelasgians; Homer, the biggest poet ever, was a Pelasgian himself or, more correctly, Albanian. All heroes of Greece in Troy were Albanians, as well as Alexander the Great, Aristotle and many other glorious men of antiquity are erroneously characterized as Greeks.[17]

This strange opinion shows how the ideology forged during the period of national revival tried to ascribe as much as possible an old origin for the Albanians, in order to support their rights and their ethnic identity. Of course, professional historians and linguists do not share such ideas. They are instead divided by a long-lasting controversy, a still open question, which concerns the Thracian or the Illyrian origin of the Albanians.[18]

The Illyrian theory is sustained by Albanian scholars because it supports the autochthony of their people in present-day Albania and moreover in Kosovo and western Macedonia. The political consequences of this idea are obvious. A linguist remarked that "many scholars in Tirana have tended to depart a priori from a theory of Illyrian continuity and Albanian autochthony and then reflect on how to prove it, working indeed conscientiously to this end."[19] Another scholar observed in his turn that those who admit the Illyrian continuity and the autochthony of the Albanians have forgotten the social and historical significance of the migrations that occurred in the early Middle Ages, when various populations came into the Balkans from the north.[20] This remark is justified for all of Southeastern Europe.

The main arguments for the ethnogenesis of the Albanians in their present country and in Kosovo are:

- the supposed Illyrian origin of the language;
- the presence of an ancient tribe named Albanoi in present-day Albania;
- the weak Romanization in Albania and Kosovo;
- the place-names of ancient origin transmitted by the Albanian language located in Albania, Kosovo, and southern Serbia;
- the existence of an archaeological culture dated to the seventh–eighth centuries ascribed to the Protoalbanians.

The small number of Greek loan words in the basic Albanian lexis and the presence of many Latin words points to the location of the ethnogenesis of the Albanians as a region far from the Greek area and at the same time subjected to Roman influence. That region was not Romanized but only influenced by the Latin language. The second issue is the Thracian versus the Illyrian origin of the Albanian language. It is true that some Albanian words and place-names descend from Illyrian, but it was proven by a great specialist in the Balkan languages, Gustav Weigand, that the language itself was not of Illyrian stock.[21] Many linguists (not only Albanians) tried to establish a link between Illyrian and Albanian, but they did not achieve clear results. In fact, the phonetics and the main part of the lexis are of Thracian origin and for this reason are akin with the Dacian substratum of the Romanian language.[22]

The Illyrian tribe Albanoi and the place Albanopolis (names recorded by Ptolemy, *Geographia*, III. 12. 20) could be located near Krujë,[23] but nothing proves a relation with the medieval Albanians, whose name appears for the first time in the eleventh century in Byzantine sources. The name given by the Albanians themselves is Shkipëtari ("eagles"), but they are recorded in medieval sources with the names Arbanitai, Arberi. The names Arbër ("Albanian") and Arbëri ("Albania") are used now by the Albanians who immigrated to southern Italy, but not by those from Albania. The origin of this ethnic name is the word *arbër*, which comes from the Indo-European root *alb-* = "mountain, tableland."[24]

The territory of Albania was not entirely Romanized, although it was included from an early period in the Roman state (168 BCE). Only in the plains and on the seashore was Romanization quite successful. Latin inscriptions were discovered in this region. There are no proofs for the survival of the Illyrian language in the Late Roman period (as some Albanian philologists supposed in order to establish a link with the future Albanian language). The surviving Illyrian person names and the representations of Illyrian popular dress on tombstones are not enough to prove the so-called resistance against Romanization.[25] The continuous use of the names *Illyricum* and *Illyri* in late ancient writings does not prove the perpetuation of the non-Romanized Illyrians, as some researchers have supposed.[26] Like the same name *Illyrioi* used by the tenth–twelfth-century Byzantine authors for the Serbians, the late ancient name Illyri was an archaism that did not reflect the real existence of an Illyrian people. On the other hand, it is certain that the region traversed by Via Egnatia (by the center of Albania) was strongly Romanized. Being an important trading route, *Via Egnatia* attracted Latinophone people from different Roman provinces. Having a great strategic value, this zone was colonized with Roman settlements. The mapping of Latin inscriptions and Roman settlements clearly shows the Romanization of this area.[27] We can therefore conclude that only the northern mountain region of Albania (Mati) remained outside Romanization.

Romanian philologist H. Mihăescu has shown that the Latin influence was exerted over the Albanian language in another area than the primary homeland of the Romanian language. The Latin words common to Albanian and Romanian are less than the words that survived only in Albanian and in the Western Romance languages (45 versus 163). This means that the Albanian language evolved in a region with quite strong relations with the Western Romance languages and without a direct contact with the area where the Romanian language was born. H. Mihăescu located this region in present-day Albania, in Kosovo, and in the western part of Macedonia, up to Prishtina and Bitolia.[28] Based on the comparison of the Latin words of Romanian and Albanian, linguist Cătălina Vătăşescu remarked that Albanian was influenced by a disappeared Romance language, other than Dalmatian and Romanian.[29]

Several place-names and river names of Roman origin survived in Albania. Transmission through a Slavic language is excluded, but borrowing from the speakers of a Romance language, during the early Middle Ages, can be taken into consideration. This was the solution proposed by Yugoslavian linguist Ivan Popović; he said that the surviving Roman people left the names to the Slavs and then the Albanians took them from the Slavs.[30] His ideas were rejected by Albanian scholars,[31] but recently it was shown that a local Roman population that survived at least until the seventh century transmitted some place-names in Albania. Some of these names of minor importance (small hills, rivulets) are very significant for the intermediary position of this language, between the Romanian and the Western Romance languages. For instance, the place-names Shkortull (from Lat. *curtus*) and Volpul (from Lat. *vulpes*) have the suffix -*ul*, which is specific for Romanian, in combination with the evolution from *u* to *o*, which occurred in the Western Romance area.[32] This Latin-speaking population could be the missing link by which the Latin words were passed down to Albanian.

This does not mean that Latin place-names are a majority in Albania. A recent study on the river names in Albania has shown that a great part of them are of Albanian origin. The Slavic names are more widespread in the southern half of Albania, a plain region previously Romanized, where the Slavs preferred to settle during the seventh century. This southern area suffered a deep Slavic influence, while the north kept many Albanian names. The terms for the mountain trees are Albanian, while those for the species from the plain are mostly foreign.[33] This research proves that Albanians lived for a long time in the Mati tableland, where they imposed their names, while the Slavs did the same thing in the plain region of Albania.

Did the Albanians' ancestors live in Mati since the Roman period? Archaeology was used to prove this, by means of the supposed common elements between the ancient Illyrians and the Albanians. According to Albanian historians, the missing link is the Komani-Krujë culture (seventh–eighth centuries), which is represented by finds from fortresses, open settlements, and cemeteries. The exhumed cemeteries and the open and fortified settlements of the Komani-Krujë culture (Krujë, Durrës, Dalmace, Shurdhah, Aphiona, etc.) contain many objects of Byzantine fashion (belt buckles, fibulae, earrings, coins), imported from Byzantine towns or made in local workshops. The Christian character is sure, at least for some graves. Many graves were protected with stones and bricks (a funeral rite of Roman origin). The cemeteries are usually located near fortresses and churches. The Komani-Krujë culture was widespread in the northern part of Albania, but also in Kosovo, southern Albania, and Epirus. The official interpretation is that this culture was created on an Illyrian background by the ancestors of the Albanians, who lived without interruption in all these regions.[34]

On the basis of the supposed ethnic features of this culture, the Albanian homeland was located near Krujë, in the rocky region crossed by the river Mati, that was not Romanized and colonized in the Roman period. The same zone was identified with the so-called Arbanon, a region recorded since the eleventh century by Byzantine authors.[35] As a matter of fact, the real location of Arbanon was south of the Shkumbin valley. Alain Ducellier postulates that in this area survived the ancestors of the Albanians when the neighboring areas were occupied by the Slavs. In this region called Arbanon they were subject to certain Byzantine influences.[36] Therefore, according to this theory, the Albanians are autochthonous in their present country. The central part of Albania was also the source from whence the Albanians spread to the north and south.

As concerns the Komani-Krujë culture, the situation is more complicated than Albanian historians believe. Serbian archaeologist Vladislav Popović[37] supposed that this culture was created by a Roman and urban population, which cannot be identified with the Proto-Albanians. According to him, this culture belonged to the Roman population living along *Via Egnatia*. This area remained until the seventh–eighth centuries under a strong Byzantine influence. The area of this culture is nearly the same as that where Latin was spoken in antiquity (defined on the basis of inscriptions). The region was Romanized. On the other hand, in the same area many present place-names of Latin origin are known. It is therefore possible that the Komani-Krujë culture was the archaeological expression of a Roman, not Proto-Albanian, population.

This theory was of course rejected by the official Albanian archaeologists,[38] but their arguments are not convincing. They cannot explain the large amount of Byzantine and Christian objects in the environment of this culture. A pastoral population like the Albanians was not able to create a culture of Byzantine urban fashion. The assertion[39] that Albanians developed an urban civilization in the early Middle Ages and that they peopled the late Roman fortified settlements is fanciful.

In 2002, the young Albanian archaeologist Etleva Nallbani received from the Sorbonne her PhD for a dissertation entitled "La civilisation de Komani de l'antiquité tardive au haut Moyen Âge: étude du mobilier métallique" (not yet published). The main ideas were summarized in two short studies (one of them published in a Croatian scientific journal).[40] She has abandoned the traditional theory put forward by Albanian archaeology, that the Komani-Krujë culture is Proto-Albanian. Instead, she emphasizes the integration in the Byzantine civilization and the urban roots of this civilization. This new approach is shared by British archaeologist William Bowden, who concludes that the archaeological evidence does not support a single ethnic identification. On the contrary, it suggests that the appearance of the rich graves reflected significant social changes and that these communities "were participating in a European-wide medium of funerary practice, rather than constructing an identity that consciously expressed their difference from their neighbors."[41]

Sometimes, Albanian historians and linguists maintain that the area of the Albanian ethnogenesis includes not only the Mati tableland, but also all of present-day Albania together with Kosovo and some parts from Macedonia and Montenegro.[42] The genesis of the Albanians in Albania, Kosovo, and the western part of Macedonia (the Roman provinces Epirus Nova, Epirus Vetus, Praevalitana, and Dardania, Macedonia) is also supposed by some foreign linguists and historians.[43]

Some major ancient place-names from Albania, Kosovo, and southern Serbia were transmitted by the Albanian language, not by a Slavic path: Dyrrachion > Durrës, Lissus > Lesh, Scodra > Shkodër, Isamnus > Ishëm, Mathis > Mati, Drinus > Drin, Naissus > Niš, Scupi > Shkup, Scardus > Shar, Astibos > Shtip. They prove that the ancestors of the Albanians were already present in southern Serbia and Macedonia at least since the seventh century and that the Slavs took the names from them. For this reason some researchers hold that the ethnogenesis area of the Albanians includes a region located north of their present homeland, a region where they lived even before the settlement of the Slavs.[44]

In antiquity, the territory of Kosovo belonged to the regions of Dardania and Paeonia. Dardania was an area mixed between Thracians and Illyrians. The Paeonae were Thracians. I. I. Russu defined with great precision the spreading areas of the Thracian and Illyrian tribes. It can be observed that the western part of the present Kosovo province was peopled by Illyrians, while the east was Thracian. Places like Prishtina and Tetovo are located just on the blurred line between these territories.[45] The Dardanians are often considered to be a tribe with an intermediary position between Thracians and Illyrians.[46]

Dardania (Kosovo) was seen as the homeland of the future Albanians, where they lived without any break.[47] The name of Dardanians was put in relation with the Albanian word dardhë ("pear"), whose meaning can also be found in the Slavic place-name Kruševac. The Dardanians were shepherds; their cheese (caseus dardanicus) was well-known in the Roman period, as was the cheese prepared by the Vlach shepherds in medieval Byzantium and Dalmatia.[48] The continuity of traditional occupations in this mountain region is obvious, but it was not linked to a specific ethnicity. Dardania was indeed a less Romanized area because the geographical conditions were improper for urbanization.[49] It is possible that the ancestors of the Albanians were the inhabitants of Dardania, that is in Kosovo, in the Roman period, but there are also other possibilities.

The Romanization of the plain areas of the Illyrian provinces contradicts all the hypotheses based on the descent of the Albanians from a population that lived there. The primary homeland of the Albanians should be searched for in an isolated area, were Romanization was not achieved and where geographic conditions allowed the survival of a pastoral population influenced by Roman civilization, but not entirely Romanized. This region can be found in the rockiest parts of the Balkan Peninsula or even outside the Roman Empire (as we shall see below). The theory of ethnogenesis in the Mati tableland is suitable from this point of view, but the arguments presented above show its inconsistency, because the Komani-Krujë culture does not bring clear evidence for Illyrian–Albanian continuity in Mati.

Romanian linguist Alexandru Philippide reaches the conclusion that the Albanians emerged as a new people in the non-Romanized enclave located in Bosnia between the rivers Vrbas (at west) and Drina (at east). He theorizes that the Albanians descended from the Pannonians, an Illyrian tribe that also inhabited that area.[50] In fact, the Pannonians lived in another area to the north. It is otherwise true that the region proposed by Philippide was less Romanized. This theory, now forgotten, was based only on the identification of an area that was not Romanized.

German linguist Gottfried Schramm postulated recently that Albanians are the inheritors of the Bessi, a Thracian tribe that was not Romanized because it lived in the mountain regions of the provinces Dacia Mediterranea and Dardania. This means that the homeland of the Albanians should be located in southern Serbia, Kosovo, and western Macedonia. Schramm explains the survival of the Bessian language by early conversion to Christianity, in the late fourth century, through the mission of St. Nicetas of Remesiana. He supposes that St. Nicetas translated the Holy Bible into the Bessian language. According to this theory, the Bessi were deported at the beginning of the ninth century by the Byzantine army from Bulgaria to the center of present-day Albania, with the purpose of fighting against Bulgaria and strengthening the defense of the newly established province of Dyrrachion. The Bessi were previously persecuted by Bulgarians because of their Christian faith. In their new homeland, the ancestors of the Albanians took the geographical term Arbanon as their ethnic name. They assimilated the local populations of Greek, Roman, and Slavic origins.[51]

The descent of the Albanians from Bessi is also claimed by a Polish linguist in a short paper that invites researchers to debate this issue,[52] and it was also suggested in an old study about the Aromanians.[53]

It is true that some unclear data about the survival of the Bessian language until the sixth century exist,[54] but nothing proves that a great number of non-Romanized Bessi still existed until the ninth century. As Cătălina Vătășescu remarks, the survival of the genuine language as a result of Christianization is unthinkable. All the known cases show that conversion to Christianity strengthened Romanization. So, at least a part of the theory expressed by Schramm does not hold up. The Christian Latin words in Albanian belong to several periods of influence, which are not easy to put into a chronological frame. Their origin is sometimes disputable.[55] An interesting example is *qishë* "church," derived by Schramm from the Latin *ecclesia*.[56] There is also another point of view, which says that this Albanian word came from the Italian *chiesa*.[57] In this case, the word could be easily explained as a testimony of the conversion to the Catholic rites of a part of the Albanian people, during the eleventh–twelfth centuries.

The idea of Albanian–Romanian symbiosis in the mountains between Shtip and the western border of Bulgaria is not justified. Schramm took this idea from the old theory developed by Robert Roesler (1871) and Gustav Weigand (1895), also shared by some other linguists. Although it is certain that the common Albanian-Romanian words could be explained as Dacian survivals in Romanian, Schramm continues to put forth the obsolete idea that these words show that Romanians lived together with Albanians during the early Middle Ages. (In other works, Schramm tries to give new arguments for the politically biased theory of the late immigration of Romanians from the Balkans to their present country.)[58] C. Vătăşescu rejects the theory of "Romanian-Albanian symbiosis," because the common elements are less significant than the differences between these languages.[59]

A viewpoint quite similar to that of G. Schramm is held by Bulgarian linguist Vladimir Georgiev. Based on the similarities between Romanian and Albanian, he concludes that the latter derived from the Gaetic language spoken in Moesia and that the ancestors of the Albanians came from the Morava basin and from Banat,[60] but this theory has no support in historical sources.

An older theory first expressed by Romanian scholars Bogdan Petriceicu Hasdeu (1876, 1901), Vasile Pârvan (1906), and Sextil Puflcariu (1910) was resumed by Ion I. Russu.[61] In a posthumous book, Russu theorized that the Albanians descend from the tribe of Carpi (free Dacians from Moldavia). The Carpi indeed colonized an area on Roman soil after the end of the third century. The main idea of this theory is based on the supposition that a large group of people could not escape Romanization if they lived inside the Roman Empire. For this reason, only an immigrated people from Barbaricum could be considered the ancestor of the Albanians. The Carpic origin could easily explain the likeness between the Romanian and Albanian languages and even the partial Romanization of the Albanians. The tribe of Carpi was influenced by Roman civilization in its North-Danubian homeland. This influence continued to be exerted after they settled inside the Roman Empire, but their original language was preserved. Migration toward the southwestern part of the province Moesia Superior and toward Dardania could be dated in the fourth–sixth centuries, that is before the arrival of the Slavs. In the new homeland, the inheritors of the Carpi took a new ethnic name. Russu supposed that this migration was peaceful and slow, because the Carpi remained a sedentary people.

The major problem with the theory expressed by Russu is the lack of data about the intermediary places occupied by the ancestors of the Albanians, between Danube and their present country. On the other hand, this theory explains the affinities of the Albanian language with the Romanian, better than the so-called Albanian–Romanian symbiosis in the triangle Niš–Skopje–Sofia. The common Romanian-–Albanian elements are in this case the result of the common substratum. Settled in Dardania (Kosovo) and in western Macedonia by the sixth century, the ancestors of the Albanians were able to borrow many Greek and especially Latin words, together with the local toponymy, before the Slavic invasions. This explains the transmission of several ancient place-names and river names through the Albanian language, without a Slavic intermediary form. It could be supposed that the Albanians were pushed by Slavic invasions from Dardania and Macedonia toward the west and southwest, to the higher regions. Linguist G. Ivănescu remarked that a compromise could be made between the ethnogenesis of the Albanians into a region not Romanized and the ethnogenesis in Dardania (Kosovo): he maintains that the ancestors of the Albanians arrived in Albania from a non-Romanized zone of Dardania, before or during the period when the Slavs began their migrations.[62]

Even if I. I. Russu was right, it seems possible that the Albanians were present in the central part of the Balkan Peninsula before the Slavic invasions. Because their forefathers were Thracians or Dacians subjected to a partial Romanization, they are kin to the Romanians. Albanians living in Kosovo from ancient times has not been excluded, but this theory needs more proof. They survived because they took refuge in the mountains of northern Albania, escaping from Slavization. Historical sources record Albanians in that mountain area since the eleventh century. They may have begun to people the plain areas as early as the ninth century. V. Popović supposes that the conversion of the Albanians to a sedentary way of life was due to the economic and military needs of the newly established Byzantine province Dyrrachion, founded at the beginning of the ninth century.[63] In these circumstances, the Albanian tribes became step-by-step a significant proportion of the population of the plain areas, surpassing the Slavic and Romance populations.

The Albanian ethnogenesis remains an open question that will continue to fuel the propagandistic fight for Kosovo. Because no theory can be considered certain so far, discussions about the original homeland of the Albanian people could include Kosovo with a certain probability, giving strong proof to the Albanian claims.

THE BULGARIANS

One of the most fanciful ethnogenetic theories with political aims was the autochthony of the Bulgarians in the Balkan Peninsula. It is really difficult to believe that some authors affirmed that Bulgarians lived in Macedonia since classical antiquity, that Zeus was a name of Bulgarian origin, and that St. Paul christened the Macedonian Bulgarians. Yet, one of the founders of Bulgarian historiography, Gheorghi Sava Rakovski (1821–1867), launched this theory of the presence of Bulgarians in Macedonia before the Common Era, in a book published in 1859. Romantic historiography was the source of many fanciful ideas and even falsified texts in order to prove preconceived ideas. If we take into account their age, we can regard Rakovski's ideas with indulgence. More strange is that similar opinions were resumed and developed in the interwar period in a book published in Germany by Gantscho Tzenoff, *Die Abstammung der Bulgaren und die Urheimat der Slaven* (The Origin of the Bulgarian and the Homeland of the Slavs), Berlin-Leipzig, 1930. According to Tzenoff (1875–1952), the Bulgarians were the heirs of the Thracians and Macedonians. The obvious purposes of this theory were to demonstrate the prior residence of Bulgarians in Macedonia and to support the revisionist policy followed by Bulgaria in those years, namely to justify Bulgarian claims over all of Macedonia, a region which was a matter of dispute between Bulgaria, Serbia, and Greece. Of course, scientists were astonished by this theory.[64] In the same interwar period, Bulgarian scholar Vladimir Georgiev maintained that the Ionians and the Achaeans were Thracians, not Greeks. It was an idea that would be later contradicted by the decipherment of the Mycenian writing in the 1950s, which attest to an archaic form of the Greek language. The hidden reason of this study was the justification of Bulgarian claims over Macedonia, because the theory of the Thracian descent had already been expressed.[65]

The Rakovski–Tzenoff theory was much too exaggerated to be accepted as official, but Bulgarian historiography developed in the Communist period an ideology of Thraco-Bulgarian continuity which, besides some correct ideas, includes some political exaggerations. This moderate version of the theory of Bulgarian autochthony holds that the Bulgarians are mainly the descendants of Slavized Thracians, minimizing the truth that the Thracians were in fact Romanized during the long Roman domination. This theory, which became official, was presented in the most important productions of Bulgarian historians published since the 1960s. The Bulgarian nationalist historiography of the Zhivkov regime glorified medieval history, propounding many exaggerated ideas like the denial of the role of the Romanians in the creation of the second Bulgarian empire. After a short period when the canons of "proletarian internationalism" were strictly applied, Bulgarian historians received permission to resume the nationalist ideas proclaimed before by "bourgeois" authors like Petăr Mutafčiev.[66] In contrast with the interwar period, during the Zhivkov regime and after the fall of the Communism the illusory Thracian–Bulgarian continuity was emphasized.

Thracology became a national concern in Bulgaria. Bulgaria organized the first international Thracological congress in 1972. Later, it established an Institute of Thracology, which produced valuable scientific works of history, archaeology, and linguistics, but which was also a support for the official doctrine of Bulgarian ethnogenesis developed in the entire area peopled by Thracian tribes, including Macedonia. The Thraco-Bulgarian ideology remained alive after the fall of the Communist regime. Released from Marxist constraints, it continues to be offered in different works and scientific meetings that contribute to the historical justification of the nationalist ideology of a Great Bulgaria extended from the Danube Delta to the Aegean Sea.

THE SERBS AND THE CROATS

In 1601–1604, Croat priest Ivan Tomko Marnavić expressed the bizarre idea that the emperor Justinian was a Slav. This Catholic clergyman was an interesting personage. Later appointed bishop of Bosnia and adviser of the emperor Ferdinand II of Habsburg (1619–1637), he also had a hobby: the falsification of chronicles and documents. One of these Slavonic apocryphal texts was ascribed to a certain Bogomil, the teacher of the emperor Justinian; it was also affirmed that the emperor was of Slavic descent and that his original name was Upravda ("justice"). Its forgery was demonstrated in 1887, after a long period when many Slavic authors admitted without any doubt that Justinian was of Slavic origin.[67] These fanciful assertions intended to ascribe to the Slavs a prestigious origin. As a matter of fact, an antique noble origin was sought for the Serbs even in the age of Stephen Dušan. In a Slavonic translation of the universal history of Zonaras made around 1350 it was written that the Dacians and their king Decebalus were Serbians, as well as the Roman emperor Licinius, who was born in the region.[68] This invention of an ancient origin coincided, not surprisingly, with the imperial age of Serbia.

Other Croatian authors from the sixteenth–eighteenth centuries claimed that their people descended from the Illyrians. In *Oratio de origini successibusque Slavorum* (1525), Dominican friar Vinko Pribojević (Vincentius Priboevius) launched for the first time the Pan-Illyrian theory, which said that many historical figures like Alexander the Great and St. Hieronymus were Illyrians, that is Slavs or Croats. He believed that the Slavs were the native population of the Balkan Peninsula and that Dalmatia was the cradle of the Slavs. These ideas were developed by other Croatian writers, among whom were Marnavić and also Benedictine monk Mauro Orbini, who theorized that the Slavs were the Goths and that they were the most important European race.[69] This was the prototype of the theory of the Germanic origin of the Croats, an idea that would be developed in the twentieth century in special political circumstances. Another Dominican monk, Juraj Križanić, used the same theory of the Illyrian origin of the Slavs in order to justify Panslavism. He wrote in 1663 that the noble origin of the Slavs should be an incentive for the fight against

Ottoman domination and against German cultural influence. He wished the unification of all the Slavs under the protection of the Russian tzar if he would convert to Catholicism. In all these cases, the anti-Ottoman function of the Illyrian theory is obvious. In 1839, the Illyrian ideology was revived as an instrument of Russian Panslavism by Ljudevit Gaj (1809–1872), who considered the Slavs to be descended from the Illyrians and natives of the Balkan Peninsula. He distinguished two Slavic groups: Illyro-Russians and Czecho-Poles, providing in this way a "reason" for Russian expansion in the Balkan Peninsula. L. Gaj dreamed of a Great Illyria that would embrace all the Balkan Slavs.[70]

Of course, the Romanized Illyrians contributed to the ethnogenesis of the Croats and the Serbs, but this does not mean that these peoples are Illyrians. Historical science has long since abandoned such conceptions born before modern times. The fantastic ideas about the Slavic autochthony in the Balkan Peninsula are similar to those expressed about the Bulgarians, but older. They did not provide justifications for the conflicts between the Serbs and the Croats, but they opened a long tradition of claiming Illyrian heritage, continued by the Albanians who pretend the same exclusive Illyrian origin. For the Serbs and the Croats, the politization of theories about ethnogenesis took another way in the twentieth century, because this Illyrian ideology was a support for their unity, not for discord.

After the achievement of the unification of the Serbo-Croatian space in 1918, the political, religious, and cultural tensions between the Serbs and the Croats became more and more accentuated. This required a historical background that included the denial of a common origin. The ideology that aimed to separate the Croats and the Serbs from the point of view of their ethnogenesis was born in the interwar period and was revived after 1989.

The first separatist theory tried to demonstrate that the Croats descended from the Ostrogoths who lived in Croatia in the fifth century. It was first formulated in a minimal form in 1908 by G. Ruggeri, director of the Naples Anthropological Institute, who made a study of physical anthropology of the Croatian population that seemed to demonstrate a Germanic, not Slavic origin. Orbini's obsolete ideas were thus revived with scientific proof. We can suppose that in 1908 this theory could justify the domination of Austro-Hungary over Croatia. The idea still remained after the formation of the kingdom of the Serbs, Croatians, and Slovenians (since 1929, Yugoslavia). For instance, Croatian historian G. Rus maintained in several works published in 1931–1932 that his people descended from the Goths. The theory of Germanic origin was supported especially by Croatian historian Milan Šufflay, who was killed in 1931 by the Serbian terrorist organization "Young Yugoslavia" for this "crime" against the Yugoslavian idea.[71]

The "Gothic" theory has no serious scientific proofs. The data taken from some eleventh–twelfth-century sources are too confusing, while the anthropological data are not reliable enough, since the Croats were mixed with the German population in the Middle Ages. It is possible that some Ostrogoths remained in Croatia until the seventh century, but this does not mean that the Croats are a people of Germanic origin. This theory has justified the affiliation of Croatia to the Germanic cultural and political space. In the interwar period, this was a support for German expansionism toward the Balkans, which was also founded on the manipulation of history.[72] Of course, the theory established a deep rift between the Croats and the Serbs. The latter belong to the "inferior Slavic race," while the Croats were of superior Germanic stock. It is not surprising that a group of Muslim Bosnians sent a memorandum to Hitler in November 1942, which proclaimed that they were of Gothic origin.[73]

The second theory that postulates a non-Slavic origin of the Croats is more reliable, since it is based on disputable but not improbable data. It started with the discovery of the similarity between the names Hrvati (Croats) and Harahvati, an Iranian tribe. Since it is known that peoples of Iranian origin lived in the North-Pontic steppe (Scythians, Sarmats, Alans), it was supposed that the seventh-century Croats were also of Iranian origin, namely a mixture of Iranian, Slavic, Gothic, and Uralo-Altaic elements arrived in their present country from the so-called White Croatia recorded by Constantine Porphyrogenitus. This would mean that the Croats were significantly different from the Serbs, a purely Slavic people.[74] According to Constantine Porphyrogenitus, the Croats were led by a chief called Chrovatos, whose name was inherited by the people. Byzantinist Henri Grégoire has tried to identify this Chrovatos with Kuvrat, the ruler of the Protobulgarians who rebelled against the Avars, recorded by other sources in the first third of the seventh century.[75] As a matter of fact, now it is certain that Kuvrat lived in the North-Pontic steppes, not in Pannonia. He was the father of Asparuch, the ruler of the Protobulgarian group that immigrated to Moesia.[76] Chrovatos was an invented eponym hero, like other such mythical ancestors of the European peoples.[77] The name Hrvat itself was explained by the Iranian language as "warriors clad with horn-armor."[78] The real purpose of the theory, which is semi-official in Croatia and in the Croatian diaspora, is the justification of the historical fracture between Croats and Serbs.[79]

More recently, the Iranian theory received new proof from the genetic research conducted by Andrija-Željko Lovrić from the Bosković Institute in Zagreb, which demonstrates that three quarters of the present Croats have genetic links with peoples the southwestern Asia. This theory was presented at a symposium held in Zagreb on June 24th, 1998, whose works were published in a volume edited by writer Zlatko Tomičić and by Andrija-Zeljko Lovrić: *The Old-Iranian Origin of Croats. Symposium Proceedings*, Zagreb: Cultural Center of Islamic Republic of Iran in Croatia, 1999 (abstracts of the papers are available on several sites, such as www.dalmatiahus.com/Media/croats2.pdf). However, most professional historians are skeptical in this respect.[80]

It seems that the solution of the problem of the origin of the name Croati was given by researchers Otto Kronsteiner and Walter Pohl. Because they were not recorded in the sources as a distinct ethnicity before the end of the Avarian kaganate, it was supposed that this population took the name of a group of warriors from the Avarian confederacy. Those Chrovatoi had a Türkic name, *char-vata*, which means "free warriors." They became the masters of a Slavic group at the periphery of the Avarian kaganate, which acquired independency after 800. The name Chrovatoi was next assumed by the entire population.[81] A Turkish scholar also claimed that the first Croatian and Serbian polities were established by Türkic warriors from the Avarian kaganate and that they "initiated the process of the formation of the Croat nationality," like the Protobulgarians.[82] Another Türkic group subordinated to the Avars, the Kutrigurs, settled in Bosnia. It seems that their name was inherited by the Kotromanić dynasty, which descends from a family of rulers from the period of the Avarian domination. The name of this group was recorded in Herzegovina even in two fifteenth-century sources (Kuduger).[83]

In conclusion, the existence of a Türkic kernel around which Croatian ethnicity was formed could be accepted. Even so, this does not mean that the present Croatians are not Slavs and brothers of the Serbs. The Bulgarians inherited too the name of a Türkic people that was assimilated by the Slavs. As in Bulgaria, the non-Slavic warrior elite was assimilated, but at a slower pace, because the name "Croat" continued to be used only by a small number of noble families until the fifteenth century, while the common people were called Slavs (Slovjani).[84]

A possible Serbian reply to these theories is the idea that the Serbs came to their present homeland before the Croats, that is before the seventh century. Serbian archaeologist Djordje Janković tried to prove that the Serbs settled this territory as early as the fifth century and that they became Christians in the sixth century. It is not possible to make such clear-cut distinctions among the Slavs in the sixth century.[85] Even more fantastic, Stjepan Pantelić held that the Slavic homeland could be located in Dalmatia, and that the Illyrian tribe of Veneti recorded by the ancient sources between Pannonia and the Adriatic Sea was in fact Slavic. In his opinion, the Slavs departed to the north in the first century CE and returned to the primary homeland in the sixth century.[86] These fanciful ideas developed the theory expressed by Heinrich Kunstmann, who maintained that a part of the Slavs settled in the Balkan Peninsula in the sixth century returned to the north in Hungary, Slovakia, and Poland.[87]

Summing up, we can observe that Croatian historical propaganda is interested in emphasizing the non-Slavic heritage, while the Serbian one insists on an earlier presence in the present homeland. In both cases, ethnic identity is defined by early medieval facts that could bolster the interethnic conflicts.

THE VLACHS (AROMANIANS)

The Roman origin of the Aromanians was denied in order to justify the assimilationist policy of the Greek state as concerns this minority. Because it is obvious that the Vlachs or Aromanians speak a language of Latin origin, the idea that they are in fact Romanized Greeks was advanced. It seems that the first Greek author that put forward the idea of the descent of the Aromanians from some Romanized Greeks was Constantine Koumas (1777–1836), in *Historiai ton anthropinon praxeon* (The History of the Human Actions), Vienna, 1832.[88] Much earlier, Byzantine writers—who had no political interest in supporting the assimilation of the Aromanians by the Greeks—recognized that the Vlachs were a different people of Latin origin. Of course, their ideas reflected the level of the knowledge of that period, but they were generally right. For instance, Ioannes Kinnamos recorded around 1180 the tradition that the Vlachs descended from Roman colonists arrived from Italy. Even the common Greek people knew that the Aromanians were Roman colonists, as is evidenced in a document from 1221.[89] Laonicos Chalcocondyles (circa 1423–circa 1490) knew too the Roman origin of that Vlach people "which is spread from Dacia to Pindus and Thessaly."[90]

The idea of the Greek origin of the Aromanians continued to be put forth by many Greek historians and linguists during the nineteenth and twentieth centuries. The main works are those of M. Chrysochoos (*The Vlachs and the Koutzovlachs*, Athens, 1909) and A. Keramopoulos (*Who Are the Koutzovlachs*, Athens, 1939).[91] The ideas advanced by Keramopoulos were immediately rejected by Theodor Capidan, a distinguished Aromanian linguist, who showed their political reasons.[92] Keramopoulos claimed without valid proof that the forts attested to in Macedonia in the sixth century were garrisoned with Greeks and that these soldiers became shepherds after the breakdown of the military organization. They would be the ancestors of the Vlachs, whose name was derived by Keramopoulos from *fellah*—an idea that belongs to the prehistory of linguistic science. The same author believed that the name *armân* or *aromân* renders only the political meaning of the name Romanus (*cives Romanus*). In fact, *român/ aromân* has an ethnic significance, even if it comes from *Romanus*.

One of the greatest Greek historians of the twentieth century, Apostolos E. Vacalopoulos, accepted the theory of the Greek origin of the Vlachs, but he also agreed that some of them came from the Danubian area during the Slavic invasions.[93]

In the last decades, the Greek author Achilles Lazarou has published a book and several studies that recycle the old theory that the Vlachs are the inheritors of the ancient Romanized Greeks.[94] In his PhD dissertation, Lazarou developed the ideas previously expressed by Keramopoulos in a manner that seems to be convincing at first glance. He makes an accurate description of the Romanization process in Macedonia, but he does not say anything about the possibility that the Vlachs could descend from non-Greek ethnies like Thracians, Illyrians, or colonists who came from other provinces. Lazarou made a wide analysis of the Aromanian dialect (considered by him a distinct language from the Romanian and the Dalmatian), but this analysis was after a short time dismantled by linguist Matilda Caragiu-Marioțeanu, who showed that most of the Greek loan words of Aromanian are not ancient, but taken in modern times, as a result of the cohabitation of the two peoples.[95] Lazarou held that the name Armâni does not prove a relationship with the North-Danubian Romanians because it inherits the political name *Romani* evolved as *Romaioi* in the Byzantine period. This resumes the older point of view expressed by Keramopoulos and rejected by Capidan.

Lazarou's ideas have obvious political implications, because they could justify the official policy of present-day Greece, which does not recognize the existence of the Vlach minority. Being in his conception Greek, the Aromanians are not a real ethnic minority. The single good point of his book is the gathering of a large amount of data.

These Greek authors accepted the autochthonous origin of the Aromanians, but in order to prove their Greek origin and to separate them from the Romance family. The idea of autochthony was sustained with other purposes and other arguments by several authors of Aromanian origin: historians and linguists like Theodor Capidan, Neagu Djuvara, Cicerone Poghirc, Nicolae Saramandu, Nicolae-Șerban Tanașoca, and Matilda Caragiu-Marioțeanu. They brought consistent proof for the existence of a local Romance cradle in Macedonia and for the position of Aromanian in the Latin family: a dialect of the Romanian language, not a distinct language.[96]

The theory of Aromanian autochthony is not an instrument of political propaganda, since the Aromanians from Greece, the Former Yugoslavian Republic of Macedonia (FYROM), Serbia, Bulgaria, and Albania have no intention of creating their own state or organizing separatist actions. The single function of this theory is to defend the cultural identity of the Aromanian minorities living in these Balkan states.

Besides these scientific contributions, the idea of autochthony was sustained in some writings that have no relation with real historical science. They are, however, important for our research, because they display a naïve attempt to find a justification for the rights of the Aromanians over Macedonia. The first is the PhD. dissertation obtained with the qualification "très honorable" by Nicolae Caranica at the University of Besançon in 1990, under the direction of Pierre Lévêque (a reputable specialist in the history of ancient Greece). The author imagines an absurd theory of the Pelasgic origin of the Vlachs, under the inspiration of the fantastic ideas of Nicolae Densuşianu, a Romanian historian who published in 1913 a huge book that claimed that prehistoric Dacia was the hearth of the entire European civilization founded by the Pelasgians. In this view, the Aromanians would be the heirs of the oldest Europeans, who spoke in classical antiquity a so-called Proto-Latin language, the mother of the Indo-European languages.[97] It is unthinkable that such a text was accepted as a PhD dissertation. Similar ideas are held by a dilettante from FYROM, Branislav Stefanoski, in several works published in his country and in Romania. Electronics engineer, poet, painter, apiculturist, and historian, this author believes that the Aromanians are pure Thracians, the heirs of the ancient Macedonians, the oldest Balkan population. The "proof" relies on the same pretended "Proto-Latin" character of the Aromanian language, which is in his mind the mother of the Indo-European languages. The Aromanians were not Romanized and they kept over millennia the ancestral language. In another book, Stefanoski assumes the Pelasgian theory (perhaps under the influence of Caranica).[98]

The Greek dilettant of Aromanian origin Sokrates N. Liakos (a military topographer) has published at his own expenses several pamphlets that try to demonstrate that the Aromanians are the heirs of the ancient Macedonians, Romanized during the Roman domination. He relies on some fanciful etymologies that cannot be accepted. On the other hand, he proclaims that all the Romanians spread from Macedonia, including those from present-day Romania.[99] A similar point of view was supported by a Macedonian Slavophone historian, who believes that the Vlachs descend from the ancient Macedonians who retreated into the mountains after the arrival of the Slavs.[100]

In conclusion, we can see that, in the Balkan states, *theories about ethnogenesis were much more biased by political interests than in other European countries.* They were and still are *used as weapons of historical propaganda, because they could justify mastership over the disputed territories.*[101] The Albanians, Bulgarians, Greeks, and Aromanians insist on their continuity in those regions (Macedonia and Kosovo), while the Croats tried to legitimate the conflicts with the Serbs by the "discovery" of a different ethnic origin.

NOTES

1. See a presentation of the author and of his work in F. J. Frost, Fallmerayer Revisited, *Migrations 1989*, 109–114.

2. P. Charanis, The Formation of the Greek People, in S. Vryonis Jr. (ed.), *The "Past" in Medieval and Modern Greek Culture* (Byzantina kai Metabyzantina, I), Malibu, CA, 1978, 96.

3. See for this C. Carras, Greek Identity: A Long View, *Balkan Identities*, 315–319.

4. For Fallmerayer's theory and its political implications, see S. G. Xydis, Medieval Origins of Modern Greek Nationalism, BS, 9, 1 (1968), 3; G. Veloudis, Jakob Philipp Fallmerayer und die Entstehung der neugriechischen Historismus, SOF, 29, 1970, 43–90; J. V. A. Fine Jr., *The Early Medieval Balkans. A Critical Survey from the Sixth to the Late Twelfth Century*, Ann Arbor, MI, 1991, 59–64; V. Traikov, *Curente ideologice şi programe din mişcările de eliberare naţională din Balcani până în anul 1878*, Bucureşti, 1986, 247; B. G. Spiridonakis, *Grecs, ocidentaux et Turcs de 1054 à 1453, quatre siècles de relations internationals*, Thessalonique, 1990, 27–29; M. W. Weithmann, Interdisziplinäre diskrepanzen in der "Slavenfrage" Griechenlands, ZB, 30, 1 (1994), 85–86; F. Curta, Barbarians in Dark-Age Greece: Slavs or Avars? in Ts. Stepanov & V. Vachkova (eds.), *Civitas divino-humana. In honorem annorum LX Georgii Bakalov*, Sofia 2004, 513–514; F. Curta, L'administration Byzantine dans les Balkans pendant la "grande brèche": Le temoignage des sceaux. *Bizantinistica. Rivista di Studi Bizantini e Slavi*, serie seconda, 6 (2004), 157.

5. R. J. H. Jenkins, *Byzantium and Byzantinism*, University of Cincinnati, OH, 1963, 21–42.

6. P. Charanis, Observations on the Demography of the Byzantine Empire, in *Proceedings of the XIIIth International Congress of Byzantine Studies*, London–Oxford, 1967, 462; P. Charanis, Observations on the History of Greece during the Early Middle Ages, BS, 11, 1 (1970), 28–34; P. Charanis, On the Demography of Medieval Greece, a Problem Solved, BS, 20, 2 (1979), 216–218.

7. M. Vasmer, *Die Slaven in Griechenland*, Berlin, 1941.

8. G. G. Arnakis, Byzantium and Greece. A Review Article. A Propos of Romilly Jenkins, Byzantium and Byzantinism, BS, 4, 2 (1963), 396–397; Weithmann 1994a, 86.

9. See Charanis 1970, 27, footnote 96.

10. E. Gamillscheg, *Über die Herkunft der Rumänen*, Berlin, 1940.

11. Charanis 1970, 33–34; Charanis 1978, 93–97; J. Koder, Zur Frage der Slavischen Siedlungsgebiete im mittelalterlichen Griechenland, BZ, 71, 2 (1978), 315–331; M. Graebner, The Slavs in Byzantine Empire. Absorption, Semi-Autonomy and the Limits of Byzantinization, BB, 5 (1978), 48–54; Charanis 1979, 193–218; Weithmann 1994a, 91–93, 104; M. W. Weithmann, Politische und ethnische Veränderungen in Griechenland am Übergang von der Antike zum Frühmittelalter. *Die*

Kultur Griechenlands (1994), 24–26; J. Karayannopoulos, Zur Frage der Slavenan-siedlung im griechischen Raum, in A. Hohlweg (ed.), *Byzanz und seine Nachbarn* (Südost–Europa Jahrbuch, 26), München, 1996, 177–218.

12. A. E. Vacalopoulos, *Origins of the Greek Nation: The Byzantine Period, 1204–1461*, New Brunswick, NJ, 1970, 3–5; J. Herrin, Aspects of the Process of Hel-lenization in the Early Middle Ages, *The Annual of the British School of Archaeology at Athens*, 68 (1973), 120–126; M. Dunn, Evangelisation or Repentance? The Re-Christianisation of the Peloponnese in the Ninth and Tenth Centuries, in D. Baker (ed.), *Renaissance and Renewal in Christian History. Papers Read at the Fifteenth Sum-mer Meeting and the Sixteenth Winter Meeting of the Ecclesiastical History Society*, Ox-ford, 1977, 78–86; Graebner 1978, 50–51; Charanis 1978, 93–94; Fine 1991, 64.

13. M. Nystazopoulou–Pelekidou, *Les Slaves dans l'Empire Byzantin*, in *The 17th International Byzantine Congress. Major Papers*, New Rochelle, 1986, 360–361; G. L. Huxley, *Monemvasia and the Slavs: A Lecture on Some Works of Historical Geography in the Gennadius Library of the American School of Classical Studies at Athens*, Athens, 1988, 15; J. Koder, Anmerkungen zu graikóo, *Vyzantina*, 21, 2000, 199–202.

14. Charanis 1979, 218.

15. W. Bowden & R. Hodges, Balkan Ghosts? Nationalism and the Question of Rural Continuity in Albania, in N. Christie (ed.), *Landscapes of Change. Rural Evo-lutions in Late Antiquity and the Early Middle Ages*, Aldershot, 2004, 195–199.

16. M. Aref, *Albanie (Histoire et langue) ou l'incroyable odysée d'un peuple préhel-lenique*, Paris, 2003.

17. K. Giakoumis, Fourteenth-Century Albanian Migration and the 'Relative Autochthony' of the Albanians in Epeiros. The Case of Gjirokastër, BMGS, 27 (2003), 173, footnote 7.

18. See detailed presentations of the historiography at E. Çabej, Le problème du territoire de la formation de la langue Albanaise, AIESEEB, 10, 2 (1972), 71–82; H. Mihăescu, *La romanité dans le Sud-Est de l'Europe*, Bucureşti, 1993, 78–88; I. I. Russu, *Obârşia tracică a românilor şi albanezilor. Clarificări comparativ-istorice şi etnologice*, Cluj-Napoca, 1995, 21–36.

19. R. Elsie, Hydronimica Albanica—A Survey of River Names in Albania, ZB, 30, 1 (1994), 3.

20. Russu 1995, 27.

21. G. Weigand, Sind die Albaner die Nachkommen der Illyrer oder der Thraker?, *Balkan-Archiv* (Leipzig), 3 (1927), 227–251.

22. G. Schramm, *Anfänge des albanischen Christentums. Die frühe Bekehrung der Bessen und ihre langen Folgen*, Freiburg im Briesgau, 1994, 18–40; Russu 1995, 29–36.

23. E. Çabej, L'ancien nom national des Albanais, SA, 9, 1972, 1, 33–34; K. Bozhori, À propos de l'extension du nom Arbanon à l'époque Byzantine, CIEB XIV, vol. II (1975), 308; Mihăescu 1993, 68; N. Malcolm, *Kosovo. A Short History*, New York, 1999, 29.

24. M. Tadin, Les "Arbanitai" des chroniques Byzantines (XIe–XIIe s.), CIEB XV, vol. IV (1980), 315; Mihăescu 1993, 69; Russu 1995, 29; Malcolm 1999, 29.

25. As considers S. Anamali, Des Illyriens aux Albanais, AIESEEB, 10, 2 (1972), 109–111.

26. S. Anamali, The Illyrians and the Albanians, in *Kosova 1993*, 11.

27. Mihăescu 1993, 70–78; C. Poghirc, Romanisation linguistique et culturelle dans les Balkans. Survivances et evolution, *Les Aroumains,,* 36–39.

28. Mihăescu 1993, 66–68, 90.

29. C. Vătăşescu, *Vocabularul de origine latină din limba albaneză în comparaţie cu româna,* Bucureşti, 1997.

30. I. Popović, Slaven und Albaner in Albanien und Montenegro. Zum Problem der Slavisch–Albanischen Sprachchronologie, *Zeitschrift für Slavische Philologie,* 26 (1957–1958), 301–324.

31. See Çabej 1972, 91–92.

32. I. Popović, Byzantins, Slaves et autochtones dans les provinces de Prévalitaine et Nouvelle Epire, in *Villes et peuplement dans l'Illyricum protobyzantin. Actes du colloque organisé par l'École Française de Rome (Rome, 12–14 Mai 1982)* (Collection de l'École Française de Rome, 77), Rome, 1984, 226–227; I. Popović, L'Albanie pendant la Basse Antiquité, *Les Illyriens 1988,* 275–276.

33. Elsie 1994, 3–43.

34. See especially: S. Anamali, La nécropole de Krujë et la civilisation du haut moyen âge en Albanie du Nord, SA, 1 (1964), 149–181; Idem, Le problème de la civilisation haute-médiévale Albanaise à la lumière des nouvelles découvertes archéologiques, SA, 3, 1 (1966), 199–211; Idem, De la civilisation haute-médiévale Albanaise, in *Les Illyriens et la genèse des Albanais. Travaux de la session du 3–4 mars 1969,* Tirana, 1971, 183–189; S. Anamali & H. Spahiu, Une nécropole albanaise à Kruje, *Iliria,* 9–10 (1979–1980), 79–92; F. Tartari, Un cimetière du Haut Moyen Âge à Durrës, *Iliria,* 14, 1(1984), 227–250; H. Spahiu, Éléments de la tradition antique dans la culture des nécropoles du Haut Moyen Âge Albanais, *Iliria,* 16, 1 (1986), 268–269.

35. G. Stadtmüller, Forschungen zur Albanischen Frühgeschichte, AECO, 7, 1–3 (1941), 1–196; Anamali 1972, 127; W. Zeitler, Das lateinische Erbe im Albanischen und die älteren Wohnsitze der Albaner, ZB, 14 (1978), 205–206.

36. A. Ducellier, L'Arbanon et les Albanais au XIe siècle, TM, 3 (1968), 365–368.

37. Popović 1984, 214–244; Popović 1988, 251–283. Some doubts about the Proto-Albanian character of the Komani-Krujë culture were already expressed by J. Kovačević (Les Slaves et la population dans l'Illyricum, *Berichte 1973,* vol. 2, 151). Dj. Janković (*Scientific Discussion on Noel Malcolm's Book "äosovo. A Short History"* (London, Macmillan, 1998, 492). October 8, 1999, Institute of History of the Serbian Academy of Sciences and Arts [www.rastko.org.yu/kosovo/istorija/ malkolm/djankovic-facts.html], 1999) suggested that the culture was introduced by the people that came from Pannonia under the leadership of Kuver, taking into account the presumed relation with a treasure found at Vrap, in the area of the Komani-Krujë culture, ascribed by some researchers to this chief. The date and the significance of the treasure are still disputed, while the analogies with the artifacts from the Avarian cemeteries could be explained as a result of a common Byzantine influence.

38. Anamali 1993, 13–15.

39. A. Buda, Les Illyriens du sud, un problème d'historiographie, AIESEEB, 10 (1972), 2, 68.

40. E. Nallbani, Résurgence des traditions de l'Antiquité tardive dans les Balkans occidentaux: Étude des sépultures du nord de l'Albanie, *Hortus Artium*

Mediaevalium. Journal of the International Research Center for Late Antiquity and Middle Ages, 10 (2004), 25–42; Eadem, Transformations et continuité dand l'Ouest des Balkans: Le cas de la civilisation de Komani (VIe–IXe siècles), in *L'Illyrie méridionale et l'Épire dans l'Antiquité. IV. Actes du IVe Colloque international de Grenoble, 10–12 octobre 2002*, Paris, 2004, 481–490.

41. W. Bowden, The Construction of Identities in Post-Roman Albania, in L. Lavan & W. Bowden (eds.), *Theory and Practice in Late Antique Archaeology*, Leiden, 2003, 57–78 (quotation at 75); Bowden & Hodges 2004, 199–200.

42. See especially: Anamali 1972, 118–122; Çabej 1972, 85–99; S. Pollo & A. Puto, *The History of Albania from Its Origins to the Present Day*, London, 1981, 31; Çabej 1993, 22–24.

43. N. Jokl, Albaner, *Eberts Reallexikon für Vorgeschichte*, I (1924), 84–94; M. Gyóni, La transhumance des Valaques Balcaniques au Moyen Âge, ByzSl, 12 (1951), 41–42; P. Ivić, Balkan Slavic Migrations in the Light of South Slavic Dialectology, *Aspects 1972*, 70; C. Tagliavini, *Le origini delle lingue neolatine*, Bologna, 1972, 188–189; A. Rosetti, *Istoria limbii române, I. De la origini până la începutul secolului al XVII-lea. Ediție definitivă*, București, 1986, 197; H. Barić, Some Thoughts on the Early Habitat of the Albanians in the Balkan Peninsula, *Kosova 1993*, 31–32.

44. Çabej 1972, 80, 85–89; S. Pulaha, *L'autochtoneité des Albanais en Kosove et le prétendu exode des Serbes à la fin du XVIIe siècle*, Tirana, 1985, 13; N. Reiter, Alte Reikte in Balkansprachen, *Die Völker 1987*, 74; Mihăescu 1993, 86; Çabej 1993, 22–23.

45. I. I. Russu, Granița etnică între traci și illiri. Cercetări epigrafice și onomastice, *Anuarul Institutului de Studii Clasice* (Cluj-Sibiu) IV (1944), 73–147. See also Mihăescu 1993, 68.

46. F. Papazoglu, *The Central Balkan Tribes in Preroman Times*, Amsterdam, 1978, 195–200.

47. Gyóni 1951, 42; Ivić 1972, 70; Anamali 1993, 5–18 (especially 6–7); H. Islami, Anthropogeographic Research in Kosova. An Aperçu on the Work "Kosovo" by Academician Atanasije Urosevic, *Albanians 1985*, 486; Pulaha 1985, 10–15; Malcolm 1999, 39–40.

48. Gyóni 1951, 41; Z. Mirdita, A propos de la romanisation des Dardaniens, SA, 9 (1972), 2, 287–298.

49. Z. Mirdita, On the Problem of the Romanization of the Dardanians, in *Albanians 1985*, 179–194.

50. A. Philippide, *Originea românilor*, vol. II. *Ce spun limbile română și albaneză*, Iași, 1927, 761–802.

51. Schramm 1994, 121–169. The theory was already expressed in G. Schramm, *Anfänge des albanischen Christentums. Die frühe Bekehrung der Bessen und ihre langen Folgen*, Freiburg im Briesgau, 1986, 115–122. Criticisms were expressed by C. Vătășescu, Les débuts de la christianisation des Albanais. A propos du livre de Gottfried Schramm . . . , RESEE, 33 (1995), 3–4, 315–321; G. Hoxha, book review in *Iliria*, 23, 1–2 (1998), 328–333; Malcolm 1999, 35–38.

52. K. T. Witczak, Were the Bessans Ancestors of the Albanians? A New Opinion on the Ethnogenesis of the Albanian Nation, *Thraco-Dacica*, 16 (1995), 309–312.

53. A. J. B. Wace & M. S. Thompson, *The Nomads of the Balkans. An Account of Life and Customs among the Vlachs of Northern Pindus*, London, 1914, 267.

54. I. I. Russu, *Elementele traco-getice în Imperiul Roman şi în Byzantium (veacurile III–VII). Contribuţie la istoria şi romanizarea tracilor.* Bucureşti, 1976, 161–162.

55. Vătăşescu 1997, 496–497.

56. G. Schramm, *Ein Damm bricht. Die römische Donaugrenze und die Invasionen des 5.–7. Jahrhunderts im Lichte von Namen und Wörtern*, München, 1997, 344–362. See also E. Banfi, Cristianizzazione nei Balcani e formazione della lega linguistica Balcanica, ZB, 23, 1 (1987), 7.

57. Mihăescu 1993, 46.

58. Schramm 1986, 104–125.

59. Vătăşescu 1997.

60. V. Georgiev, Sur l'éthnogenèse des peuples Balkaniques. Le Dace, l'Albanais et le Roumain, *Studii clasice*, 3 (1961), 23–37; Idem, The Genesis of the Balkan Peoples, SEER, 44 (1966), 103, 285–297.

61. Russu 1995.

62. G. Ivănescu, *Istoria limbii române*, Iaşi, 1980, 58–59.

63. Popović 1984, 231; Popović 1988, 279.

64. S. P. Kyriakides, *The Northern Ethnological Boundaries of Hellenism*, Thessaloniki, 1955, 13–15; N. Ş. Tanaşoca, O problemă controversată de istorie Balcanică, participarea românilor la restaurarea ţaratului Bulgar, *Răscoala 1989*, 159, footnote 13.

65. V. Georgiev, *Die Träger der kretisch-mykenischen Kultur, ihre Herkunft und ihre Sprache*, Sofia, 1937. See also N. Andriotes, *The Language and the Greek Origin of the Ancient Macedonians*, Thessaloniki, 1978, 18.

66. For the political manipulation of medieval history in Communist Bulgaria, see M. Pundeff, Nationalism and Communism in Bulgaria, SOF, 29 (1970), 161–162.

67. Kyriakides 1955, 14; Russu 1976, 90–91.

68. B. I. Bojović, Historiographie dynastique et idéologie politique en Serbie au Bas Moyen Âge. Essai de synthèse de l'idéologie de l'Etat médiéval Serbe, SOF, 51 (1992), 44, footnote 56.

69. In *Il regno degli Slavi*, 1601. According to a forgery used by Orbini, Alexander the Great had some relations with the Slavs. This text was invoked by B. Vishinski, The Gratitude of Alexander the Great to the Slavs, *Macedonian Review* (Skopje), 21, 3 (1991), 127–130, as proof of the Slavic origin of the ancient Macedonians.

70. R. Lauer, Genese und Funktion des Illyrischen Ideologems in den südslawischen Literaturen (16. bis Anfang des 19. Jahrhunderts), in K.-D. Grothusen (ed.), *Ethnogenese und Staatsbildung in Südosteuropa*, Göttingen, 1974, 116–143; Traikov 1986, 162–168; A. Stipcević, *The Question of Illyrian-Albanian Continuity and Its Political Topicality Today* (www.alb-net.com/illyrians.htm); N. Malcolm, *Storia di Bosnia dalle origini ai giorni nostril*, Milano, 2000, 28.

71. S. Guldescu, *History of Medieval Croatia*, The Hague, 1964, 317–320.

72. This was the reason why the journal *Südost–Deutsche Forschungen* (the future *Südost Forschungen*) was founded at München in 1936. The indisputable scientific value of this periodical does not exclude its primary political aim, to support the Balkan policy of the Nazi regime. Another similar review was *Deutsche Forschung im Südosten* (issued in 1942). A. Pippidi, Changes of Emphasis, Greek Christendom, Westernization, South-Eastern Europe, and Neo-Mittel Europa,

Balkanologie, 3, 2 (1999), 103, remarked too the relationship between this use of the term *south-east* and the idea of the German vital space.

73. Malcolm 2000, 28–29.

74. The link between the names Hrvati and Harahvati was proposed by S. Sakać, Iranische Herkunft des kroatischen Volksnamen, *Orientalia Christiana Periodica*, 15 (1949), 313–340. A similar hypothesis was held by G. Vernadsky, The Origin of the Name Rus', SOF, 15 (1956, 171 (from the Iranian word *xvarva*, "sun"). For the theory of the Iranian origin, see also Guldescu 1964, 33–42; O. Karatay, Ogur Connection in the Croatian and Serbian Migrations, in G. H. Celâl, C. C. Oguz, & O. Karatay (eds.). *The Turks*, vol. 1, Ankara, 2002, 554.

75. H. Grégoire, L'origine et le nom des Croates et des Serbes, *Byzantion*, 17 (1945), 91–116.

76. V. Popović, Koubrat, Kouber et Asparouch, *Starinar* (Belgrade) , 37, 1986, 127–128; W. Pohl, *Die Awaren. Ein Steppenvolk in Mitteleuropa, 567-822 n. Chr,.* München, 1988, 261–268.

77. P. J. Geary, *The Myth of Nations: The Medieval Origins of Europe*, Princeton, NJ, 2002, 36, 148, 171.

78. Z. Golab, *The Origins of the Slavs. A Linguist's View*, Columbus, 1991, 324–327.

79. Malcolm 2000, 30–31.

80. R. Katičić, Die Anfänge des Kroatischen states, in H. Friesinger & F. Daim, *Die Bayern und ihre Nachbarn*, I (DAW, 179), Wien, 1985, 309 considered improbable the Iranian origin of the Croats.

81. O. Kronsteiner, Gab es unter den Alpenslawen eine Kroatische ethnische Gruppe?, WSJ, 24 (1978), 137–157; W. Pohl, Das Awarenreich und die "Kroatischen" Ethnogenesen, in H. Friesinger & F. Daim (eds.), *Die Bayern und ihre Nachbarn*, I (DAW, 179, 1985), 293–298. The theory was also accepted by Geary 2002, 148, but denied by A. Tietze, Kroaten ein türkisches Ethnonym?, WSJ, 25 (1979), 140.

82. Karatay 2002, 557–560.

83. Karatay 2002, 559–560; O. Karatay, Contribution to the Debates on the Origin of the Medieval Bosnian Royal Dynasty Kotromanids, in *Eran und Aneran. Webfestschrift Marshak. Studies presented to Boris Ilich Marshak on the Occasion of His 70th Birthday.* Electronic Version, Buenos Aires (www.transoxiana.org/Eran/Articles/karatay.pdf), 2003, 6, 13–15.

84. J. V. A. Fine Jr., 2000, 208–218.

85. D. Janković, Pogreb Srba u ranom srednijem veku, in *Works of the VIth International Congress of Slavic Archaeology*, vol. 1: *Problems of Slavic Archaeology*, Moscow 1997, 382–393; D. Janković, *Srpske gromile*, Belgrade, 1998; Dj. Janković, *The Serbian Questions in the Balkans*, Faculty of Geography, Belgrade (www.rastko.org.yu/arheologija/djankovic-serbs_balkans.htm), 1995; Janković 1999.

86. S. Pantelić, Die neue Version der Migration der Kroaten, Duleben und Wolinjanen, in *Works of the VIth International Congress of Slavic Archaeology*, vol. 3: *Ethnogenesis and Ethnocultural Contacts of the Slavs*, Moscow, 1997, 242–250.

87. H. Kunstmann, *Die Slawen: Ihre Name, ihre Wanderung nach Europa und die Anfänge der russischen Geschichte in historisch–onomastischer Sicht*, Stuttgart, 1996

and previous papers published especially in the journal *Die Welt der Slawen* (München).

88. Vacalopoulos 1970, 13; A. Lazarou, *L'Aroumain et ses rapports avec le Grec*, Thessalonique, 1986, 103.

89. P. Ş. Năsturel, Les Valaques Balkaniques aux Xe–XIIIe siècles (Mouvements de population et colonisation dans la Romanie Grecque et Latine), BF, 7 (1979), 94–95, 97, 102–105.

90. E. Stănescu, Byzance et les Pays Roumains aux IXe–XVe siècles, CIEB XIV, vol. I, 429.

91. T. J. Winnifrith, *The Vlachs, the History of a Balkan People*, London, 1987, 42.

92. Th. Capidan, *L'origine des Macédo-Roumains. Réponse à M. le professeur Kéramopoulos de l'Académie d'Athènes*, Bucarest, 1939. A. Keramopoulos continued to support this theory in other works, published between 1945 and 1953.

93. Vacalopoulos 1970, 13–14.

94. Lazarou 1986.

95. M. Caragiu-Marioţeanu, À propos de la latinité de l'aroumain (à la lumière des dernières recherches), *Revue Roumaine de Linguistique*, 33, 4 (1988), 237–250.

96. See chapter 1, footnote 76.

97. N. Caranica, *Les Aroumains, recherche sur l'identité d'une ethnie*, Besançon, 1990.

98. B. C. Stefanoski, *Limba traco-dacă, fundul a limbilor indo-europene*, Casa Gramosta, Tetova, 1993; Idem, *Geneza limbii armâne-macedonene*, ed. Mirton, Timifloara, 1995; Idem, *Pelasghyi. Limbâ, carte, numâ*, Casa Gramosta, Tetova, 1998.

99. S. N. Liakos, *L'origine des Albanais et Roumains. Complement (Daco-geto-sclavinica)*, Thessaloniki, 1972. Other pamphlets are: "The Origin of the Aromanians" (1965), "The Thraco–Dacian Origin of the Albanians" (1973), and "The Illyrian Origin of the ancient Macedonians" (1980).

100. Panov 2001, 31.

101. See an overview at H. Guillorel & P. Michels, Continuité territoriale, continuité nationale: L'exemple Yougoslave, *Balkanologie*, 1, 1 (1997), 95–118.

Chapter 5

The Legitimation of Expansionism by the Abuse of History

Romanian historian Victor Papacostea emphasized that Balkan historiographies became instruments of legitimization for the political and military expansion of those states.[1] Of course, this does not concern the entire production of Balkan historians. There are enough earnest and nonbiased works, but even those could be used by propagandists as highly efficient weapons.

The irredentism and autonomist claims are often based on alleged historical rights, in most cases taken from ancient and medieval history. One of the best specialists in the Ottoman period of Balkan history (of Balkan origin himself, but living in the United States) remarks that:

> governments and peoples, particularly intellectuals [from the Balkan countries], have based their attitudes and actions on what happened, or what they believe to have happened centuries ago. The reason is that during the almost five centuries of Turkish rule the Balkan peoples had no history. . . . This obsession with the past has its ludicrous aspects. Alexander the Great is claimed by the Greeks as a Macedonian Greek. He is also claimed by the Albanians, who issued coins bearing his image. And he is claimed by the Bulgarians, who exhorted their armies in World War I "to revive the fame of the great Bulgarian, Alexander the Great." More serious have been the political repercussions of this living in the past. Peaceful inter-Balkan relations were scarcely likely in this face of simultaneous attempts to revive the medieval Greek, Bulgarian and Serbian empires. Thus historical tradition has been an

important factor, and usually a disturbing factor, in Balkan affairs in the modern period.

The same author shows how Serbia claims the frontiers of the empire of Stephen Dušan, while Bulgaria expresses similar pretensions on the basis of the maximal extent of the medieval state ruled by Symeon. In order to be better understood by a Western reader, he closes these remarks with a suggestive comparison: "one must imagine a British statesman citing the empire of Edward III as justification for claiming half of modern France."[2] The meaning of this example is that *the conquests made by medieval kingdoms cannot justify the territorial claims of the modern states.* At the same time, this reveals the differences between Western and Balkan mentalities. Only in the Balkans is medieval history still used as an instrument for contemporary policy, in the international and interethnic disputes for Kosovo, Bosnia, and Macedonia.

KOSOVO—SERBIAN OR ALBANIAN?

Kosovo is a tableland with an altitude of 300–500 m and a surface of 10.887 km^2, located between the Šar Mountains (south), Southern Morava (east), Kopaonik Mountains (north), and the Prokletije Mountains (west). In fact, the region usually called Kosovo is composed of two zones: the real Kosovo and Metohija (named after the numerous medieval monastery estates, called *metoh*). Metohija (the western part) is mainly agricultural, while Kosovo (the eastern part) has important mineral resources (silver, lead, coal) that have been exploited since the Middle Ages. The Albanian name of the Metohija plain is Dukagjini. By its position at the crossroads of the Ibar, Binačka Morava, and Vardar valleys, Kosovo has an obvious strategic importance.[3]

Serbian or Albanian rights over Kosovo were and continue to be argued on the basis of ancient and medieval history. The Serbs claim the indisputable value of their cultural heritage in Kosovo,[4] while the Albanians say they lived there before the settlement of the Slavs in the Balkan Peninsula and, anyway, before the conquest of Kosovo by Serbia. Therefore, the dispute concerns the ethnogenesis of the Albanians and the land settled by them in the period of the Slavic migrations. The still open issue of the Albanian origin is thus a propagandistic weapon used by both parties. Some scientific works dealing with this issue are undoubtedly unbiased, but others were produced under political command or under special circumstances that influenced their objectivity. The best example is the study by renowned Yugoslavian historian and archaeologist Vladislav Popović about late ancient Albania,[5] which brings valuable proof against the theory of the Albanian origin of the Komani-Krujë culture, a dogma of Albanian historiography. The study itself is serious, but we should remark that it appeared in 1988 in a collection of papers from a session organized in 1986 by the Serbian Academy of Sciences and Arts. The ultimate purpose of that session was to reject the Albanian propaganda and Albanian points of view about Kosovo. In the introduction of the volume, the deputy president of the Serbian Academy, A. Isaković, states that Yugoslavian historians should bring the study of the Albanian ethnogenesis back into the real scientific framework, because it was biased by the lack of objectivity of Albanian historians. Moreover, he affirms that a sustained campaign against Yugoslavia is carried on in Albania, remembering "the well-known events from Kosovo."[6]

The papers presented at this session had indeed a high scientific level, but the conference was organized with a political target, when the interethnic conflict of Kosovo was already fired up by the riots that occurred in 1981 at Prishtina. The Yugoslavian historians were thus determined to find various arguments against the Albanian claims on Kosovo. One of these arguments was the rejection of Albanian autochthony in Kosovo. They denied the Illyrian origin of the Dardanians and the Illyrian origin of the Albanians. The great Serbian archaeologist Milutin Garašanin, who drew up the conclusions of the above-mentioned session, affirmed that the Albanians have no historical rights in Kosovo.[7] He claims in his paper that the Dardanians were Thracians, although in his previous studies he accepted the theory of the Illyrian origin of this tribe.[8] The problem of the ethnic origin of the Albanians and of their continuity in Kosovo was discussed even at the Congress of the Serbian Communist Party in June 1982, when the speakers said that the theory of the Illyrian origin of the Albanian people is racist.

Croatian historian Aleksander Stipcević remarks that:

> In fact, the theory of Albanian autochthony has never been disputed with such determination and savagery as today, precisely when so much scientific proof has been produced in its support. Nevertheless, the number of researchers still today refusing to take into consideration the many arguments supplied by different academic disciplines has shrunk, or, more accurately, absolutely the only researchers who deny the theory of Albanian autochthony are Serbian. Serbian archaeologists and historians began long ago to dispute the autochthony theory, but this opposition increased especially after the great Albanian revolt in Kosova in 1981. It was therefore a consequence of a political event rather than of new scientific data. . . . The Serbs vigorously attacked the idea that the Dardanians were ethnically Illyrian. Not because they were led to this conclusion by scientific evidence, but purely because Kosova was "the cradle of Serbian history" and "holy soil" for the Serbs, and as such could not have been inhabited by a people that

were of Illyrian stock and hence claimed by their descendants, the Albanians.
. . . No Serbian researcher can freely express his opinion over the Illyrian-
Albanian question without exposing himself to the danger of charges of high
treason.[9]

The opposition against the Albanian autochthony led to some unthinkable exaggerations. A Serbian archaeologist tried to demonstrate that the
Albanians came from Caucasus in the seventh century. (There is indeed a
people called Albanoi attested to in Caucasus, but there is no proof for
such migration). He also claims that:

> Metohija and Kosovo, as well as the areas farther to the east and south, were
> integrated into the Serb lands not later than the seventh century. It is possi-
> ble that there lived other Slavs or autochthonous population, but this has not
> been supported by convincing evidence. The Field of Kosovo attracted the
> Serbs by its situation at a divide, its fitness for cattle-breeding, for summer
> settlements and agriculture. . . . Owing to natural and geographical circum-
> stances, this area, situated south-east of Serb lands, became the core of the
> Serb state.[10]

Yugoslavian historians fulfilled an intensive propaganda campaign in
order to convince the Western public of their rights. For instance, the massive volume entitled *Le Kosovo-Metohija dans l'histoire Serbe* (published at
Lausanne in 1990) presents the historical rights of Yugoslavia in Kosovo
with the aid of several well-informed and convincing studies that cover
the entire history of the region from the early Middle Ages to the 1980s,
emphasizing the permanence of the Serbs in Kosovo and the lack of historical rights of the Albanians over this region. During the Kosovo war,
Yugoslavian historians succeeded in publishing a very impressive catalog
of archaeological discoveries from Kosovo, dated from Neolithic times to
the Middle Ages.[11] The work indeed has scientific value, but it also has an
obvious propagandistic purpose because it shows the antiquity and
brightness of the Slavic civilization created in Kosovo.

The medieval history of Serbia is widely presented on the Internet. Several websites were dedicated to this subject during the Kosovo crisis and
after (for instance: www.kosovo.com, www.decani.yunet.com, www
.srpska-mreza.com/Kosovo). Some of them contain the texts of monographs written by Western scholars who embraced the Serbian point of
view. Among these works is Hugo Roth's *Kosovo Origins*, first printed by
"Nikola Pasić" Publishing House, Belgrade, 1996—an impartial description of the problems of the history of this region, from the origin of the
Albanians to the 1980s. These websites created in Yugoslavia or by the
Serbian diaspora give various data on the history of Kosovo, emphasizing
its glorious Middle Ages.

On the other side, Albanian historians and linguists tried to give full support to the Kosovar autonomy. During the Communist period and after, they tried to prove the autochthony of the Albanians in Kosovo (the Roman province Dardania) by linguistic and archaeological evidence. The dogma of the Illyrian origin of the Albanian people clearly has this purpose.

In 1985 the volume *The Albanians and Their Territories* was published at Tirana (there is also a German version, *Die Albaner und ihre Gebiete*). The studies were written especially by Albanian historians and linguists, but there is also a piece by Alain Ducellier, "Have the Albanians Occupied Kosova?" With his prestige as a great Byzantinist, French historian Ducellier gave great support to the viewpoints expressed by Albanian historiography. He is the author of many important studies on Albania during the eleventh–fourteenth centuries, published since the 1960s. As concerns the Kosovo problem, Ducellier upholds the rights of the Albanian population, on the basis of its autochthony and because the Albanians became a majority again during the Ottoman domination.[12]

Another collection of studies, documents, and newspaper articles entitled *The Truth on Kosova* was edited by the Institute of History of the Albanian Academy of Sciences in 1989 in Albanian and next in English, in 1993.[13] Its target was to reply to another volume, published in Belgrade in 1989, *Kosovo—Past and Present* (the original version of the volume was published in Lausanne in 1990). Among the authors who contributed to the Albanian miscellany are noted scholars like Skënder Anamali, Eqrem Çabej, and Alain Ducellier. In the final part of the volume are various texts from the 1980s concerning political attitudes supporting the autonomy of Kosovo (including an interview with Ibrahim Rugova).

This mixture of science and politics is typical for how the propaganda was understood at Tirana during the Communist regime and also after its fall. On the contrary, the volume published in Belgrade in 1988 by the Serbian Academy does not remember the present situation of Kosovo, except some brief instances in the foreword and in the conclusion. However, we should note that the historical and linguistic studies included in the volume published at Tirana in 1989 and 1993 brought important contributions to the knowledge of the medieval history of Kosovo. They are not propaganda texts, but scientific works that can be used for propagandistic purposes.

The Albanian emigration from Western Europe and the United States crossed over the opposition against the Communist regime of Albania, being involved in the propaganda for Kosovo, just after the revolts in Prishtina in 1981. The Albanian community from New York organized in November 1982 a symposium dedicated to the problem of the Kosovar Albanians; its papers were published in 1984. At the symposium Albanian specialists from the diaspora took part, as did French, German and American historians. The volume begins with a study by well-known Byzantinist and Albanologist (and Albanophile) Alain Ducellier, which explains why Albanians failed to found a powerful state in the Middle Ages; he also emphasizes the Albanian presence in Kosovo.[14] The editors (Arshi Pipa and Sami Repishti) have prophetically shown that Kosovo is "an intricate ethnic problem, which, due to its magnitude and explosive potential, may provoke serious troubles in the Balkans, thus destabilizing the *status quo* in Europe."[15] The book analyzes both the past and the present, with the purpose of legitimating the collective rights of the Albanians in Kosovo through their history. The situation of Kosovo in the Yugoslavian federation is presented from political, demographical, and economic points of view. Although the result of a scientific meeting, the volume has a clear propagandistic message, addressed to possible groups of influence able to support the autonomy or the secession of Kosovo. Among the other studies included in the book, we remember: Anton Logoreci, A Clash between Two Nationalities in Kosova (185–194), Peter Bartl, Kosovo and Macedonia as Reflected in Ecclesiastical Reports (23–40), and Hartmut Albert, Kosovo 1979, Albania 1980 (103–121). In the same year the monograph of an Albanian author who explained for the public at large the evolution of Serbian–Albanian relations in Kosovo and the theory of Albanian autochthony in Kosovo was published in New York. The book has now an online version.[16]

A scientific journal entitled *The International Journal of Albanian Studies* was founded in 1997 by a group of Albanian historians led by Shinasi A. Rama from Columbia University, New York. The journal has published studies of modern and contemporary history, but also some contributions to medieval history, like that of Selami Pulaha, On the Autochthony of Albanians in Kosova and the Postulated Massive Serb Migration at the End of the XVIIth Century, (number 2, 1998, 1), which supports the continuity of the Albanians in Kosovo from antiquity to the beginning of modern times (it is the translation of the study published at Tirana in 1985).

The Internet is also used for Albanian claims. An important website with rich data on the history of the Albanians from Kosovo, Macedonia, and Montenegro is www.albanian.com. For instance, the already quoted study of A. Ducellier about Kosovo is presented on this site.

The Serbs are not autochthonous in Kosovo, because the Slavs as a whole are not a genuine Balkan population. It is likewise true that the Albanians reached a majority in Kosovo during the Ottoman domination because they benefited from that regime. We can also remark that nobody in this quarrel speaks about the Aromanians, although this population was recorded by Serbian deeds since the first years of the Serbian domination in Kosovo. Even the family of Balšić (Balsha) seems to be of Vlach origin. Kosovo became part of Serbia only in the thirteenth century, when—it is true—it became the political and spiritual center of the state, until the end of the fourteenth century. Serbia conquered Kosovo as part of its imperial policy. This province acquired a symbolic place in the Serbian and Yu-goslavian national mythologies[17] for several reasons: in Kosovo ruled the great emperor Stephen Dušan, in Kosovo were built the most important Serbian religious monuments, and finally in Kosovo took place the heroic battle against the Ottomans in 1389. For the Serbs, as observes a Serbian Canadian scholar:

> a romantic, idealized vision of that medieval state was often proposed as a paradigm for the future in the popular discourses of politics, scholarship and literature. Among the Serbs and their neighbors this invocation of the past as a justification for present and future rights and options, the coupling of history with contemporary issues, not only durably influenced debates about choices to be made today and tomorrow, but also clouded the critical examination of historical facts.[18]

In the Serbian political conscience, Kosovo and Macedonia are still designated as Stara Srbija ("The Old Serbia"), a name that was used without justification even in some Yugoslavian scientific works.[19] Kosovo is a kind of Holy Land of the Serbs. As is remarked in a recent analysis of the development of the Serbian ethnic identity, "at the moment when Kosovo stopped being the factual homeland of Serbian people (when the Turks came), it became their mythic homeland."[20] However, somebody observed that the battle of 1389 from Kosovopolje that fueled the Serbian victimization myth was not the battle of the Serbs for the salvation of the Christian world, as is often stated, because in the confrontation fought a regional coalition that included, besides the Serbian prince Lazar Hrebel-janović, the Bosnian king Tvrtko and the Albanian rulers George II Balšić (Balsha) and Theodore II Muzaka (the latter lost four thousand men on the battlefield).[21] Therefore, Kosovo was defended both by Serbs and by Albanians.

In fact, medieval history does not allow us to decide who now has more rights in Kosovo: the Albanians, the Serbs, or maybe the Aromanians? This is the historical reality. But reality can be manipulated according to the interests of each party involved, because each can find useful and valid arguments for its point of view, Serbian or Albanian. The use and abuse of medieval history is not able to resolve the interethnic conflict of Kosovo.

THE HISTORICAL MACEDONIA—THE APPLE OF DISCORD AMONG GREECE, BULGARIA, AND SERBIA

The troubled history of Macedonia makes difficult even the definition of the limits of this region. In classical antiquity, Macedonia was located between Lychnidis (Ochrid) Lake and the Strymon (Struma) River. The early Roman province Macedonia was more extended, because it included the northern zone called Paeonia. In the Byzantine period, the name Macedonia was applied to a province (*theme*) that was nearly the same with ancient Macedonia (see p. 53).

The western parts of the present state Former Yugoslavian Republic of Macedonia (FYROM) did not belong to Roman and Byzantine Macedonia. Skopje was included in the late Roman province Dardania, and in the Byzantine period was the center of the *theme* of Bulgaria. Yet, a Greek author sustained that this region between the Axios (Vardar) River and Pindus could be called Western Macedonia, for the Byzantine period.[22] On the other hand, the FYROM (with its area of 25,713 km²) does not includes the southern and northeastern old Macedonia, owned now by Greece (34,602.5 km²) and Bulgaria (6,789.2 km²). The historical propaganda makes use of this ambiguous significance of the name Macedonia, which can be applied to the present northern Greece, but also to the state officially entitled "The Former Yugoslavian Republic of Macedonia."[23]

The position of Macedonia is the ultimate cause of the confrontations between Greeks, Bulgarians, and Serbs. Located in the center of the Balkan space at a major crossroad, Macedonia is desired by all the neighbors, and for this reason is highly vulnerable.

As a Greek historian has remarked about Macedonia:

> located on the convergent point of four conflicting national programs—Greek, Bulgarian, Serbian and Albanian—it provided a microcosm of Balkan complexities. Its geographical delimitation was uncertain and, at best, arbitrary; its ethnological composition ambiguous; and its historical legacies open to controversial and conflicting interpretations.[24]

A great contemporary Greek historian considers that Macedonia was along history and especially in the Middle Ages "a bulwark of Hellenism, assailed by successive waves of invaders from the north."[25] It is indeed true that Macedonia was since the fifth century BCE a part of the Greek world by its culture, but its ethnic configuration was not purely Greek. Macedonia was located at the crossroads between three ethnic families: Thracians, Illyrians, and Greeks. The ancient Macedonians spoke their own language. This language was used by Alexander the Great with his soldiers.[26] If some historians still consider the ancient Macedonians to be a branch of the Hellenic people, others accept that they were a distinct ethnicity, not Greek, but also different from the Thracians and the Illyrians. According to I. I. Russu, the Macedonians belonged to a group of central Balkan populations that also included the Epirots, the Dardanians, and the Paeones. Because the Dardanians were perhaps an intermediary group between Thracians and Illyrians, it can be theorized that the Macedonians occupied a median position among the three great ethnic groups (Thracians, Illyrians, Greeks).[27] The existence of a distinct Macedonian ethnicity in classical times seems to be clearly established now by the research of American archaeologist Eugene Borza, former professor at Pennsylvania State University.[28]

The claims of Yugoslavia and Bulgaria over Macedonia in its entirety were based on the argument that each of these states mastered Macedonia in different periods of the Middle Ages. Both countries emphasize the cultural side of their presence in Macedonia (the glorious age of Stephen Dušan for the Serbs, St. Clement of Ochrid for the Bulgarians). However, the remote domination of Serbia or Bulgaria over Macedonia was not enough to legitimate the expansionist ambitions of the modern states. Thus other historical arguments that are more effective because they are founded on ethnic principles were put forward.

Medieval Serbia mastered Macedonia only in a later period and for a short time (between 1282—the conquest of Skopje—and 1371—the battle of Cernomen). Before the Serbian conquest, Macedonia belonged to the Byzantine Empire, to Bulgaria, and again to the Byzantine Empire. During the Byzantine domination the Bulgarian population continued to live there, but together with Greeks, Aromanians, and later also with Albanians. The Serbs came there in the aftermath of the conquests of Stephen Dušan. Finally, the entry of Macedonia under the Ottoman domination caused new ethnic changes because of the colonizations of the Anatolian Turks and by the conversion to Islamism of some Albanians and Serbs. Macedonia was always heterogeneous, and no population had an absolute majority. It is impossible to separate the Greek territory from the Slavic territory in medieval Macedonia. Moreover, the intricate ethnic composition made uncertain the ethnic affiliation of some persons. Expressions like *Bulgaroalbanitovlachos* or *Serbalbanitobulgarovlachos* applied to Macedonian inhabitants indicate mixed marriages, but also unclear distinction between ethnies.[29] The present linguistic frontier between the FYROM and Greece was established after the changes of populations that occurred after the Balkan Wars. Now, the word *Macedonian* should be understood only as a geographical term. Macedonians are all the inhabitants of this region, regardless of their ethnic origin (Greeks, Bulgarians, Albanians, Serbs, Aromanians, Gypsies, Turks, Jews, Armenians).[30]

One of the most striking cases of manipulation of medieval history in the service of politics is the "Slavic Macedonian nation." Although this book does not deal with the contemporary history of the Balkan Peninsula, it is necessary to discuss the events that led to the imagination of the so-called Macedonian nation and to its endowment with a millenary history.

The idea of the Macedonian nation aims for the legitimation of the Yugoslavian claims over the Macedonian territories possessed by Greece and Bulgaria. The conquest of the Greek part of Macedonia was first planned by Yugoslavian prime minister Milan Stoiadinović. In 1937–1938, he declared to the Italian minister of foreign affairs Galeazzo Ciano that the "vital space" of Yugoslavia extended up to the Aegean Sea and included Thessaloniki. Later, the Cvetković cabinet, which joined the Axis on March 18, 1941, obtained the agreement of Germany for this expansion in the framework of the "New European Order," but its demise on March 27, 1941 thwarted this plan.[31] Instead, Germany gave a free hand to Bulgaria in April 1941 to occupy Macedonia east of the Strymon River. In this territory started a process of Bulgarization that provoked the reaction of the Greek resistance movement. In the summer of 1943, Bulgaria tried to extend its domination over all of Macedonia, but the Communist Yugoslavian forces started at the same time their advance in Macedonia. On August 2, 1943, the Central Committee of the Macedonian Communist Party was created at Prespa. The Yugoslavian Communists tried to strengthen their positions by attracting the population from southwestern Bulgaria (the Pirin region). Already in October 1943 it was declared that this region should be included in a Great Macedonia together with northern Greece. The Antifascist Council for National Liberation recognized the Macedonian nation on November 29, 1943. The People's Republic of Macedonia was proclaimed on August 2, 1944, during a meeting at the monastery Prohor Pcinjski (very significant for the need of a medieval justification for the existence of this state). It was a new state, built on a territory that was not before an official distinct entity within Serbia. It is obvious that the new state was a kind of magnet for the nearby territories from Bulgaria and Greece.[32]

In August 1944 the Antifascist Council of National Liberation of Macedonia decided to create an Institute for National History (it would be established in 1948).[33] The antifascist war was not yet finished, but the Yugoslavian Communist leaders were already searching for ideological weapons for the future fight for supremacy in the Balkan Peninsula. The Yugoslavian leaders, foremost of whom was Tito, claimed Greek Macedonia, stimulating the separatist movement of the Macedonian Slavophones. In a speech given in Skopje on October 11, 1945, Tito declared that:

> We will never renounce the right of the Macedonian people to be united. This is our principle and we do not abandon our principles for any temporary sympathies. We are not indifferent to the fate of our brothers in Aegean

Macedonia [the part included in Greece] and our thoughts are with them. We will steadfastly defend the principle that all Macedonians must be united in their own country.[34]

The events of 1943–1945 represented in fact the implementation in another way of an older dream of the Bulgarian Communists of the interwar period. The Comintern projected the constitution of a Communist Balkan Federation under the hegemony of Bulgaria, which would include Macedonia after its separation from the nationalist and bourgeois Yugoslavia (Bulgarian Communist Gheorghi Dimitrov had an important role in the Comintern). The Bulgarian Communists acted for the achievement of the older irredentist plans of Bulgaria. The Internal Macedonian Revolutionary Organization founded in 1893 to fight for the unification of Macedonia with Bulgaria launched terrorist actions before and after the Balkan wars of 1912–1913. In 1924 an agreement between this nationalist organization and the Comintern was achieved.[35] Even the Greek Communist Party, at the indications of dispatches from Moscow, recognized in 1934 the existence of the Macedonian Slavic nation, a fact that was contrary to Greek national interests.[36]

Therefore, the so-called Macedonian nation was a political creation that resulted from these Communist plans for the organization of a Balkan Communist Federation under Soviet hegemony. Tito undertook the idea of an autonomous Macedonia as an instrument for his own intentions for the hegemony of Belgrade in the Balkans (a Communist confederation of the Balkan Slavs). All these facts are quite similar with the place given by the Soviet Union and by the Comintern to the Soviet Autonomous Moldavian Republic, established in 1924 at Tiraspol, with the target of the separation of Bessarabia from Romania. In 1940, its administration was extended over the territory taken from Romania by the Soviets. From the very beginning, an entire ideology of Moldavian identity was imagined at Tiraspol, of a so-called Moldavian people speaking a Moldavian language, different than the Romanian language. In fact, there is no Moldavian language. In 1944, the People's Republic of Macedonia had for Belgrade the same function that the Soviet Autonomous Moldavian Republic had for Moscow between 1924 and 1940.

After the occupation of Bulgaria by the Soviet army negotiations between Tito and the Bulgarian Communist leaders were organized (in September–October 1944), which sought the inclusion of Bulgaria in the Yugoslavian federation. The plan failed because it was contrary to Soviet, American, and British interests. Yugoslavia continued its southward expansionist policy with involvement in the Greek civil war of 1945–1946. The target was the unification of the entire historical Macedonia with the republic created in 1944. Even before the civil war, the Liberation Front of the Macedonian Slavic Nation entered into conflict with the Greek Army of National Liberation in the summer and autumn of 1944. The failure of the Communist rebellion in Greece put an end to this attempt. Yet, Yugoslavia dared to ask at the Paris Peace Conference (September 6th, 1946) for the unification of Macedonia (the annexation of Greek Macedonia).[37] Bulgaria accepted giving cultural autonomy to the population from Pirin, recognizing the Macedonian identity requested by Belgrade. At the census of February 1947, most of the population from Pirin declared themselves to be Macedonian, aware of the advantages given by this status of autonomy. After Tito's dissidence, Bulgaria abandoned this policy. The idea of a Macedonian people became thus undesirable in Bulgaria.[38]

A new Slavic language called Macedonian was invented and proclaimed official within the Yugoslavian federation in 1944. This language was unknown before to linguists. In fact, this language is a western Bulgarian dialect.

The authorities of the former Socialist Republic of Macedonia began to build an entire theory of a distinct Slavic Macedonian people, different from the Serbs and the Bulgarians, but closer to the Serbs in traditions, language, and history. The first form of this theory appeared in the 1850s, under the influence of the Panslavism promoted by the Russian Empire, when some Macedonian Slavs issued the idea that they belonged to a distinct Slavic ethnicity, different than the Bulgarians', being purely Slavic and, on the other hand, distinct from the descendants of the Macedonians of Alexander the Great. One of them, George Pulevski, published in Belgrade two Macedonian dictionaries. After the liberation of Bulgaria (1878), he moved to Sofia, where he continued to sustain the Macedonian identity. This identity was not accepted by the national Bulgarian ideology for any great length of time. In 1903, the authorities forbade a book about the Macedonian identity and the existence of a Macedonian Slavic language.[39] When most of Macedonia entered Serbia after World War I, this region was subjected to a forceful colonization with Serbs. The idea of a Macedonian language was no more officially sustained, yet nor was it banned.[40] The propagandistic name that was assigned Macedonia and Kosovo was Old Serbia, labeled by Jovan Cvijic in a work on the ethnography of Macedonia published in 1907.[41]

After 1944, historians and linguists from Skopje wrote a different history of this region, in order to fit with the official position, which said that the ethnogenesis of the Macedonian Slavs began in the seventh–eighth centuries, when the first Slavic tribes arrived.[42] The early presence of the Aromanians in the region was denied in order to ensure the earlier presence of the Slavs in the region. It was affirmed that they arrived from Albania, together with the Albanians.[43] On the other hand, it was argued that the Slavs settled in Macedonia in the seventh century (or perhaps even since 586) were from the very beginning a distinct Slavic group. This is the purpose of a study published by Vladislav Popović in 1980, which ends so:

> The Slavs from Macedonia and Greece were the first who obtained the autonomy from the Avars. From a historical point of view, it is important to acknowledge that these successive stages of Slavization are the origin of the ethnic differences between the present Balkan peoples, among whom the Macedonian Slavs have a distinct place.[44]

The Slavs from Macedonia had developed their own political forms of organization since the early Middle Ages, but this process was interrupted by the Byzantine reconquest in the ninth century and soon by the Bulgarian one. Yet, some Slavo-Macedonian and Serbian historians believe that a new Macedonian state was created in 976 (or even in 969). This theory holds that the establishment of Samuel's capital at Ochrid signified the creation of a new state, other than the Bulgarian one that was defeated by John Tzimiskes in 971. This state is also seen as the superior stage of the organizational forms of the Macedonian Slavs, first appearing in the seventh century. The Old Slavonic language used by Saints Cyril and Methodius was proclaimed "the Old Macedonian language." All these reinterpretations of history made in the Communist period were maintained after 1990.[45]

The historical sources do not support such interpretations. Samuel and his heirs Gabriel Radomir and John Vladislav were Bulgarian tzars and nothing else. Samuel was not called Macedonian in the Byzantine sources. The Bulgarian tzardom that had capitals at Skopje and Ochrid was not a national state of a Macedonian people. The upheaval of local rulers from Macedonia against Byzantine power aimed for the restoration of Bulgaria to its former frontiers, which included much more territory than Macedonia. The center of this new state was in western Macedonia because this area was easier to defend. A well-balanced position is expressed instead by Serbian author Stoian Pribichevich in his presentation of Macedonian history. He agrees that the title "Tzar of the Bulgarians" held by Samuel expressed claims over all the territories peopled by Bulgarians, but also that Samuel relied on the Macedonian Slavs.[46]

Other authors express fantastic ideas about the descent of the Macedonian Slavs from the ancient Macedonians in propaganda publications of the diaspora, as well in the FYROM.[47] It is postulated that the ancient Macedonians, different than the Greeks, survived during the Roman occupation until their assimilation by the Slavs who arrived in the sixth or seventh century[48] (this is not true, because the name Macedonians was used in the ancient sources only with a geographical meaning). Much more strange are the ideas that Alexander the Great spoke a language from which descended the present Slavic Macedonian language.[49] The Pelasgian obsession is also present in these discussions of the origins of the Macedonians. One author claims that the Slavs have been autochthonous in the Balkan Peninsula since the Neolithic Age, and that they are in fact the Pelasgians, the creators of the oldest European writing. He calls upon as proof the so-called Isenbeck inscriptions on wooden material edited by A. A. Kur and J. Mirolubov (San Francisco, 1954–1959), which are most probably faked.[50]

The fanciful interpretation of some Neolithic signs made by Macedonian dilettante Vasil Ilyov led him to the conclusion that

> the Macedonians (who bear their name continually at least 5,500 years), but many other people . . . not only were they present on the Balkan spaces in prehistory as the so-called pre Slav people but they also argumentedly appear as descendants of the oldest people on these first civilisation centres and are with an alphabet, language and mythology much older than the so-called Vedic or Proto-Vedic people.[51]

His ideas were undertaken by another Macedonian author, Risto Stefov. In a work published on the Internet in 2003, he wrote that

> "the language of the Pelasgian and other Macedonian tribes, like the Payonian, Piertian, Brygian or Phrygian, Venets or Enets, etc., is in fact the language of the ancient Macedonians which dates back to prehistoric times." He also supported the idea that the present Macedonians (the Slavophones) are the direct descendants of Alexander the Great's people ("the Slav language was most probably spoken by Alexander's Macedonian soldiers and settlers and was spread throughout the vastness of the uncivilized regions of Eastern Europe and Northern Asia").[52]

Medieval history was intensively used by the authorities from Skopje in order to support the building of the new state. In October 1958 the old archbishopric of Ochrid was restored. On July 17th, 1967, the Yugoslavian state authorities declared the autocephaly of the Macedonian Orthodox Church, despite the opposition of the Serbian and Bulgarian patriarchates. The Bulgarian Church was disturbed by the confiscation of the Bulgarian spiritual center created by St. Clement at the end of the ninth century.[53] The restoration of the autocephalous archbishopric of Ochrid at the initiative of a Communist state is one of the most striking examples of manipulation of medieval history by contemporary policy. In this way was clearly affirmed the continuity with the medieval archbishopric of Ochrid founded by Samuel and recognized by Basil II. By this act, the Communist leader Tito applied a Byzantine imperial prerogative. It is interesting that the same idea of the restoration of the archbishopric of Ochrid was used one century before to legitimate Bulgarian claims over Macedonia. In 1870, the Ottoman Empire allowed the creation of a Bulgarian Church separated from the patriarchate of Constantinople (the so-called Bulgarian exarchate), that covered all the territories peopled by Bulgarians. This exarchate, considered a revival of the old archbishopric of Ochrid, was a major support for the Bulgarian national movement and at the same time a threat for Greece and Serbia, because its area included Macedonia. It was, on the other hand, a good instrument of Russian Panslavism, a way to prepare a future expansion of the Russian empire in the Balkans.[54]

In 1969, at the twenty-fifth anniversary of the Macedonian Yugoslav Republic, it was decided to publish a collection of studies (issued in 1970),[55] which presented the image of the history of this state in the historiographies of Slavic and Western countries, as well in the states for which Macedonia remained an open issue (Greece and Bulgaria). Besides the obvious interest of this survey in the research carried on in the USSR, Poland, Czechoslovakia, Bulgaria, or Greece, this volume displays the effort of building a millenary history for an artificial state. The Bulgarian and Greek works were considered constantly tendentious.[56] According to the authors, Bulgarian historiography justified the oppressive policy of Bulgaria in Macedonia, during the bourgeois regime as well as in the Communist period, except a short period between 1944 and 1948, when the policy of the Bulgarian Communist Party required the presentation of the history of Macedonia in an "internationalist" manner. The schism that occurred between Tito and the rest of the Communist leaders in 1948 led to new anti-Serbian attitudes in Bulgarian historiography and propaganda. The productions of Greek historiography were strongly criticized (in that period, the relationships between Yugoslavian Macedonia and Greece were very bad because the latter had a regime considered fascist by the Communist propaganda).

Another volume that included scientific studies about various aspects of Macedonian history, dedicated to the anniversary of the Socialist Macedonia, was published in Skopje in 1970.[57] The studies are written by competent specialists, but it is nevertheless true that the publication of this volume had propagandistic purposes. The presentation of some highlights from Macedonian history was used to illustrate the idea that this region was always a distinct entity in the Balkan Slavic world, since the seventh century.

At another level of propaganda, focused on the Western public, the Secretariat for Information of the Executive Council of the Assembly of the Socialist Republic of Macedonia published in 1969 a collection of articles about the history of Macedonia, from the Middle Ages to the present, in

English and French. The texts emphasized the continuous fight for Macedonia ethnic identity. The editors wrote in the preface that:

> The events of the last few years show that the embers of the fire still glow, that even the most minute oscillations in international politics are capable of activating afresh the well-known aspirations towards Macedonia. This is so in spite of the fact that the Macedonian nation is a member of the Yugoslav Federation, having rights equal to those of the other members. . . . It is not difficult to imagine that, within the framework of the aspirations of the neighboring Balkan states, one of their undertakings—one upon which a great deal of care and attention has been bestowed—was the attempt to take over the past of the Macedonian people, to falsify their history, to dispute the independence of their language and to underrate their cultural heritage.[58]

On the occasion of the thirtieth anniversary of the Institute for National History from Skopje (1948–1978) another volume was written, printed in 1981. The book includes translations of several studies published in the previous decades in local journals. Most of them are honest research, although the volume itself had a propagandistic purpose (the historical legitimation of the existence of the Socialist Republic of Macedonia). One could point out in this respect the two studies dedicated to Ottoman Macedonia, written by Aleksandar Stojanovski (a leading scholar in the field) and by M. Sokolovski. There are still other texts that could illustrate the wrong way of writing history. For instance, Branko Panov[59] tried to demonstrate that the Macedonian people was formed in the sixth–ninth centuries in the area occupied by the Slavs at the end of the sixth century, and that their ethnogenesis was accomplished by the creation of the state of Samuel and by the emergence of the feudal relations. The entire study is full of bizarre interpretations that show that the author wished to provide proofs for a preconceived theory.

More subtle, Stjepan Antoljak argued that local aristocrats from Macedonia rebelled first against Bulgaria in 969, and only in 976 against the Byzantine Empire.[60] In this view, the unrest meant the affirmation of the independence of the Macedonian people against the Bulgarian power center from Preslav. Indeed, some historians supposed that the presence of Bulgarian envoys at the court of German emperor Otto I at Quedlinburg in the spring of 973 could be explained by the survival of a Bulgarian state in Macedonia,[61] but there are also other possible locations of this Bulgarian power center, for instance near Sirmium, a city conquered by the Byzantine Empire only in 1018.[62] Considering the inconsistency of the available data, the existence of a primary upheaval in 969 is denied by most historians.[63] It is otherwise true that Bulgarian Macedonia was not occupied by the Byzantine army in 971, which meant that the rebellion of 976 had a good opportunity to develop, and we can even admit that the breakdown of the central power in 968–969 was the incentive for this event. Therefore, it cannot be excluded that an autonomous polity was formed as early as 969, and that this polity started the fight for liberation after the death of John Tzimiskes. The local Bulgarian aristocracy was inclined to autonomist trends and it could be theorized that the state restored after the mutiny was not centralized.[64] However, the rebellion of the local Macedonian aristocrats cannot be interpreted as an affirmation of a Macedonian ethnic identity, different from the Bulgarian ethnicity. The context in which this theory was resumed in the volume published in 1981 suggests that it became an instrument for the legitimation of Macedonian particularism in relationships with Bulgaria.

We can add that the volume published at Skopje in 1981 opened with the speech of the president of the presidium of the Socialist Republic of Macedonia, Vidoe Milevski. The Yugoslavian statesman emphasized the importance of the institute for the study of the history of the Macedonian people from the most ancient times to the present, and the attention paid by the Communist Party to this institute, since its foundation, according to the decision taken in August 1944.

The Slavo-Macedonian propaganda acted at the level of the larger public by spreading maps of Great Macedonia that included northern Greece. The diaspora is also very active. There are several publications and organizations all over the world, from Germany to the United States and Australia, that have fought since the 1960s for the creation of the Great Macedonia that should include territories from Greece and Bulgaria. The organization "Matitsa," from the Socialist Republic of Macedonia, which established links with the diaspora, has also contributed to the spread of the historical theories imagined at Skopje.[65] Now these ideas are available on the Internet. One of the most important sites is www.historyofmacedonia.org, which has a section entitled "Evidence of 2,500 years long existence of the Macedonian Nation."

For contemporary Greece, the outside Macedonia is a very sensitive issue. Greek historians were and continue to be preoccupied by the "Macedonian problem." Officially, there is no Slavic national minority in Greece, but only an ethnic group speaking a Slavic language. Macedonia always had a first rank position in the national ideology of modern Greece, because it was the most endangered province.

A short time after the creation of the Popular Republic of Macedonia, the Society for Macedonian Studies from Thessaloniki (established in 1939) organized a propagandistic and historical conference, given by S. P. Kyriakides in October 1945. The text was later published and translated into English in 1955, as a volume in a series edited by the Institute for Balkan Studies, founded first as a branch of this association.[66] The work is valuable, because it presents objectively the essential data of Macedonian history. However, the propagandistic purpose is too obvious. Kyriakides's work was a reaction to the exaggerations made by Bulgarian and Serbian historians, being at the same time an expression of Greek claims over all of Macedonia, occasioned by the creation of the Yugoslavian republic.

One of the purposes of the Institute for Balkan Studies from Thessaloniki is to counteract Slavo-Macedonian propaganda by thorough and intensive scientific activity. Besides a series of monographs with various subjects, the Institute for Balkan Studies from Thessaloniki has continued to publish since 1960 the prestigious scientific journal *Balkan Studies*. Since its first years, the journal has published studies that concern the Macedonian problem. In the first number, linguist N. P. Andriotes wrote some dense pages about the history of the name Macedonia, in order to repel the usurpation of this name by the Slavs.[67] Other studies have presented the circumstances of the creation of the People's Republic of Macedonia and the targets of Yugoslavian policy in 1944–1948. Some of the studies dedicated to the Macedonian problem were reprinted in a collection edited by the same institute in 1992 (when the dispute increased after the proclamation of the independence of Macedonia). In the preface, Basil Kondis (the director of the Institute for Balkan Studies) observed that it is necessary to react to the systematic falsification of Macedonian history carried on at Skopje.[68]

The fact that Greece succeeded in making official the bizarre name "Former Yugoslavian Republic of Macedonia" after the proclamation of the independence of this state in January 1991 shows how sensitive this issue is for Greek policy and public opinion. Ancient and medieval history had in this case a strong impact over international relations. For Greece, the name Macedonia could be only a part of the Hellenic historical and cultural heritage, a name that could not be usurped by the Slavs (and this is correct).[69]

The research on the medieval history of Macedonia conducted by Greek authors emphasizes the pure Greek or Byzantine character of the name Macedonia, in order to counteract the claims of the republic from Skopje. Sometimes, they wrote propagandistic works that criticized the points of view expressed by historians from Skopje. For instance, Byzantinist Maria Nystazopoulou-Pelekidou from Ioannina University, author of some studies about the Slavs in Greece, has also published a leaflet about the Macedonian question, in Greek and English.[70] Scientific meetings were organized with the participation of prominent scholars, for instance at Melbourne (July 1995), about "Byzantine Macedonia." The volume that was later printed includes some valuable studies about the history of Macedonia in the sixth–fourteenth centuries and about the position of this province in the framework of the Byzantine Empire. Besides some Greek historians such as Angeliki Laiou, Alkmene Stavridou-Zafraka, and

Martha Grigoriou-Ioannidou, at this conference German, British, American, and Australian Byzantinists took part.[71] The papers contributed to a better knowledge of the military and administrative organization of Byzantine Macedonia and of its economic and cultural history. The end of one of these studies is illustrative for the present conceptions of Greek historiography:

> In the light of the above, when talking today about contemporary Macedonians it would be unhistorical to ignore this Byzantine tradition and to seek to connect them directly with antiquity. The Macedonians of today are the successors of the Macedonians of Byzantium.[72]

At the vulgarization level, a book by Nikolaos Martis presents the "falsification of Macedonian history." The author (lawyer and politician, former head of the Ministry for Northern Greece and born in Macedonia) has dedicated the book to the "Macedonian president of the Hellenic Republic, Constantinos Caramanlis."[73] The political message of the entire book is obvious. The author presents the place of ancient Macedonia in Greek history and civilization, insisting that the Slavs are newcomers in Macedonia. He points out the various exaggerations of Serbian and Bulgarian historians, such as the Bulgarian state restored by Samuel was a "national" Macedonian tzardom. Martis denounces the irredentism manifested since the 1970s by the Socialist Republic of Macedonia toward northern Greece, a policy based on faked historical arguments, namely on the fiction of the so-called Macedonian nation.

When Anastasia Karakasidou (Politicizing Culture: Negating Ethnic Identity in Greek Macedonia, *Journal of Modern Greek Studies*, 11, 1 [1993], 1–28) held that Slavophones from northern Greece are subjected to forced assimilation by the Greek state and that they are a specific Slavic Macedonian ethnicity, the reply came very soon. The fact coincided with the claims of the authorities from Skopje for the name Macedonia. In the same year, her assertions were fiercely denied in a long and well-informed study published in *Balkan Studies*,[74] which shows that Karakasidou has abandoned any scientific objectivity, becoming a supporter of the interests of a certain political conception, and that she ignores many historical facts. The promptness of this reply shows how much importance is given to historical arguments in the dispute for Macedonia. Anastasia Karakasidou maintains the iconoclast opinion in the volume *Fields of Wheat, Hills of Blood: Passages to Nationhood in Greek Macedonia, 1870–1990* (Chicago, 1997), that appeared only after difficult fights with the Greek diaspora from the United States.

The propagandistic war is also conducted on the Internet. For instance, the site www.real.macedonia.gr counteracts the falsification of Macedonian history by Macedonian Slavs, with many data provided by medieval history. Another site, www.macedonian-heritage.gr, includes, besides news about recent events, electronic versions of some studies on Macedonian history and on the "Greek struggle in Macedonia in the twentieth century."

The Hellenic character of Alexander the Great's Macedonia has an important place in Greek propaganda. The discovery of the luxurious royal graves from Vergina (the capital of the ancient Macedonian kingdom) in 1977 and in the following years provided spectacular proof that stimulated the national pride of the Greeks.[75] A volume edited by M. B. Sakellariou illustrates the four millennia continuity of Hellenism in Macedonia,[76] which is, however, a propagandistic exaggeration (but not so great as the absurd ideas of the descent of the Bulgarian or Macedonian Slavs from the Macedonians of Alexander the Great).

Bulgaria was also disturbed by the usurpation of Macedonian history by authorities from Skopje. In this case one could observe how the attitude toward Macedonia evolved according to the relationships between the Communist countries. The policy promoted between 1944 and 1948 by Bulgarian leader Gheorghi Dimitrov led to the toleration and even stimulation of the cultural autonomy of Bulgarian Macedonia (Pirin). Later, the dissidence of Tito caused a new rivalry between Bulgaria and Yugoslavia that especially concerned Macedonia. Since the 1960s, the Communist regime from Sofia developed a nationalist policy that sought legitimation in the medieval past and even in ancient history (see the previous chapter). In this context, Macedonia became in the official theory a part of the territory where the Bulgarian people were born (this is only partially true). As in Greece, Bulgaria did not express open territorial claims over Yugoslavian Macedonia after 1944, but it has affirmed historical rights by an increasing number of studies on the Macedonian past.[77] Bulgaria recognized after a short time the independence of the FYROM (on September 8th, 1991), but not the existence of a distinct Macedonian nation.[78]

Of course, the Bulgarians are right when they affirm the Bulgarian character of the state organized by Samuel in Macedonia, but this truth is used to support the ideology of Great Bulgaria, as well as the period of the maximal extension of this state during the reign of Symeon. On the other hand, some Bulgarian historians and linguists tried to demonstrate that the Slavic place-names from Greece are in fact Bulgarian and that they prove the extension of the Bulgarian population up to Peloponnesus. The fallacy of this theory was demonstrated by Greek linguist Phaedon Malingoudis, who showed that the Slavs settled in Greece in the seventh century evolved distinct from the ancestors of the Bulgarians, being finally assimilated by the Greeks.[79]

The official theory about the area of the Bulgarian ethnogenesis is presented, for instance, in a book written by Dimiter Angelov, a leader of

Communist Bulgarian historiography (also translated in the former East Germany). He affirms that Macedonia was one of the three heart zones of the Bulgarians, together with Moesia and Thrace. The synthesis between the Proto-Bulgarians and the Slavs was achieved in each of these zones. The participation of the Greek and Roman populations at the formation of the Bulgarian people is not mentioned, but it is emphasized that the annexation of Macedonia by Boris accomplished the unification of the Bulgarian ethnogenesis area, and that the missionary activity of St. Clement of Ochrid gave to Macedonia a very important place in the history of medieval Bulgaria.[80] In this way, as in Serbian propaganda, Macedonia received a symbolic central position in Bulgarian history, although from the geographical point of view this region is marginal.

NOTES

1. V. Papacostea, La Péninsule Balkanique et le problème des études compares, *Balcania*, 6 (1943), XI.

2. L. S. Stavrianos, *The Balkans since 1453*, New York, 1959, 13–15. See also the similar remarks of another Greek historian, specializing in contemporary history: E. Kofos, National Heritage and National Identity in Nineteenth– and Twentieth–Century Macedonia, *European History Quarterly*, 19, 2 (1989), 229.

3. B. I. Bojović, Le passé des territoires, Kosovo-Metohija (XIe–XVIIe siècle), BS, 38, 1 (1997), 31; S. Ćirković, Le Kosovo-Metohija au Moyen Âge, *Kosovo 1990*, 22; N. Malcolm, *Kosovo. A Short History*, New York, 1999, 1–10.

4. Especially the monasteries and churches from Peć (1250), Gračanica (1321), and Dečani (1327).

5. V. Popović, L'Albanie pendant la Basse Antiquité, *Les Illyriens 1988*, 251–283 (a slightly changed form of V. Popović, Byzantins, Slaves et autochtones dans les provinces de Prévalitaine et Nouvelle Epire, in *Villes et peuplement dans l'Illyricum protobyzantin. Actes du colloque organisé par l'École Française de Rome [Rome, 12–14 Mai 1982]* (Collection de l'École Française de Rome, 77), Rome, 1984).

6. A. Isaković, in *Les Illyriens 1988*, 7–8.

7. M. Garašanin, in *Les Illyriens 1988*, 369–375.

8. A. Stipcević, *The Question of Illyrian-Albanian Continuity and Its Political Topicality Today* (www.alb-net.com/illyrians.htm).

9. Stipcević. This author has published several volumes about the Illyrians, among them *The Illyrians, History and Culture*, New Jersey, 1977.

10. Dj. Janković, *Scientific Discussion on Noel Malcolm's Book "Kosovo. A Short History" (Macmillan, London 1998, 492)*, October 8th, 1999, Institute of History of the Serbian Academy of Sciences and Arts (www.rastko.org.yu/kosovo/istorija/malkolm/djankovic-facts.html), 1999.

11. *The Archaeological Treasures of Kosovo and Metohija from Neolithic to the Early Middle Ages*, Belgrad, 1998.

12. A. Ducellier, Have the Albanians Occupied Kosova? *Kosova 1993*, 63–68.

13. *Kosova 1993.*

14. A. Ducellier, Genesis and Failure of the Albanian State in the Fourteenth and Fifteenth Century, in A. Pipa & S. Repishti (eds.), *Studies on Kosova*, Boulder, New York, 1984, 3–22.

15. *Studies on Kosova*, ed. by A. Pipa & S. Repishti, Boulder, New York, 1984, V.

16. S. S. Juka, *The Albanians in Yugoslavia in Light of Historical Documents*, New York (online version at www.alb-net.com/juka2.htm), 1984.

17. For the Kosovo myth, see M. Bakić-Hayden, National Memory as Narrative Memory. The Case of Kosovo, *Balkan Identities*, 25–40.

18. M. V. Dimić, *Who Is a Serb? Internal Definitions and External Designations*, www.kakanien.ac.at/beitr/fallstudie/MDimic1.pdf, 9 (revised edition of the paper published in E. Waugh & M. V. Dimić [eds.], *Diaspora Serbs: A Cultural Analysis*, Edmonton, Alberta, 2004).

19. H. Islami, Anthropogeographic Research in Kosova. An Aperçu on the Work "Kosovo" by Academician Atanasije Urosevic, *Albanians 1985*, 477–484.

20. D. Gavrilović, Elements of Ethnic Identification of the Serbs, *Facta Universitatis. Series: Philosophy, Sociology and Psychology* (Niš), 10, 2 (2003), 725–727.

21. A. Doja, Formation nationale et nationalisme dans l'aire de peuplement albanais, *Balkanologie* (Paris), 3, 2 (1999), 37.

22. N. Nerantzi-Varmazi, Western Macedonia in the Twelfth and Thirteenth Centuries, *Byzantine Macedonia*, 2000, 192.

23. The political fight around the name of this state is presented in the collection of studies *Athens–Skopje: An Uneasy Symbiosis, 1995–2002*, Athens, 2003. A good overview of the Macedonian problem at J. Engström, The Power of Perception: The Impact of the Macedonian Question on Inter-Ethnic Relations in the Republic of Macedonia, *The Global Review of Ethnopolitics*, 1, 3 (2002), 3–17.

24. Kofos 1989, 230.

25. A. E. Vacalopoulos, *History of Macedonia, 1354–1833*, Thessaloniki, 1973, 5.

26. Plutarch, *Alexandros*, LI.

27. I. I. Russu, Macedonica. Osservazioni sulla lingua e l'etnografia degli antichi Macedoni, *Ephemeris Dacoromana*, 8 (1938), 105–232. See also I. I. Russu, Granița etnică între traci și illiri. Cercetări epigrafice și onomastice, *Anuarul Institutului de Studii Clasice* (Cluj-Sibiu), IV (1944), 79–95.

28. See for instance his paper *Who Were (and Are) the Macedonians?*, presented at the 1996 Annual Meeting of the American Philological Association (www.makedonika.org/ borza.htm).

29. Dj. S. Radojičić, "Bulgaroalbanitoblahos" et "Serbalbanitobulgaroblahos"— deux caractéristiques ethniques du Sud-Est européen du XIVe et XVe siècle. Nicodim de Tismana et Grégoire Camblak, *Romanoslavica*, 13 (1966), 77–79; P. Ş. Năsturel, Les Valaques Balkaniques aux Xe–XIIIe siècles (Mouvements de population et colonisation dans la Romanie Grecque et Latine), BF, 7 (1979), 111.

30. N. K. Martis, *The Falsification of Macedonian History*, Athens, 1984, 86; E. Kofos, The Macedonian Question: The Politics of Mutation, BS, 27, 1 (1986), 170.

31. E. Kofos, *Nationalism and Communism in Macedonia, Civil Conflict, Politics of Mutation, National Identity*, Thessaloniki, 1964, 95–97.

32. E. Kofos, The Making of Yugoslavia's People's Republic of Macedonia, BS, 3, 2 (1962), 379–389; Kofos 1964, 97–153; S. Pribichevich, *Macedonia. Its People and*

History, Philadelphia: Pennsylvania State University Press, 1982, 150–151; Martis 1984, 83–84; Kofos 1986, 152–154; B. Kondis, The Macedonian Question as a Balkan Problem in the 1940's, BS, 28, 1 (1987), 153–154; I. Stefanidis, *Macedonia in the 1940s*, in I. Hassiotis & I. Koliopoulos (eds.), *Modern and Contemporary Macedonia*, II, Thessaloniki, 1992, 104–137.

33. M. Apostolski, in *Macédoine 1981*, 6.

34. Kofos 1962, 393; Pribichevich 1982, 154.

35. Pribichevich 1982, 120–122, 139–140.

36. Kofos 1964, 25, 66–89; Kofos 1989, 243.

37. Kofos 1962, 391–394; Kofos 1964, 154–187; Kofos 1986, 155–157; Kondis 1987, 155–156; S. Sfetas, Autonomist Movements of the Slavophones in 1944: The Attitude of the Communist Party of Greece and the Protection of the Greek–Yugoslav Border, BS, 36, 2 (1995), 297–317.

38. Kofos 1962, 389–391; Kofos 1964, 189–191; Pribichevich 1982, 153; Martis 1984, 84; Kondis 1987, 157.

39. Pribichevich 1982, 112–113.

40. Kofos 1964, 46–47; Pribichevich 1982, 115; Kofos 1989, 239–242.

41. See P. Stephenson, The Byzantine Frontier in Macedonia, *Dialogos. Hellenic Studies Review*, 7 (2000), 31–32 for the political consequences of Cvijic's work.

42. For instance: D. Taškovski, *The Macedonian Nation*, Skopje, 1976; B. Panov, Toward the Ethnogenesis of the Macedonian People, *Macédoine 1981*, 37–47.

43. J. Trifunovski, Die Aromunen in Mazedonien, *Balcanica*, 2 (1971), 337–347.

44. V. Popović, Aux origines de la Slavisation des Balkans: La constitution des premières Sklavinies Macédoniennes vers la fin du VIe siècle, *Académie des Inscriptions et Belles-Lettres. Comptes Rendus des séances de l'année 1980s, 1* (Paris) (Janvier–Mars), 1980, 257.

45. The criticism of this theory at Kofos 1986, 159; Kofos 1989, 239–245; M. Nystazopoulou–Pelekidou, *The "Macedonian Question," a Historical Review*, Corfu (electronic version: www.hri.org/docs/macque), 1992, chapter "The 'Macedonian Question': The Question and the Position of Skopje."

46. Pribichevich 1982, 87.

47. Kofos 1989, 260–261 and footnote 64.

48. Panov 2001, 28–31.

49. D. M. Perry, Crisis in the Making? Macedonia and Its Neighbors, *Südost–Europa. Zeitschrift für Gegenwartsforschung*, 43, 1–2 (1994), 41–42.

50. R. Peschich, On the Scent of Slavic Autochthony in the Balkans, *Macedonian Review* (Skopje), 19, 2–3 (1989), 115–119 (also in *Zavicaj. Casopis Matice Iseljenika Srbije*, 36 [May–August 1989], 344–347).

51. V. Ilyov, *Macedonian Artifacts, Ancient Inscriptions and Their Translations* (www.unet. com. mk/ancient–macedonians–part2/index.html).

52. R. Stefov, *History of the Macedonian People from Ancient Times to the Present* (www.maknews.com/html/articles/stefov), 2003, Part 1, Part 15.

53. C. Papastathis, L'autocéphalie de l'Église de la Macédoine Yugoslave, BS, 7, 1 (1968), 151–154; S. Dimevski, The Archbishopric of Ohrid, in *From the Past of the Macedonian People*, Skopje, 1969, 71–72; M. Pundeff, Nationalism and Communism in Bulgaria, SOF, 29 (1970), 165; Martis 1984, 83, 91; Kofos 1986, 160; Kofos 1989, 245.

54. Kofos 1964, 13–16; Dimevski 1969, 69–70; Pribichevich 1982, 114; V. Traikov, *Curente ideologice şi programe din mişcările de eliberare naţională din Balcani până în anul 1878*, Bucureşti, 1986, 335–337; Kofos 1989, 238; Engström 2002, 5.

55. *The Foreign and Yugoslav Historiography of Macedonia and the Macedonian People*, Skopje: Institute of National History, 1970.

56. L. Doklestić, O. Ivanoski, & V. Brezoski, *Bulgarian Post-War Historiography about the History of the Macedonian Peoples*, ibidem, 59–101; K. Bitoski, T. Simovski, *Greek Historiography on Macedonia Published after the Second World War*, ibidem, 121–145.

57. *Macédoine 1970*.

58. *From the Past of the Macedonian People*, Skopje, 1969, II.

59. Panov 1981, 37–47 (the paper was first published in 1972).

60. S. Antoljak, Die Schaffung und Erweiterung des Kerns des Staates Samuels in der Periode von 969 bis 976, in *Macédoine 1981*, 49–66 (with previous bibliography). See also Idem, Die Wahrheit über den Aufstand der Comitopulen, in *Actes du IIe Congrès International des Études du Sud–Est Européen* (Athènes), 2 (1972), 379–384.

61. H. D. Döpmann, Wechselbeziehungen zwischen Otto I. und Bulgaren auf dem Hintergrund der Deutsch–Byzantinischen Beziehungen, in J. Dummer & J. Irmscher (eds.), *Byzanz in der Europäischen Staatenwelt. Eine Aufsatzsammlung* (BBA, 49), Berlin, 1983, 47, 50; M. De Vos, *Un demi-siècle de l'histoire de la Macédoine (975–1025)* (Thèse de doctorat du IIIe cycle, Institut National des Langues et Civilizations Orientales), Paris, 1977, 39, 45.

62. M. Ljubinković, *L'Illyricum et la question romaine à la fin du Xe siècle et au début du XIe siècle. Autour de l'Eglise autocéphale de l'État de Samuel*, "Italia Sacra," Padova, 22 (= *La Chiesa greca in Italia dall'VII al XVI secolo*, III), 1973, 949–950; V. Popović, Episkopiska sednata u Srbiji od IX do XI veko (Les évêchés médiévaux sur le territoire de la Serbie (IXe–XIe siècles), *Godišnjak Grada Beograda*, 25 (1978), 36–39.

63. D. Anastasijević, L'hypothèse de la Bulgarie Occidentale, in *L'art byzantin chez les Slaves. Les Balkans. Premier recueil dédié à la mémoire de Théodore Uspenskij*, I, Paris, 1930, 20–36; J. Ferluga, *Byzantium on the Balkans. Studies on the byzantine Administration and the Southern Slavs from the VIIth to the XIIth Centuries*, Amsterdam, 1976, 354; E. Stănescu, Byzantinovlachica. I. Les Vlaques à la fin du Xe siècle–début du XIe siècle et la restauration de la domination Byzantine dans la Péninsule Balkanique, RESEE, 6, 3 (1968), 409–412.

64. J. V. A. Fine Jr., *The Early Medieval Balkans. A Critical Survey from the Sixth to the Late Twelfth Century*, Ann Arbor, MI, 1991, 188–189; G. Nikolov, The Bulgarian Aristocracy in the War against the Byzantine Empire (971–1019), *Byzantium 2001*, 142.

65. Kofos 1986, 162–163, 171.

66. S. P. Kyriakides, *The Northern Ethnological Boundaries of Hellenism*, Thessaloniki, 1955. For the history of the "Society for Macedonian Studies," see http://vu.hyper.net/ems.

67. N. P. Andriotes, History of the Name 'Macedonia,' BS, 1 (1960), 143–148.

68. B. Kondis, in *Macedonia, Past and Present*, Thessaloniki, 1992, 9–10.

69. For the Greek (and Bulgarian, Serbian, and Albanian) attitudes toward the proclamation of the FYROM, see O. Popa, At the Dawn of the Hope: The Building

of Macedonian National Identity, *Central European Issues. Romanian Foreign Affairs Review*, 3, 2 (1997), 132–159.

70. Nystazopoulou–Pelekidou 1992.

71. *Byzantine Macedonia.*

72. I. Tarnanidis, The Macedonians of the Byzantine Period, in *Byzantine Macedonia*, 49.

73. Martis 1984, 11.

74. C. G. Hatzidimitriou, Distorting History: Concerning a Recent Article on Ethnic Identity in Greek Macedonia, BS, 34, 2 (1993), 315–351.

75. Kofos 1989, 262. It has to be observed that Martis 1984 includes a large number of pages (20–70) about pre-Roman history.

76. *Greek Lands in History: Macedonia, 4000 Years of Greek History and Civilization*, Athens, 1983.

77. Kofos 1986, 165–166.

78. Engström 2002, 3.

79. Malingoudis 1983, 109–110.

80. D. Angelov, *Die Enstetehung des bulgarischen Volkes*, Berlin, 1980, 95.

Chapter 6

Conclusion

The great obsession of Balkan policy and propaganda was and continues to be ethnic purity (of the Serbs, Croats, Bulgarians, Albanians, and Greeks). *This ethnic purity is an illusion in this most mingled European region, the scene of a long series of ethnic and cultural changes, where there are no pure ethnies and races.* It is not a coincidence that the conflict areas of the Balkan Peninsula were the most affected by the ethnic, demographic, and religious changes. Indeed, the central parts of the Balkan Peninsula (Macedonia and Kosovo) were since late antiquity and the early Middle Ages the most ethnically and linguistically mixed. A linguist holds that Macedonia and Kosovo display the same heterogeneity in the fifth–eighth centuries that exists in modern times.[1] Bosnia had even before the Ottoman conquest a mottled population, composed of Catholic Croats, Orthodox Serbs, and also Romanians. The installation of the Ottoman administration increased this variety with the appearance of a strong Muslim community, born especially from converted Serbs and Croats. Serbian and Croatian historians try to argue the right of each party for Bosnia in its entirety. In fact, Bosnia was always a contact and middle zone between West and East. Someone called it a "border area" like Alsace and Lorraine.[2]

In Kosovo, the demographic proportions between Albanians and Serbs varied to a great degree throughout history. It is possible that the ancestors of the Albanians lived there in the sixth–seventh centuries, that is before the installation of the Slavs. Later, their number increased at the same time as Serbia began its expansion in Kosovo, in the twelfth–thirteenth centuries. Finally, the Albanians acquired the first position because they were the profiteers of the Ottoman domination. The turning point of the demographic proportion between Albanians and Serbs was surpassed at the end of the seventeenth century, when a part of the Serbian population departed in exile. But we should not forget that the Aromanians also lived in Kosovo. Few authors speak about them when discussing the ethnic composition of this conflict area, although they are attested to in Kosovo by the oldest Serbian documents concerning this region. One possible reason is that there is no "homeland" state which they could join. A British author (who published a very interesting book about the Aromanians) wrote that:

> I would like to suggest a much greater Vlach element in the Balkans during the Middle Ages than has been commonly allowed. If this existed, the extreme nationalist claims of Balkan nations to parts of Macedonia on the grounds of history are obviously of less account.[3]

Macedonia suffered the most intensive ethnic series of changes, because all the Balkan powers and all the powers involved in the Balkan region aimed to own it, from Roman antiquity to the present. Great Serbia, Great Bulgaria, Great Greece, even Great Albania, and of course Great Macedonia, as they were dreamed by modern nationalists, intersected in Macedonia. Macedonia is the key to the Balkan Peninsula. *To master Macedonia means to control the main roads that cross the peninsula from west to east, and north to south,* the roads that intersect in Macedonia and that have sea access by Thessaloniki. This fact is still valid, because the Morava–Vardar corridor preserves its old strategic and economic value. The Romans, the Bulgarians, the Byzantines, and the Ottomans tried one after another to ensure and strengthen their mastership over Macedonia, through forced or voluntary colonizations combined with the deportation of the natives, and by the fortification of the region. Ancient, medieval, and modern history show that *the conquest of Macedonia opened the way to the domination of the entire Balkan Peninsula for any external power that held it.* Macedonia was the base of Roman expansion toward the north,[4] while the Ottoman Empire was able to conquer Serbia and Bulgaria just after penetrating Macedonia. Later, during World War I, the opening of a new front at Thessaloniki supported the advance of the Entente armies toward Bulgaria and Austro-Hungary.

The location of Macedonia at the intersection of the spheres of influence led to the well-known ethnic mosaic, which in turn created the conditions for the conflicting situations. For the first time in the twentieth century, this potential for conflict exploded with the Balkan wars of 1912–1913, which involved all the Balkan countries and Romania (the latter aimed for national rights for the Aromanians). The remarks of Nicolae Iorga at the beginning of this book were occasioned by these wars. Future events confirmed the trends observed for the medieval history of Macedonia.

Unlike Western Europe, where the kingdoms evolved from feudal fragmentation to centralization and next to national states, *the Balkan medieval states evolved toward separatism. These centrifugal trends are specific for the region. All the states that attained a certain extension then reached the stage of devolution.* The centrifugal trends were often fired up by the ruthless financial policy of the central authorities. It was remarked that "the powerful central authority is specific for all the societies with a Byzantine pattern, based on a complicated tax collection system and on the lack of the privileges of the town citizens."[5] *The extreme centralization, more or less related to the oriental despotism, stimulated the unrest of the peripheral areas and of those who felt themselves to be marginal.* The geographic environment and the entire historical tradition favored the centrifugal or secessionist movements and particularism. This should be a lesson for the present.

The unifications of the Balkan space were made only by outside powers both in the Roman and the Ottoman periods. As an American historian of Greek origin has observed, "this Balkan unity in the past has not risen from within but has been forced from without by foreign conquerors, first the Romans and then the Turks."[6] A similar idea was previously expressed by Nicolae Iorga: the unifications of the Balkan space made from outside by the Romans, Byzantines, and Ottomans sought the pacification of this space, in order to secure the travel roads.[7] Bulgaria and Serbia were not able to achieve this unity.

In a paper presented at a round table dedicated to the "historical origins of the Yugoslavian crisis" organized by the Institute for South-East European Studies from Bucharest in February 1991, Romanian historian Andrei Pippidi concluded that the shattering of the former federation was also caused by the so-called instrumentalization of history, that is by the manipulation of different historical items (usually medieval), used as sources of legitimation for separatist policy and for conflicts with the neighbors:

> In quest for legitimacy, Macedonia invokes the empire of Samuel, Slovenia the 7th century principality of Carantania, the Albanians claim their autochthony, Croatia claims the independency, naming Tomislav II his nominal king Aimone of Savoia, because a Tomislav I ruled in the 10th century.[8]

Indeed, *nationalist historical mythology is one of the causes of the conflicts that beset Bulgaria, Serbia, Croatia, and Greece in the twentieth century.* As Victor Papacostea has remarked, "the small Balkan nations engaged in great

imperialist actions based on the myth of the chosen nation."[9] In this way
appeared a Greek, a Serbian, and a Bulgarian imperialism. All of them
pursued the conquest of or hegemony over the entire Balkan Peninsula,
because all of them tried to restore the Byzantine model. As another historian, Alain Ducellier, has observed, "these nations are more contracted
or expanding empires than nations-states organized according to our criteria."[10] We saw how the official historiography of the Balkan countries
has legitimated policy with arguments that are medieval not only by
content, but also by form. By form, because this kind of imperialism
expressed nostalgia for the Byzantine ideal, and not the demographic,
economic, or military power of a state.

In fact, the historical arguments are only a source of confusion if they
are applied to the situation of the Balkan Peninsula. *Only the present ethnic
configuration could be the starting point for the resolution of the international
disputes.* Otherwise, each party involved in such a dispute or in a war will
have the same equal arguments to support its claims, since each party is
somehow right, depending on the historical period chosen to be invoked
as support for those claims.

In a study dedicated to the medieval history of Kosovo, the same Alain
Ducellier argued that "there is no solid argument today to determine the
nationality of this or that region, especially in the Balkans, except the existence there of a recognized national majority."[11]

We will close in the same way as we began, with another fragment from
the works of Nicolae Iorga, written just during World War I, in the opening course organized by the Institute of South-East European Studies in
1916:

> What happened before the beginning of the modern times could not be in-
> voked by anyone in the Balkan Peninsula as a support for his rights in the
> present or future conflicts. . . . If the Balkan nations do not want to decay to
> a weak territorial situation, unable of initiatives and development, which
> will allow the expansion and political domination of the stronger neighbors,
> they should acknowledge that only by a detached and full of sacrifices quest
> of their real and present interests, that leaves aside all the deceptive fogs of
> the past and all the dangerous illusions of the future, could be established a
> modern order in the Balkans, right for all, which today does not exist, but
> which should be tomorrow.[12]

*History could not be used for the legitimation of the present frontiers of the
Balkan countries, because the past is giving to all, that is to nobody, different and
contradictory arguments for each disputed zone.* As an American historian
writes in a recent work dealing with the misperceptions of the European
ethnic origins,

those who claim that their actions are justified or compelled by history have no understanding of change, the very essence of human history. The history of the peoples of Europe in the early Middle Ages cannot be used as an argument for or against any of the political, territorial and ideological movements of today.[13]

Usually, the appeal to history led to the justification of wars, but we think that the same history should be used only to explain the origin of the conflict areas from Bosnia, Kosovo, and Macedonia.

NOTES

1. N. Reiter, Alte Reikte in Balkansprachen, *Die Völker 1987*, 75.

2. L. S. Stavrianos, *The Balkans since 1453*, New York, 1959, 235.

3. T. J. Winnifrith, *The Vlachs, the History of a Balkan People*, London, 1987, 38.

4. As has also observed A. Lazarou, *L'aroumain et ses rapports avec le Grec*, Thessalonique, 1986, 33–34.

5. T. Teoteoi, Civilizaţia statului Asăneştilor între Roma şi Bizanţ, *Răscoala 1989*, 81.

6. Stavrianos 1959, 4.

7. N. Iorga, *Ce este Sud-Estul European*, Bucureşti, 1940, 11.

8. A. Pippidi, De la Kosovo la Sarajevo, *Sud-Estul şi contextul european. Buletin*, 1 (1994), 26.

9. V. Papacostea, La Péninsule Balkanique et le problème des études compares, *Balcania*, 6 (1943), X–XI.

10. A. Ducellier, Structures politiques et mentales de longue durée dans les Balkans, *Historiens-Géographes*, 337 (Octobre 1992), 105.

11. A. Ducellier, Have the Albanians Occupied Kosova? *Kosova 1993*, 63.

12. N. Iorga, *Ilusii şi drepturi naţionale în Balcani. Lecţie de deschidere la Institutul de Studii Sud-Ost Europene*, Vălenii de Munte, 1916, 10, 33–34.

13. P. J. Geary, *The Myth of Nations: The Medieval Origins of Europe*, Princeton, NJ, 2002, 173.

Abbreviations
(Journals and Collections
of Studies)

AECO   *Archivum Europae Centro-Orientalis*, Budapest
AIESEEB   *Association Internationale d'Études du Sud-Est Européen. Bulletin*, Bucarest
Albanians 1985   The Albanians and Their Territories, Tirana, 1985
Les Aroumains   Les Aroumains (Centre d'Etude des Civilisations de l'Europe Centrale et du Sud-Est. Cahier no. 8), Paris, 1989
Aspects 1972   H. Birnbaum and S. Vryonis Jr. (eds.), *Aspects of the Balkans, Continuity and Change. Contributions to the International Balkan Conference Held at UCLA, 1969*, The Hague, 1972
Balkan Identities   M. Todorova (ed.), *Balkan Identities. Nation and Memory*, London, 2004
Balkans 1963   C. Jelavich and B. Jelavich (eds.), *The Balkans in Transition. Essays on the Development of Balkan Life and Politics since the Eighteenth Century*, Berkeley, CA, 1963
BB   *Byzantinobulgarica*, Sofia
BBA   *Berliner Byzantinische Arbeiten*, Berlin
BBRF   *Buletinul Bibliotecii Române din Freiburg*, Freiburg
BCH   *Bulletin de Correspondance Hellénique*, Paris
Berichte 1973   Berichte über den II Internationalen Kongress für Slawische Archäologie, 3 vol., Berlin, 1973
BF   *Byzantinische Forschungen*, Amsterdam
BHR   *Bulgarian Historical Review*, Sofia

BMGS   *Byzantine and Modern Greek Studies*, Birmingham
BNJ   *Byzantinisch-Neugriechische Jahrbücher*, Athens
BS   *Balkan Studies*, Thessaloniki
BSl   *Balcanoslavica*, Belgrade
Byzantine Macedonia   J. Burke and R. Scott (eds.), *Byzantine Macedonia. Identity, Image and History. Papers from the Melbourne Conference, July 1995* (Byzantina Australiensia, 13), Melbourne, 2000
Byzantium and Serbia   Byzantium and Serbia in the 14th Century. National Hellenic Foundation, Institute for Byzantine Research (International Symposium, 3), Athens, 1996
Byzantium 2001   G. Prinzing, M. Salamon, and P. Stephenson (eds.), *Byzantium and East Central Europe. Papers of a Symposium, Krakow, 24–26 September 2000*, Krakow, 2001
ByzSl   *Byzantinoslavica*, Prague
BZ   *"Byzantinische Zeitschrift,"* München
Carter 1977   F. W. Carter, ed., *An Historical Geography of the Balkans*, London, 1977
CIAS III   *Rapports du IIIe Congrès International d'Archéologie Slave*, 2 vol., Bratislava, 1979–1980
CIEB XIV   *Actes du XIVe Congrès International des Études Byzantines*, 3 vol., Bucarest, 1974–1976
CIEB XV   *Actes du XVe Congrès International d'Études Byzantines*, 4 vol., Athènes, 1976
DAW   *Österreichische Akademie der Wissenschaften, Philosophisch-Historische Klasse, Denkschriften*, Wien
Die Kultur Griechenlands   R. Lauer and P. Schreiner (eds.), *Die kultur Griechenlands in Mittelalter und Neuzeit. Bericht über des Kolloquium der Südosteuropa-Kommission, 28–31 Oktober 1992* ("Abhandlungen der Akademie der Wissenschaften. Philolosophishe-Historische Klasse," 3 Folge, 212), Göttingen, 1994
Die Völker 1987   B. Hänsel (ed.), *Die Völker Südosteuropas im 6. bis 8. Jh.*, München, 1987
DOP   Dumbarton Oaks Papers, Washington, DC
EB   *Études Balkaniques*, Sofia
EH   *Études Historiques*, Sofia
Europe 1968   *L'Europe aux IXe–XIe siècles. Aux origines des etats nationaux*, Varsovie, 1968
Gli Slavi   *Gli Slavi occidentali e meridionali nell'alto medioevo* (Settimane, 30, 1982), Spoleto, 1983
GRBS   *Greek, Roman and Byzantine Studies*, Durham, NC
INMV   *Izvestija na Narodnija Muzej*, Varna
JÖB   *Jahrbuch der Österreichischen Byzantinistik*, Wien
Kosova 1993   *The Truth on Kosova*, Tirana, 1993

Kosovo 1990 R. Samardžić et alii, *Le Kosovo-Metohija dans l'histoire Serbe*, Lausanne, 1990

Les Illyriens 1988 *Les Illyriens et les Albanais. Serie de conferences tenues du 21 Mai au 4 Juin 1986* (Academie Serbe des Sciences et des Arts. Colloques scientifiques, vol. 39, Classe des Sciences Historiques, vol. 10), Belgrade, 1988

Macédoine 1970 *La Macédoine et les Macédoniens dans le passé. Recueil d'articles scientifiques*, Skopje, 1970

Macédoine 1981 *Macédoine (Articles d'histoire)*, Institut d'Histoire Nationale, Skopje, 1981

Migrations 1989 Ivan Ninić (ed.), *Migrations in Balkan History*, Belgrade, 1989

NCMH II R. McKitterick (ed.), *The New Cambridge Medieval History, vol. II, c. 700–c. 900*, Cambridge, 1995

NCMH IV D. Luscombe and J. Riley-Smith (eds.), *The New Cambridge Medieval History, vol. IV/2, c. 1024–c. 1198*, Cambridge, 2003

NCMH V D. Abulafia (ed.), *The New Cambridge Medieval History, vol. V, c. 1198–c .1300*, Cambridge, 1999

Răscoala 1989 *Răscoal şi statul Asăneştilor. Culegere de studii*, coord. E. Stănescu, Bucureşti, 1989

RdI *Revista de Istorie*, Bucureşti

RESEE *Revue des Études Sud-Est Européennes*, Bucarest

RHC *Revue d'Histoire Comparée*, Paris

RHSEE *Revue Historique du Sud-Est Européen*, Bucarest

RRH *Revue Roumaine d'Histoire*, Bucarest

SA *Studia Albanica*, Tirana

SBS *Studies in Byzantine Sigillography*, Washington, DC

SEER *The Slavonic and East European Review*, London

Settimane *Settimane di Studio del Centro Italiano di Studi sull'Alto Medioevo*, Spoleto

SOF *Südost-Forschungen*, München

TM *Travaux et Mémoires*, Centre de Recherche d'Histoire et Civilisation Byzantines, Paris

Völker 1959 *Völker und Kulturen Südosteuropas. Kulturhistorische Beiträge*, München, 1959

VV *Vizantijskij Vremennik*, Moscow

WSJ *Wiener slavistisches Jahrbuch*, Wien

ZB *Zeitschrift für Balkanologie*, Wiesbaden

ZRVI Zbornik Radova Vizantološkog Instituta, Belgrade

Bibliography

Ahrweiler, H. (1976). Recherches sur la société byzantine au XIe siècle: Nouvelles hiérarchies et nouvelles solidarités. TM, 6, 99–124.

Anamali, S. (1972). Des Illyriens aux Albanais. AIESEEB, 10, 2, 101–129.

———. (1993). The Illyrians and the Albanians. *Kosova 1993*, 5–18.

Andonova-Hristova, M. (2003). Modèles historiques de coexistence pacifique entre musulmans et chrétiens orthodoxes pendant les periodes Byzantine et Post-Byzantine. ByzSl, 61, 229–264.

Angelov, D. (1956). Certains aspects de la conquête des peuples balkaniques par les Turcs. ByzSl, 17, 2, 220–275.

———. (1980). *Die Entstehung des Bulgarischen Volkes*. Berlin.

Angold, M. (1975). Byzantine "nationalism" and the Nicaean Empire. BMGS, 1, 49–70.

———. (1984a). *The Byzantine Empire, 1025–1204. A political history*, London, New York.

———. (1984b). Archons and dynasts: Local aristocracies and the cities of the later Byzantine Empire. In M. Angold (Ed.), *The Byzantine aristocracy, IX to XIII centuries* (BAR International Series, 221) (pp. 236–253). Oxford.

———. (1985). The shaping of the medieval Byzantine city. BF, 10, 1–37.

———. (1999). Byzantium in exile. NCMH V, 543–568.

Antoljak, S. (1970). Die Makedonische Sklavinien. *Macédoine 1970*, 27–44.

Antonijević, D. (1989). Cattlebreeders' migrations in the Balkans through centuries. *Migrations 1989*, 147–156.

Argyriou, A. (1994). Peuples orthodoxes et musulmans dans les Balkans. *Contacts. Revue Française de l'Orthodoxie, 46*, nr. 168, 243–258.

Arnakis, G. (1963). The role of religion in the development of Balkan nationalism. *Balkans 1963*, 115–144.

Avraméa, A. (1997). *Le Peloponnèse du IVe au VIIIe siècle. Changements et persistances.* Paris.

———. (2001). Les Slaves dans le Péloponnèse. In E. Kountoura-Galaki (Ed.), *The Dark Centuries of Byzantium (7th–9th c.)* (pp. 293–302). Athens.

Bádenas de la Pena, P. (2000). La composante religieuse dans les conflits balkaniques. AIESEEB, 30, 151–161.

Balivet, M. (1993). Aux origines de l'Islamisation des Balkans Ottomans. *Revue des mondes Musulmans et de la Méditerranée, 66*, Octobre, 11–20.

Bănescu, N. (1946). *Les duchés byzantins de Paristrion (Paradounavon) et de Bulgarie.* Bucarest.

Banfi, E. (1987). Cristianizzazione nei Balcani e formazione della lega linguistica Balcanica. ZB, 23 1, 4–18.

Barnea, I., & Ştefănescu, şt. (1971). *Din istoria Dobrogei*, vol. III. Bucureşti.

Bartusis, M. (1998). The settlement of Serbs in Macedonia in the era of Dušan's conquests. In H. Ahrweiler & A. E. Laiou (Eds.), *Studies on the internal diaspora of the Byzantine Empire* (pp. 151–159). Washington, DC.

Bataković, D. T. (1992). *The Kosovo Chronicles*, Belgrade (online version: members .tripod. com/Balkania/resources/history/kosovo_chronicles).

Beldiceanu, N. (1957). La région de Timok-Morava dans les documents de Mehmed II et de Selim I. *Revue des Études Roumaines, 3–4*, 111–129.

———. (1975). Les Valaques de Bosnie à la fin du XVème siècle et leurs institutions. *Turcica. Revue d'Etudes Turques, 7*, 122–134.

———. (1984). Însemnări asupra românilor din Balcani în lumina documentelor otomane. BBRF, 11 (15), 3–14.

Beševliev, V. (1981). *Die Protobulgarische periode der Bulgarischen Geschichte.* Amsterdam.

Bojović, B. I. (1992). Historiographie dynastique et idéologie politique en Serbie au Bas Moyen Âge. Essai de synthèse de l'idéologie de l'etat médiéval serbe. SOF, 51, 29–49.

———. (1997). Le passé des territoires, Kosovo-Metohija (XIe-XVIIe siècle). BS, 38, 1, 31–61.

Bowden, W., & Hodges, R. (2004). Balkan ghosts? Nationalism and the question of rural continuity in Albania. In N. Christie (Ed.), *Landscapes of change. Rural evolutions in late antiquity and the early Middle Ages* (pp. 195–222). Aldershot.

Bozhori, K. (1975). À propos de l'extension du nom Arbanon à l'époque byzantine. CIEB XIV, vol. II, 307–313.

Božić, I. (1968). La formation de l'etat serbe aux IXe–XIe siècles. *Europe 1968*, 133–147.

Braudel, F. (1966). *La Méditerranée et le monde méditerranéen a l'époque de Philippe II*, 2 vol. Paris.

Brezeanu, S. (1999). *Romanitatea orientală în evul mediu. De la cetăţenii romani la naţiunea medievală.* Bucureşti.

Budak, N. (1990). Die südslawischen Ethnogenesen an der östlichen Adriaküste im frühen Mittelalter. In *Typen der Ethnogenese unter besonderer Berücksichtigung der Bayern*, I (DAW, 201) (pp. 129–136). Wien.

———. (2000). Slavic ethnogenesies in modern Northern Croatia. In R. Bratož (Ed.), *Slowenien und die Nachbarländer zwischen Antike und karolingischer Epoche. Anfänge der slowenischen Ethnogenese* (Situla, 39) (vol. I, pp. 395–401). Ljubljana.

Bulin, H. (1968). Aux origines des formations étatiques des Slaves du Moyen Danube au IXe siècle. *Europe 1968*, 149–204.

Çabej, E. (1972). Le problème du territoire de la formation de la langue albanaise. AIESEEB, 10, 2, 71–99.

———. (1993). The problem of the autochthony of Albanians in the light of place-names. *Kosova 1993*, 19–25.

Cankova-Petkova, G. (1973). De nouveau sur Kékaumenos. BHR, 1, 3, 61–77.

———. (1980). Les forces centrifuges et centripètes à Byzance du début du régne d'Isaak Ange (L'insurection des Asénides et la révolte d'Alexis Branas). CIEB XV, vol. IV, 55–64.

Capidan, Th. (1927). Românii nomazi. Studiu din viaţa românilor din sudul Peninsulei Balcanice, Dacoromania" (Cluj), 4, 2, 183–352.

———. (1943). *Limbă şi cultură.* Bucureşti.

Caragiani, I. (1929). *Studii istorice asupra românilor din Peninsula Balcanică.* Bucureşti.

Carras, C. (2004). Greek identity: A long view. *Balkan Identities*, 294–326.

Castellan, G. (1991). *Histoire des Balkans (XIVe–XXe siècle).* Paris.

Cazacu, M. (1989). Les Valaques dans les Balkans occidentaux (Serbie, Croatie, Albanie, etc.). La Pax ottomanica (XVème–XVIIème siècles). *Les Aroumains*, 79–93.

Chadwick, H. (2003). *East and West: The making of a rift in the church. From apostolic times until the Council of Florence.* Oxford.

Charanis, P. (1959). Ethnic changes in the Byzantine Empire in the seventh century. DOP, 13, 25–44.

———. (1961). The transfer of population as a policy in the Byzantine Empire. *Comparative Studies in Society and History, 3,* 2, 140–154.

———. (1970). Observations on the history of Greece during the early Middle Ages. BS, 11, 1, 1–34.

———. (1978). The formation of the Greek people. In S. Vryonis Jr. (Ed.), *The "past" in medieval and modern Greek culture* (Byzantina kai Metabyzantina, I) (pp. 87–101). Malibu, CA.

———. (1979). On the demography of medieval Greece, a problem solved. BS, 20, 2, 193–218.

Cheynet, J. C. (1990). *Pouvoir et contestations à Byzance (963–1210).* Paris.

———. (1991). La politique militaire byzantine de Basile II à Alexis Comnène. ZRVI, 29–30, 61–73.

———. (1993a). Points de vue sur l'efficacité administrative entre les Xe–XIe siècles. BF, 19, 7–16.

———. (1993b). Le rôle de l'aristocratie locale dans l'état (Xe–XIIe siècle). BF, 19, 105–112.

———. (2001). Les transferts de population sous la contrainte à Byzance. *Travaux et Recherches de l'Université de Marne-la-Vallée, 7,* 45–69.

Čirković, S. (1988). Les Albanais à la lumière des sources historiques des Slaves du Sud. *Les Illyriens 1988*, 341–359.

———. (1990). Le Kosovo-Metohija au Moyen Âge. *Kosovo 1990*, 21–39.

————. (1996). Between kingdom and empire: Dušan's state (1346–1355) reconsidered. *Byzantium and Serbia*, 110–20.

Čorović-Ljubinković, M. (1972). Les Slaves du centre balkanique du VIe au IXe siècle. BSl, 1, 43–54.

Curta, F. (2001). *The making of the Slavs. History and archaeology of the lower Danube region c. 500–700.* Cambridge.

————. (2004a). Barbarians in Dark-Age Greece: Slavs or Avars? In Ts. Stepanov & V. Vachkova (Eds.), *Civitas divino-humana. In honorem annorum LX Georgii Bakalov* (pp. 513–550). Sofia.

————. (2004b). L'administration byzantine dans les Balkans pendant la "grande brèche": Le temoignage des sceaux. *Bizantinistica. Rivista di Studi Bizantini e Slavi*, serie seconda, 6, 155–189.

Cvijić, J. (1918). *La Péninsule Balkanique. Géographie humaine.* Paris.

De Vos, M. (1977). *Un demi-siècle de l'histoire de la Macédoine (975–1025)* (thèse de doctorat du IIIe cycle, Institut National des Langues et Civilizations Orientales). Paris.

Diaconu, P. (1970). *Les Petchénègues au Bas-Danube.* Bucarest.

Dimevski, S. (1969). The Archbishopric of Ohrid. In *From the past of the Macedonian people* (pp. 55–72). Skopje.

Dimnik, M. (2003). Russia, the Bulgars and the southern Slavs, 1024–c.1200. NCMH IV, 254–276.

Ditten, H. (1993). *Ethnische Verschiebungen zwischen der Balkanhalbinsel und Kleinasien vom Ende des 6. bis zum zweiten Hälfte des 9. Jahrhunderts* (BBA, 59). Berlin.

Djuvara, N. (1991). Sur un passage controversé de Kekaumenos. RRH, 30, 1–2, 23–66.

Doja, A. (1999). Formation nationale et nationalisme dans l'aire de peuplement albanais. *Balkanologie, 3* (Paris), 2, 23–43.

Döpmann, H.-D. (1981). Zum Streit zwischen Rom und Byzanz um die Christianisierung Bulgariens. *Palaeobulgarica, 5*, 1, 62–73.

Dragojlović, D. (1989). Migrations of the Serbs in the Middle Ages. *Migrations 1989*, 61–66.

Dragomir, S. (1944). La patrie primitive des Roumains et ses frontières historiques. *Balcania, 7*, 1, 63–101.

————. (1959). *Vlahii din nordul Peninsulei Balcanice în evul mediu.* Bucureşti.

Ducellier, A. (1968). L'Arbanon et les Albanais au XIe siècle. TM, 3, 353–368.

————. (1979). Les Albanais du XIe au XIIIe siècle: Nomades ou sédentaires? BF, 7, 23–36.

————. (1981). *La façade maritime de l'Albanie au Moyen Âge. Durazzo et Valona du XIe au XVe siècle.* Thessalonique.

————. (1984). Genesis and failure of the Albanian state in the fourteenth and fifteenth century. In A. Pipa & S. Repishti (Ed.), *Studies on Kosova.* Boulder, New York.

————. (1993). Have the Albanians Occupied Kosova? *Kosova 1993*, 63–68.

————. (1999). Albania, Serbia and Bulgaria. NCMH V, 779–795.

Dujčev, I. (1971). *Medioevo bizantino-slavo*, vol. III. Roma.

Dvornik, F. (1970). *Byzantine mission among the Slavs. SS Constantine-Cyril and Methodius.* New Brunswick, NJ.

Elsie, R. (1994). Hydronimica Albanica—A survey of river names in Albania. ZB, 30, 1, 1–46.

Engström, J. (2002). 7, 3–17.

Ferjančić, B. (1988). Les Albanais dans les sources byzantines. *Les Illyriens 1988,* 303–322.

Ferluga, J. (1976). *Byzantium on the Balkans. Studies on the byzantine administration and the southern Slavs from the VIIth to the XIIth centuries.* Amsterdam.

———. (1979). Quelques problèmes de la politique byzantine de colonisation au XIe siècle dans les Balkans. BF, 7, 37–56.

———. (1983). Gli Slavi del Sud ed altri gruppi etnici di fronte a Bisanzio. *Gli Slavi,* 303–343.

———. (1985). Aufstände im Byzantinischen Reich zwischen den Jahren 1025 und 1081. Versuch einer Typologie. *Rivista di Studi Bizantini e Slavi, 5* (Bologna), 137–165.

———. (1998). Die byzantinischen Provinzstädte im 11. Jahrhundert. In J. Jarnut & P. Johanek (Eds.), *Die Frühgeschichte der europäischen Stadt im 11. Jahrhundert* (Veröffentlichungen des Instituts für vergleichende Städtgeschichte in Münster, 43) (pp. 359–374). Köln.

Fine, J. V. A., Jr. (1975). *The Bosnian church. A new interpretation.* New York.

———. (1991). *The early medieval Balkans. A critical survey from the sixth to the late twelfth century.* Ann Arbor, MI.

———. (1994). *The late medieval Balkans. A critical survey from the late twelfth century to the Ottoman conquest.* Ann Arbor, MI.

———. (2000). Croats and Slavs: Theories about historical circumstances of the Croats' appearance in the Balkans. BF, 26, 205–218.

Frashëri, K. (1985). The territories of the Albanians in the XVth century. *Albanians 1985,* 207–226.

Frazee, C. A. (1993). The Balkans between Rome and Constantinople in the early Middle Ages, 600–900 AD. BS, 34, 2, 213–228.

Gashi, S. (1985). The presence of the Albanian ethnos in Kosova during the 13th–14th centuries in the light of the Serbian Church sources. *Albanians 1985,* 247–286.

Geary, P. J. (2002). *The Myth of nations: The medieval origins of Europe.* Princeton, NJ.

Giakoumis, K. (2003). Fourteenth-century Albanian migration and the 'relative autochthony' of the Albanians in Epeiros. The case of Gjirokastër. BMGS, 27, 171–184.

Gjuzelev, B. (1991). *Die Bulgarisch-Albanische Ethnische Grenze während des Mittelalters (6.-15. Jh.).* EB, 27, 3, 78–91.

———. (1977). *Das Papstum und Bulgarien im Mittelalter (9.-14. Jh.).* BHR, 5, 1, 34–58.

Golab, Z. (1991). *The origins of the Slavs. A linguist's view.* Columbus.

Graebner, M. (1978). The Slavs in Byzantine Empire. Absorption, semi-autonomy and the limits of Byzantinization. BB, 5, 41–55.

Grégoire, H. (1945). L'origine et le nom des Croates et des Serbes. *Byzantion,* 17, 88–118.

Guldescu, S. (1964). *History of medieval Croatia*. The Hague.

Gyóni, M. (1945). L'oeuvre de Kekauménos, source de l'histoire roumaine. RHC, 23, n.s., vol. 3, 1–4, 96–180.

———. (1951). La transhumance des Valaques balcaniques au Moyen Âge. ByzSl, 12, 29–42.

Haldon, J. F. (1997). *Byzantium in the seventh century. The transformation of a culture*. Cambridge.

Hammond, N. G. L. (1976). *Migrations and invasions in Greece and adjacent areas*. Park Ridge, NJ.

Herrin, J. (1973). Aspects of the process of Hellenization in the early Middle Ages. *The Annual of the British School of Archaeology at Athens*, 68, 113–126.

Hoffman, G. W. (1977). The evolution of the ethnographic map of Yugoslavia. *Carter 1977*, 437–499.

Hoffmann, J. (1974). *Rudimente von Territorialstaaten im byzantinischen Reich. Untersuchungen über Unabhängigkeitsbestrebungen und ihr Verhältnis zu Kaiser und Reich* (Miscellanea Byzantina Monacensia, 17). München.

Hussey, J. M. (1986). *The Orthodox Church in the Byzantine Empire*. Oxford.

Inalcik, H. (1954). Ottoman methods of conquest. *Studia Islamica*, 2, 103–129.

Iorga, N. (1916). *Ilusii şi drepturi naţionale în Balcani. Lecţie de deschidere la Institutul de Studii Sud-Ost Europene*. Vălenii de Munte.

———. (1925). *Histoire des états balkaniques jusqu'a 1924*. Paris.

———. (1939). *Études Byzantines*, I. Bucarest.

———. (1984). *Sârbi, Bulgari şi Români în Peninsula Balcanică în evul mediu* [1915]. In Ş. Papacostea (Ed.), *Studii asupra evului mediu românesc* (pp. 51–64). Bucureşti.

Islami, H. (1985). Anthropogeographic research in Kosova. An aperçu on the work "Kosovo" by academician Atanasije Urosevic. *Albanians 1985*, 476–492.

Ivănescu, G. (1980). *Istoria limbii române*. Iaşi.

Ivić, P. (1972). Balkan Slavic migrations in the light of South Slavic dialectology. *Aspects 1972*, 66–86.

Janković, Dj. (1995). *The Serbian questions in the Balkans*. Faculty of Geography, Belgrade (www.rastko.org.yu/arheologija/djankovic-serbs_balkans.htm).

———. (1999). *Scientific discussion on Noel Malcolm's book "Kosovo. A Short History"* (Macmillan, London 1998, 492). October 8th, 1999, Institute of History of the Serbian Academy of Sciences and Arts (www.rastko.org.yu/kosovo/istorija/malkolm/djankovic-facts.html).

Jenkins, R. (1963). *Byzantium and Byzantinism*. University of Cincinnati.

Jochalas, T. (1971). Über die Einwanderung der Albaner in Griechenland. In *Dissertationes Albanicae in honorem Josephi Valentini et Ernesti Koliqi septuagenariorum* (Beiträge zur Kenntnis Südosteuropas und des nahen Orients, 13) (pp. 89–106). München.

Jordanov, I. (2003). The Katepanikion of Paradunavon according to the sphragistic data. SBS, 8, 63–74.

Juka, S. S. (1984). *The Albanians in Yugoslavia in light of historical documents*. New York (online version at www.alb-net.com/juka2.htm).

Kalić, J. (1988). La région de Ras à l'époque byzantine. In *Géographie historique du monde mediterranéen* (sous la direction de H. Ahrweiler) (pp. 127–140). Paris.

Karatay, O. (2002). Ogur connection in the Croatian and Serbian migrations. In G. H. Celâl, C. C. Oguz, & O. Karatay (Eds.), *The Turks*, vol. 1 (pp. 553–561). Ankara.

———. (2003). Contribution to the debates on the origin of the medieval Bosnian royal dynasty Kotromanids. In *Eran und Aneran. Webfestschrift Marshak. Studies presented to Boris Ilich Marshak on the occasion of his 70th birthday*. Electronic Version, Buenos Aires (www.transoxiana.org/Eran/Articles/karatay.pdf).

Katičić, R. (1985). Die Anfänge des Kroatischen staates. In H. Friesinger & F. Daim, *Die Bayern und ihre Nachbarn*, I (pp. 299–312) (DAW, 179), Wien.

Kazhdan, A. P., & Epstein, W. A. (1985). *Change in Byzantine culture in the eleventh and twelfth centuries*. Berkeley, CA.

Koder, J. (1978). Zur Frage der slavischen Siedlungsgebiete im mittelalterlichen Griechenland. BZ, 71, 2, 315–331.

Kofos, E. (1962). The making of Yugoslavia's People's Republic of Macedonia. BS, 3, 2, 375–396.

———. (1964). *Nationalism and communism in Macedonia, civil conflict, politics of mutation, national identity*. Thessaloniki.

———. (1986). The Macedonian question: The politics of mutation. BS, 27, 1, 157–172.

———. (1989). National heritage and national identity in nineteenth- and twentieth-century Macedonia. *European History Quarterly, 19*, 2, 229–267.

Koledarov, P. (1977). Ethnical and political preconditions for regional names in the central and eastern part of the Balkan Peninsula. In *Carter 1977*, 293–317.

———. (1980). Zur Frage der politischen und ethnischen Veränderungen auf dem Balkan im 7. Jahrhundert. EH, 10, 77–89.

Kondis, B. (1987). The Macedonian question as a Balkan problem in the 1940's. BS, 28, 1, 151–160.

Kostanick, H. (1963). The geopolitics of the Balkans. *Balkans 1963*, 1–55.

Kovačević, J. (1973). Les Slaves et la population dans l'Illyricum. *Berichte 1973*, vol. 2, 143–151.

Kühn, H. J. 1991. *Die Byzantinische Armee im 10. und 11. Jahrhundert. Studien zur Organisation der Tagmata*. Wien.

Kyriakides, S. P. (1955). *The northern ethnological boundaries of Hellenism*. Thessaloniki.

Lauer, R. (1994). Gräkoslawen und Germanoslawen bei Jakob Philipp Fallmerayer. *Die Kultur Griechenlands*, 31–38.

Lawless, R. I. (1977). The economy and landscapes of Thessaly during Ottoman rule. *Carter 1977*, 501–33.

Lazarou, A. (1986). *L'aroumain et ses rapports avec le grec*. Thessalonique.

Lemerle, P. (1960). Prolégomènes à une édition critique et commentée des "Conseils et Récits de Kékaumenos." *Académie Royale de Belgique. Classe des lettres. Mémoires. Collection in-8°, deuxième série*, 54, 1–120.

———. (1977). *Cinq études sur le XIe siècle byzantin*. Paris.

Liebeschuetz, W. J. H. G. (2003). The refugees and evacuees in the age of migrations. In R. Corradini, M. Diesenberger, & H. Reimitz (Eds.), *The construction of communities in the early Middle Ages. Texts, resources and artifacts* (Transformation of the Roman World, 12) (pp. 65–79). Leiden.

212   *Bibliography*

Lilie, R. J. (1985). Kaiser Heraklios und die Ansiedlung der Serben. Überlegungen zum Kapitel 32 des "De Administrando Imperio." SOF, 44, 17–43.
Ljubinković, M. (1973). Les Slaves des régions centrales des Balkans et Byzance. *Berichte 1973*, vol. 2, 173–194.
———. (1973). *L'Illyricum et la question romaine à la fin du Xe siècle et au début du XIe siècle. Autour de l'Eglise autocéphale de l'État de Samuel*, "Italia Sacra," Padova, 22 (= *La Chiesa greca in Italia dall'VII al XVI secolo*, III), 927–969.
Madgearu, A. (1997). *Continuitate și discontinuitate culturală la Dunărea de Jos în secolele VII–VIII*. București.
———. (1999). The military organization of Paradunavon. ByzSl, 60, 2, 421–446.
———. (2003). The periphery against the centre: The case of Paradunavon. ZRVI, 40, 49–56.
Makk, F. (1989). *The Árpáds and the Comneni. Political relations between Hungary and Byzantium in the 12th century*. Budapest.
———. (1999). *Ungarische Aussenpolitik (896–1196)*. Herne.
Maksimović, L. (1996). Verwaltungsstrukturen in Byzanz und in den Balkanländern. In A. Hohlweg (Ed.), *Byzanz und seine Nachbarn* (Südost-Europa Jahrbuch, 26) (pp. 47–63). München.
———. (2002). L'Empire de Stefan Dusan: Genèse et caractère. TM, 14, 415–428.
———, & Subotić G. (2001). La Serbie entre Byzance et l'Occident. In *XXe Congrès International des Études Byzantines. Pré-actes, I. Séances plénières* (pp. 241–250). Paris.
Malamut, E. (1998). Concepts et réalités: Recherches sur les termes désignant les Serbes et les pays serbes dans les sources byzantines des Xe–XIIe siècles. In *Eupsychia. Mélanges offerts à Hélène Ahrweiler* (Byzantina Sorbonensia, 16), II (pp. 439–457). Paris.
Malcolm, N. (1999). *Kosovo. A short history*. New York.
———. (2000). *Storia di Bosnia dalle origini ai giorni nostri*. Milano.
Malingoudis, Ph. (1983). Toponimy and history. Observations concerning the Slavonic toponimy of the Peloponnese. *Cyrillomethodianum* (Thessaloniki), 7, 99–111.
Martis, N. K. (1984). *The falsification of Macedonian history*. Athens.
Matschke, K. P. (1995). Grundzüge des byzantinischen Städtewesens vom 11. bis 15. Jahrhundert. In K. P. Matschke (Ed.), *Die Byzantinische stadt im Rahmen der allgemeinen Stadtentwicklung. Referate und diskussionen der Byzantinischen Fachkonferenz im Leipzig 9. bis 11. Januar 1990* (pp. 27–73). Leipzig.
Mavromatis, L. (1978). *La fondation de l'Empire serbe. Le Kralj Milutin*. Thessalonique.
Mihăescu, H. (1993). *La romanité dans le Sud-Est de l'Europe*. București.
Mihaljčić, R. (1996). Les batailles de la Maritza et de Kosovo. Les dernières décennies de la rivalité serbo-byzantine. *Byzantium and Serbia*, 97–109.
Mintsis, G. (2000). The Balkans: A term bearing a heavy politico-historical load. AIESEEB, 30, 133–150.
Murnu, G. (1984). *Studii istorice privitoare la trecutul românilor de peste Dunăre*. București.
Năsturel, P. Ș. (1978). Vlacho-Balcanica. BNJ, 22, 221–248.

———. (1979). Les Valaques balkaniques aux Xe–XIIIe siècles (Mouvements de population et colonisation dans la Romanie grecque et latine). BF, 7, 89–112.

———. (1989). Les Valaques de l'espace byzantin et bulgare jusqu'à la conquête Ottomane. *Les Aroumains*, 45–78.

Nerantzi-Varmazi, N. (2000). Western Macedonia in the twelfth and thirteenth centuries. *Byzantine Macedonia*, 192–198.

Nicol, D. M. (1976). Refugees, mixed population and local patriotism in Epiros and Western Macedonia after the Fourth Crusade. CIEB XV, vol. I, 3–33 (Idem, *Studies in late Byzantine history and prosopography*, London, Variorum Reprints, 1986, IV).

———. (1984). *The despotate of Epiros (1267–1479). A contribution to the history of Greece in the Middle Ages*. Cambridge.

———. (1993). *The last centuries of Byzantium, 1261–1453*. Cambridge.

Nikolov, G. (2001). The Bulgarian aristocracy in the war against the Byzantine Empire (971–1019). *Byzantium 2001*, 141–158.

Nystazopoulou-Pelekidou, M. (1992). *The "Macedonian question," a historical review.* Corfu (electronic version: www.hri.org/docs/macque).

Obolensky, D. (1971). *The Byzantine commonwealth. Eastern Europe 500–1453*. London.

Oikonomides, N. (1976). La décomposition de l'Empire Byzantin à la veille de 1204 et les origines de l'Empire de Nicée: À propos de la "Partitio Romaniae." CIEB XV, vol. I, 3–28 (Idem, *Byzantium from the ninth century to the fourth crusade: Studies, texts, monuments*. Hampshire, Variorum, 1992, XX).

———. (1996a). The medieval Via Egnatia. In E. Zachariadou (Ed.), *The Egnatia under Ottoman rule (1380–1699). Halcyon days in Crete II: A symposium held in Rethymnon (9–11 January 1994)* (pp. 9–16). Rethymnon (Idem, *Social and Economic Life in Byzantium*, Variorum, Ashgate, 2004, XXIII).

———. (1996b). *Emperor of the Romans—Emperor of the Romania*. In *Byzantium and Serbia*, 121–128.

Ostrogorsky, G. (1956). *Histoire de l'État byzantin*. Paris.

———. (1967). Problèmes des relations byzantino-serbes au XIVe siècle. In *Proceedings of the XIIIth International Congress of Byzantine Studies* (pp. 41–55) (Oxford, September 5–10, 1966). London, Oxford.

———. (1971). Observations on the aristocracy in Byzantium. DOP, 25, 3–32.

Palikruševa, G. (1970). Islamisation de la région Reka dans le nord-est de la Macédoine. *Macédoine 1970*, 135–147.

Panaitescu, P. P. (1969). *Introducere la istoria culturii românești*. București.

Panov, B. (1981). Toward the ethnogenesis of the Macedonian people. *Macédoine 1981*, 37–47.

Papacostea, Ş. (1993). *Românii în secolul al XIII-lea. Între cruciată și imperiul mongol*. București.

Papacostea, V. (1943). La Péninsule Balkanique et le problème des études compares. *Balcania*, 6, III–XXI.

Philippide, A. (1927). *Originea românilor, vol. II. Ce spun limbile română și albaneză*. Iași.

Pillon, M. (2002). L'exode des "Sermésiens" et les grandes migrations des Roumains de Pannonie durant le Haut Moyen Âge. EB, 38, 3, 103–141.

Pippidi, A. (1994). De la Kosovo la Sarajevo. *Sud-Estul şi contextul European. Buletin, 1*, 17–26.

———. (1999). Changes of emphasis, Greek Christendom, westernization, South-Eastern Europe, and Neo-Mittel Europa. *Balkanologie, 3*, 2, 93–106.

Poghirc, C. (1989). Romanisation linguistique et culturelle dans les Balkans. Survivances et evolution. *Les Aroumains*, 9–44.

Pohl, W. (1988). *Die Awaren. Ein Steppenvolk in Mitteleuropa, 567-822 n. Chr.* München.

Pollo, S., & Puto, A. (1981). *The history of Albania from its origins to the present day.* London.

Popa, O. (1997). At the dawn of the hope: The building of Macedonian national identity. *Central European Issues, 3*, 2, 132–159.

Popović, V. (1975). Les témoins archéologiques des invasions avaro-slaves dans l'Illyricum byzantin. *Mélanges de l'École Française de Rome. Antiquité, 87*, 1, 445–504.

———. (1980). Aux origines de la Slavisation des Balkans: La constitution des premières Sklavinies Macédoniennes vers la fin du VIe siècle. *Académie des Inscriptions et Belles-Lettres. Comptes Rendus des séances de l'année 1980*, 1 (Paris) (Janvier–Mars), 230–257.

———. (1984). Byzantins, Slaves et autochtones dans les provinces de Prévalitaine et Nouvelle Epire. In *Villes et peuplement dans l'Illyricum protobyzantin. Actes du colloque organisé par l'École Française de Rome (Rome, 12–14 Mai 1982)* (Collection de l'École Française de Rome, 77). Rome, 181–243.

———. (1986). Koubrat, Kouber et Asparouch. *Starinar, 37* (Belgrade), 127–133.

———. (1988). L'Albanie pendant la Basse Antiquité. *Les Illyriens 1988*, 251–283.

Pranvera, B. (1993). Kosova under the Albanian feudal state of the Balshes. *Kosova 1993*, 55–62.

Pribichevich, S. (1982). *Macedonia. Its people and history.* Philadelphia: Pennsylvania State University Press.

Prinzing, G. (1972). *Die Bedeutung Bulgariens und Serbiens in den Jahren 1204-1219 in Zusammenhang mit der Entstehung und Entwicklung der byzantinischen Teilstaaten nach der Einname Konstantinopels infolge des 4. Kreuzzuges.* München.

Pulaha, S. (1985). *L'autochtoneité des Albanais en Kosove et le prétendu exode des Serbes à la fin du XVIIe siècle.* Tirana.

———. (1993). On the presence of Albanians in Kosova during the 14th–17th centuries. *Kosova 1993*, 33–47.

Pundeff, M. (1968). National consciousness in medieval Bulgaria. *SOF, 27*, 1–27.

———. (1970). Nationalism and communism in Bulgaria. *SOF, 29*, 128–170.

Puşcariu, S. (1926). *Studii istro-române*, vol. II. Bucureşti.

Reiter, N. (1987). Alte Relikte in Balkansprachen. *Die Völker 1987*, 69–84.

Rosetti, A. (1986). *Istoria limbii române, I. De la origini până la începutul secolului al XVII-lea. Ediţie definitivă.* Bucureşti.

Runciman, S. (1990). *The fall of Constantinople, 1453.* Cambridge.

Russu, I. I. (1944). Graniţa etnică între traci şi illiri. Cercetări epigrafice şi onomastice. *Anuarul Institutului de Studii Clasice, IV* (Cluj-Sibiu), 73–147.

———. (1976). *Elementele traco-getice în Imperiul Roman şi în Byzantium (veacurile III–VII). Contribuţie la istoria şi romanizarea tracilor.* Bucureşti.

———. (1995). *Obârşia tracică a românilor şi albanezilor. Clarificări comparativ-istorice şi etnologice*. Cluj-Napoca.

Sacerdoţeanu, A. (1939–1940). Mouvements politiques et sociaux de la Péninsule Balkanique dans la seconde moitié du XIe siècle. *Balcania*, 2–3, 83–106

Samardžić, R. (1989). Migrations in Serbian history (the era of foreign rule). *Migrations 1989*, 83–89.

Savvides, A. G. C. (1987). Internal strife and unrest in later Byzantium, XIth–XIIth centuries (A.D. 1025–1261). The case of urban and provincial insurrections (causes and effects). *Symmeikta. Ethnikon Idryma Ereynon. Kentron Vyzantinon Ereynon*, 7 (Athens), 237–273.

———. (1998). Splintered medieval Hellenism: The semi-autonomous state of Thessaly (A.D. 1213/1222 to 1454/1470) and its place in history. *Byzantion, 68*, 2, 406–418.

Schmitt, J. (1989). Die Balkanpolitik der Arpaden in den Jahren 1180–1241. *Ungarn-Jahrbuch. Zeitschrift für die Kunde Ungarns und verwandte Gebiete*, 17 (München), 25–52.

Schramm, G. (1986). Frühe Schicksale der Rumänen. Acht Thesen zur Lokalisierung der lateinischen Kontinuität in Südosteuropa (II). ZB, 22, 1, 104–125.

———. (1994). *Anfänge des albanischen Christentums. Die frühe Bekehrung der Bessen und ihre langen Folgen*. Freiburg im Briesgau.

Shepard, J. (1995). Slavs and Bulgars. NCMH II, 228–248.

———. (1999). Bulgaria: The other Balkan 'empire'; Byzantium expanding, 944–1025. In T. Reuter (Ed.), *The new Cambridge medieval history, vol. III, c. 900–c.1024* (pp. 553–623). Cambridge.

Simeonova, L. (1998). *Diplomacy of the letter and the cross: Photios, Bulgaria and the Papacy, 860s–880s*. Amsterdam.

Skendi, S. (1956). Religion in Albania during the Ottoman rule. SOF, 15, 311–327.

Soulis, G. (1984). *The Serbs and Byzantium during the reign of Tsar Stephen Dushan (1331–1355) and his successors*. Washington, DC.

Spiridonakis, B. G. (1990). *Grecs, ocidentaux et Turcs de 1054 à 1453, quatre siècles de relations internationals*. Thessalonique.

Stadtmüller, G. (1955). Die Islamisierung bei den Albanern. *Jahrbücher für Geschichte Osteuropas, 3*, 4, 404–429.

Stănescu, E. (1966). La crise du Bas-Danube byzantin au cours de la séconde moitié du XIesiècle. ZRVI, 9, 49–73.

———. (1989). Premisele răscoalei Asăneştilor. Lumea românească sud-dunăreană în veacurile X–XII. *Răscoala 1989*, 11–36.

Stavrianos, L. S. (1959). *The Balkans since 1453*. New York.

Stavridou-Zafraka, A. (1992). Slav invasions and the theme organization in the Balkan Peninsula. *Vyzantiaká*, 12 (Thessaloniki), 165–179.

Stefov, R. (2003). *History of the Macedonian people from ancient times to the present* (www.maknews.com/html/articles/stefov).

Stephenson, P. (2000). *Byzantium's Balkan frontier, a political study of the northern Balkans, 900–1204*. Cambridge.

———. (2003). The Balkan frontier in the year 1000. In P. Magdalino (Ed.), *Byzantium in the year 1000* (The Medieval Mediterranean: Peoples, Economies and Cultures, 400–1500, vol. 45) (109–133). Leiden.

Stipcević, A. *The question of Illyrian-Albanian continuity and its political topicality today* (www.alb-net.com/illyrians.htm).

Stoianovich, T. (1967). *A study in Balkan civilization.* New York.

Sugar, P. F. (1977). *Southeastern Europe under Ottoman rule, 1354–1804.* Seattle, WA.

Tadin, M. (1980). Les "Arbanitai" des chroniques byzantines (XIe–XIIe s.). CIEB XV, vol. IV, 315–330.

Tagliavini, C. (1972). *Le origini delle lingue neolatine.* Bologna.

Tanaşoca, A. (1981). Autonomia vlahilor din Imperiul Otoman în secolele XV–XVII. RdI, 34, 8, 1513–1530.

Tanaşoca, A., & Tanaşoca, N. Ş. (1994). Vlaques et Croates aux XIVe–XVe siècles: Les Keglević contre les Silanić. RESEE, 32, 1–2, 123–128.

———. (2004). *Unitate romanică şi diversitate balcanică. Contribuţii la istoria romanităţii balcanice.* Bucureşti.

Tanaşoca, N. Ş. (1989). O problemă controversată de istorie balcanică, participarea românilor la restaurarea ţaratului bulgar. *Răscoala 1989,* 153–181.

———. (2001). Aperçus of the history of Balkan Romanity. In R. Theodorescu & L. Conley Barrows (Eds.), *Politics and culture in southeastern Europe* (pp. 97–174). Bucharest.

Tăpkova-Zaimova, V. (1980). La population du Bas-Danube et le pouvoir byzantin (XIe–XIIe s.). CIEB XV, vol. IV, 331–339.

———. (1993). L'administration byzantine au Bas-Danube (fin du Xe–XIe siècle). ByzSl, 54, 1, 95–101.

Teoteoi, T. (1989). Civilizaţia statului Asăneştilor între Roma şi Bizanţ. *Răscoala 1989,* 70–102.

Todorova, M. (1997). *Imagining the Balkans.* Oxford.

Traikov, V. (1986). *Curente ideologice şi programe din mişcările de eliberare naţională din Balcani până în anul 1878.* Bucureşti.

Treadgold, W. (1988). *The Byzantine revival, 780–842.* Stanford, CA.

———. (1997). *A history of the Byzantine state and society.* Stanford, CA.

Tričković, R. (1990). Au-devant des plus dures épreuves: Le XVIIe siècle. *Kosovo 1990,* 88–129.

Vacalopoulos, A. E. (1970). *Origins of the Greek nation: The Byzantine period, 1204–1461.* New Brunswick, NJ.

———. (1973). *History of Macedonia, 1354–1833.* Thessaloniki.

Vasić, M. (1985). *Der Islamisierungsprozess auf der Balkanhalbinsel* ("Zur Kunde Südosteuropas," II/14). Graz.

Vătăşescu, C. (1997). *Vocabularul de origine latină din limba albaneză în comparaţie cu româna.* Bucureşti.

Vilfan, S. (1983). Evoluzione statale degli Sloveni e Croati. *Gli Slavi,* 103–140.

Vryonis, S. Jr. (1972). Religious changes and patterns in the Balkans, 14th–16th centuries. *Aspects 1972,* 151–176.

Wace, A. J. B., & Thompson, M. S. (1914). *The nomads of the Balkans. An account of life and customs among the Vlachs of Northern Pindus.* London.

Wasilewski, T. (1964). Le thème byzantin de Sirmium-Serbie au XIe et XIIe siècles. ZRVI, 8, 2, 465–482.

———. (1971). Stefan Vojislav de Zahumlje, Stefan Dobroslav de Zéta et Byzance au milieu du XIe siècle. ZRVI, 13, 109–126.

Weithmann, M. W. (1978). *Die slawische Bevölkerung auf der griechischen Halbinsel. Ein Beitrag zur historischen ethnographie Südosteuropas.* München.

———. (1994a). Interdisziplinäre diskrepanzen in der "Slavenfrage" Griechenlands. ZB, 30, 1, 85–111.

———. (1994b). Politische und ethnische Veränderungen in Griechenland am Übergang von der Antike zum Frühmittelalter. *Die Kultur Griechenlands,* 13–30.

Whittow, M. (1996). *The making of Byzantium, 600–1025.* Berkeley, CA.

Winnifrith, T. J. (1987). *The Vlachs, the history of a Balkan people.* London.

Wolff, R. L. (1949). The "Second Bulgarian Empire." Its origin and history to 1204. *Speculum,* 24, 167–206.

Xhufi, P. (1993). Albanian heretics in the Serbian medieval kingdom. *Kosova 1993,* 48–54.

———. (1996–1997). Religione e sentimento religioso in Albania durante il Medioevo. AIESEEB, 26-27, 41–49.

Xydis, S. G. (1968). Medieval origins of modern Greek nationalism. BS, 9, 1, 1–20.

Zirojević, O. (1990). Les premiers siècles de la domination étrangère. *Kosovo 1990,* 40–87.

Živojinović M. (1996). La frontière serbo-byzantine dans les premières décennies du XIVe siècle. *Byzantium and Serbia,* 57–66.

Indexes

Geographical Index

219

People and Persons Index

Author Index (except those quoted only in endnotes with their works)

About the Author

Alexandru Madgearu (born 1964, Bucharest) received his Ph.D. in medieval history from the University of Bucharest in 1997 with a dissertation on the archaeology of the Lower Danubian area in the 6th–8th centuries. He is currently working as researcher at the Institute for Defence Studies and Military History (Bucharest, Romania), being specialized in late ancient and early medieval history. His works include other four books and more than 60 papers published in different academic journals and collections of studies in Romania, Italy, Greece, Bulgaria, Czech Republic, Great Britain, and Serbia. The works concern various aspects of the military and political history of the Southeastern European region. In 2002–2003, he was a Fulbright visiting scholar at Ohio State University.